W9-AOX-820

How to write simulations using microcomputers

HOW TO WRITE SIMULATIONS USING MICROCOMPUTERS

D. Ellison and J.C. Tunnicliffe Wilson

McGRAW-HILL Book Company (UK) Limited

London · New York · St Louis · San Francisco · Auckland · Bogotá
Guatemala · Hamburg · Johannesburg · Lisbon · Madrid · Mexico
Montreal · New Delhi · Panama · Paris · San Juan · São Paulo
Singapore · Sydney · Tokyo · Toronto

Published by
McGRAW-HILL Book Company (UK) Limited
MAIDENHEAD · BERKSHIRE · ENGLAND

British Library Cataloguing in Publication Data

Ellison, D.
    How to write simulations using microcomputers.
    1. Digital computer simulation
    2. Microcomputers
    I. Title   II. Wilson, J. Tunnicliffe
    001.4'24   QA76.9.C65

    ISBN 0-07-084722-3

Library of Congress Cataloging in Publication Data

Ellison, D.
    How to write simulations using microcomputers.
    Bibliography: p.
    Includes index.
    1. Digital computer simulation.   2. Microcomputers.
    I. Wilson, J. Tunnicliffe.   II. Title.
    T57.62.E44   1984   001.4'24   84–10011
    ISBN 0-07-084722-3

1234AP 8654

Typeset by Oxprint Ltd, Oxford
Printed and Bound in Great Britain by
Whitstable Litho Ltd., Whitstable, Kent

Contents

Preface

The traditional simulator or operational researcher for many years has used mainframe machines and mainframe languages to carry out his simulations. He may not realize the restrictions these impose on him—having to share a large remote machine with other programmers; the lack of portability of computers; the lack of interactive graphics; the slowness of debugging in many mainframe languages. And he may not have realized that all these problems can be avoided by using a suitable microcomputer. He may have dismissed these as toys. However, we show that this is not the case, that useful interactive simulation models can be quickly built and used on microcomputers.

We have aimed this book at two groups of people. First, those already experienced in simulating on a mainframe, in a business or industrial environment, and who are used to developing their models in, say, FORTRAN, or perhaps in a simulation language such as GPSS, ECLS or GASP. The second group consists of those who already have a microcomputer and may be less familiar with simulation but would like to put their machines to this serious use.

Because there are so many different microcomputers with new ones becoming available all the time, it is impossible to give full details for writing simulations on every micro. We have used the BASIC language as it is common to every micro, and we give working programs for the PET and the Apple II. The programs are in modular form, each module being explained in detail so that users of other machines can easily translate the BASIC to fit their own systems. This also allows easy modification where desired without confusing the whole structure.

Chapter 1 introduces graphics and breaks new ground in the ways of presenting simulation results. Traditional simulation languages provide tables of statistics and histograms, usually without any obvious time dependency. Moving interactive graphics change this—you can show objects moving round the screen and control their progress by using the games paddles; or you can display graphs of simulation variables, a form the brain can assimilate much more readily than piles of statistics. This lack of emphasis on statistics is intentional. Of course, if you are still interested in collecting and analyzing statistics, you are encouraged to develop the necessary software for yourself.

The activity approach to simulation is presented in Chapter 2, with simple models showing how to use the executive whose structure and programs are detailed in Chapter 3. We start with the simple traditional A-B-C structure and extend it step-by-step to include (i) moving pictures (2.2. and 3.2); (ii) graphical displays and interactive facilities (2.3 and 3.3); and, (iii) the combination of continuous and discrete happenings (2.4 and 3.4). The presentation is in the form of pseudocode and also the actual BASIC code. In this way, the ideas behind the executives can be understood independently of the programming languages used, and, thus, converting to another language should be a fairly straightforward task.

Chapter 4 contains illustrative working examples for the various executives and gives some feel for the range and types of problems that can be tackled on a microcomputer.

Acknowledgements

Grateful thanks are due to our typists Pam Waring, Claire Wildsmith and Margaret Ball all of whom had to endure the eccentricities of a wayward word processor. This work was developed during the last two years of the Centre in Simulation at Lancaster University and we express our gratitude for the use of facilities there and for the help of John Crookes and Mike Simpson and to the SRC who funded the Centre. The initial versions of the simple executive and the warehouse example (4.2) were written by John Crookes.

1. Introduction to simulation and microcomputer graphics

1.0 Introduction

You may be familiar already with the technique of simulation on large computers, or with microcomputer applications in other areas; but for those people for whom these topics are new ground we include, in this chapter, brief introductions with references for more detailed study if desired.

We believe that the use of microcomputers for simulations will increase rapidly as they become more powerful, and as the potential of interacting with a simulation model as it runs is recognized. This interaction is made possible by the presentation of a graphical display (which may be coloured) unfolding on a video screen, a medium which is instantly attractive, and further very powerful in explaining your simulation to both technically skilled and unskilled people. This must be contrasted with the output from a conventional simulation, often a long strip of computer paper folded into a pile several centimetres thick. It will contain many histograms and pages of indigestible statistics.

Those of you who have simulated on large computers will have experienced the hours of frustration waiting for the computer to produce the results to your programs. Even for a modest program and working a solid five-day week, several months may elapse before your ideas are successfully embodied in a working simulation. On a microcomputer, the same project will take only days, with the added bonus of a large reduction in costs.

Lastly, your microcomputer is easily portable—you can carry the whole thing along with you. If you need to show your simulation to someone in the next building or the next town you can easily take the whole system there, a suitcase in one hand and a TV in the other.

In this chapter, then, we begin with a short look at what we, in this book, mean by simulation. We follow this with sections on the advantages and disadvantages of simulating using microcomputers. The rest of the chapter concentrates on the use of graphics on a microcomputer and how we exploit these facilities to observe a simulated system as it changes and to produce moving records of the changing system.

1.1 What we mean by simulation

It is very hard to give an adequate definition of simulation; there are so many different interpretations, some loose, others more or less precise.

One could start with the subterfuge of so many authors by quoting the dictionary definition; but this would convey overtones of 'counterfeit and feigning', certainly not an auspicious opening for us as we wish simulation to throw illumination on the real world, rather than to obscure it.

We could try a second tack and quote as many definitions as one can find in the literature, but again, this would fail as there are so many interpretations.

What we shall do is give Shannon's definition (Shannon, 1975) which contains most of the important points for a general definition and then narrow his field down to what we mean by simulation. 'Simulation is the process of designing a model of a real system and conducting experiments with this model for the purpose of either understanding the behaviour of the system or of evaluating various strategies for the operation of the system.'

For us, in our narrower sense, simulation is a method of studying systems or organization in industry, business, social services, etc. We wish to answer questions about the system. For example, in planning a warehouse for storing cans of paint, how many metres of shelving are needed, how many fork lift trucks for efficient operation, will maintaining a constant temperature be economical, and so on and so on. The principles and techniques of simulation are fully discussed by Pidd (1983).

We first develop a model (on paper) whose kernel consists of logical statements and/or mathematical equations describing the behaviour of the real system. Except for a few simple systems, a computer will be needed to deal with the interplay arising from these equations and statements and to display the results. For us this means a microcomputer. The model is thus translated into a computer program and this is often loosely referred to as a simulation model or a computer model. Indeed, we shall use the phrase 'running a simulation' to mean a microcomputer run of this program. Simulation is the process of developing and running such a program with the intention of gaining experience and knowledge of the real system by modifying the computer model or experimenting with it.

We are also rather circumspect in the domain of models—we shall be dealing with ones which are popularly known as 'discrete', 'continuous', and 'combined' models. Note these terms describe the model and not the real system, and it may be possible for the same system to be cast either as a discrete or as a continuous model. For example, consider the planes landing at London Airport. We may be interested only in the number of planes landing; this variable varies discretely with time. In this case we can use a discrete model. However, our interest may be in the distance between aircraft, a variable which varies continuously with time, and so we adopt a continuous model. If we are interested in both together, then we could well develop a combined model.

Note in this example, as in most simulation problems, time is the independent variable; the others are functions of time and are the dependent variables.

Continuous models

Continuous models are characterized by continuous changes in their variables. The ones we consider are the solutions of ordinary differential equations, which are integrated numerically.

A very simple example is the simple pendulum—well-remembered from schooldays—which consists of a weight attached to one end of a string whose other end is fixed. The weight swings back and forth, the motion, for small angles x, being described by

$$\ddot{x} = -(g/l)x$$

where g is the acceleration due to gravity and l the length of string. The solution of this equation for small x is easily found so that the motion of the pendulum is known at all times. Thus, for example, if we are interested in the times when the pendulum is stationary we can easily find them from the simple model—and probably without a computer! Figure 1.1 shows a characteristic output from a continuous model presented as a graph. Compare this with those below. More substantial examples of systems which can be modelled continuously are the flights of projectiles, space rockets, the growth of biological populations and weather systems.

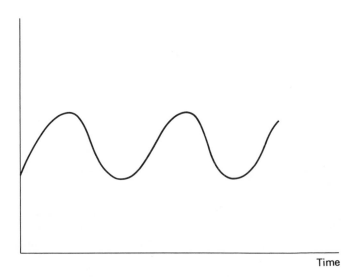

Time

Fig. 1.1 Graph of output from a continuous model.

Discrete models

The essential ingredients which characterize discrete models are:

1. They involve discrete entities.
2. The dependent variables usually change discontinuously or in jumps.
3. Events occur at scheduled discrete times—i.e., between consecutive events nothing is deemed to change, so a continuous time is not required.

Thus, for example, in a supermarket, which we are modelling to discover how many checkout tills are needed at various busy times of day or week, the discrete entities may be the customers, the trolleys, and the checkout girls.

3

The dependent variables would include the lengths of the queue at each till and at the meat counter. The events could be a customer arriving and a customer leaving. Such arrivals are usually scheduled by sampling from some statistical distribution which reflects the real arrival rate. The customers will leave after reaching the front of the queue and being served for some time at the till or counter. Suppose, at some point in the model, the next event is due in two minutes—since nothing else of interest will change until then, simulation time can be advanced directly to that next event; thus simulation time jumps along in this discrete fashion.

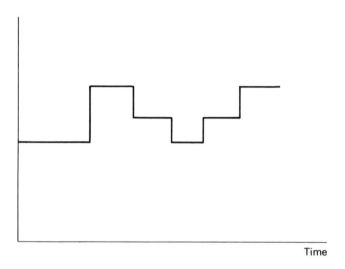

Time

Fig. 1.2 Graph of output from a discrete model.

Figure 1.2 shows a typical graph from a discrete model. Discrete models are used in great variety: air traffic control, ambulance dispatching, bank operations, distribution systems, job shop scheduling, steel plants, computers, and so on.

Combined models

Combined models contain a combination of continuous and discrete elements, in the sense that the dependent variables of the model may involve continuous or discrete changes or a combination of the two and that the events may be either discrete or continuous in nature.

Events may be scheduled, as in the description of discrete simulation above, or, in the continuous case, unscheduled but determined as a result of some threshold being attained. For example, consider the temperature of a room (which varies with internal and external heating conditions). A thermostat may switch the heating on when the temperature falls below 18 °C. The model cannot predict the time of occurrence of this event, since the equations are too involved; instead the temperature is determined at consecutive small

4

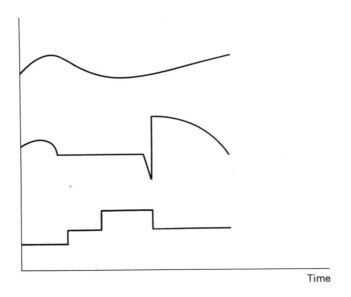

Time

Fig. 1.3 Graphs of output from a combined model.

intervals of time. After each time step the question: IS TEMPERATURE BELOW 18 °C? is asked, and the stepping process is continued until it is. This then determines the time of this so-called 'state' event. Discrete (scheduled events) take place when, for example, the time clock switches the heating on or off.

A combined model then involves two types of event: discrete and state.

Examples of systems that have been treated as combined models are the chemical reactors of Sec. 4.4, oil delivery by tankers from wells and unloading them at refineries, heating ingots in soaking pits, fouling of pipes in a chemical distillation process, and district heating.

Stochastic variation

Stochastic or, if you prefer it, random variation is an important facet of most discrete models. Such variation arises, for example, in the arrival patterns of patients at a doctor's surgery, the number of passengers waiting for a bus, the frequency of breakdown of machines, the probability of thunderstorms, and so on. However, we must point out that stochastic variation is not always present in a model and, indeed, in this book we do not discuss it in detail. (See Pritsker and Pegolen, 1979.)

In practice, arrival rates, for instance, are found numerically from an appropriate probability distribution whose form may be found by observations of the real system being modelled. For example, Poisson distributions are commonly found in batch arrivals of various sizes and negative exponential distributions in the variable time interval between individual arrivals.

5

1.2 Why simulate on microcomputers?

Simulation on a mainframe machine is something of a last resort—it is time-consuming and expensive. Many mainframe simulations produce results which are obtainable from simple calculations and produce them too late for the relevant decision making. On a microcomputer the position is different as the simulation display can prove as useful as the final results. The communication possible with a moving display enables important points to be accepted when no calculations would be believed. The reality of the model is there for all to see with no requirement of numeracy or computer skills. The results too are available much more quickly. Simulation then is useful both as a method of studying a problem beyond mere analytic techniques and, on a microcomputer, as a means of demonstrating to a wide audience how a system may operate in differing circumstances.

Displays to watch the action as it happens

We have developed two types of display for the video screen of the microcomputer, both changing with simulated time as the model proceeds and neither of which is available with any mainframe simulation package.

A 'picture' display can represent the current state of the model at any simulated time. With high resolution colour graphics a detailed picture can be drawn showing the precise state of a complex system, but it is often useful to simplify the picture to emphasize the important points. Figure 4.13 shows the display used for the warehouse model of Sec. 4.2 with one shape representing each component being moved. Colour and rotation of the shape are used to give additional information about the component and the lifting table it occupies—for example, the component destination and the movement of the lifting table. From this display it is easy for those familiar with the warehouse to recognize the truth (or otherwise!) of the model and appreciate the changing circumstances as they are simulated.

A more advanced display is the use of graphs to show both the current state of the model and also its immediate history. Only selected variables can be displayed to indicate the state of the model, so this display is appropriate for the user who wishes to make a detailed study of the model behaviour, probably having used a picture display of the same model to check its moment-by-moment changes. Figures 1.1–1.3 illustrate the graphs obtained from different types of models.

Interacting with the model as it runs

With the graphical display it is easy to see when a model is approaching an unsatisfactory state, possibly becoming unstable or hopelessly congested. Using the paddles to alter model variables the position may be remedied and sensible values quickly found to give an acceptable model state.

Another use of interaction is experimenting by changing a variable (via a paddle) to see the effect on the model as it runs.

6

Perhaps the most important form of interaction is that demonstrated by the example of Sec. 4.5 where a simulated valve is operated via a paddle. This manual operation allows the model user to develop control rules for the operation of the valve, using the simulation display. These control rules can later be built into the model and tested.

Speed of development

Development of successful working programs on microcomputers is very quick. We performed a small experiment (as part of the development of the example in Sec. 4.5) which showed that elapsed time in writing simulations on mainframe can be ten times that on micros! and that actual (programming) time can differ by a ratio of 2:1. The reasons for this are the convenience of microcomputers; easy access, at any time and any place (almost); quickness in modifying programs, because of the interpretive BASIC; and personal access—i.e., individual machines are so cheap that you can have your own, without the need to share it. You can easily take a micro home with you if you wish, and no time at all is taken in walking to them. This last remark is pertinent—the experiment on the mainframe computer showed that walking to the terminal occupied 15 per cent (4.5 hours made up of 3-minute journeys) of the total time spent developing the program!

To change a line of program, all you have to do is type in the new line and run again. No time is wasted in compilation, nor in whiling away the infamous turnaround time associated with mainframes. Further, in debugging, diagnostic print statements are easily inserted, and values of variables can be printed out at will, when the program stops; again, no waiting for turnaround.

Convenience

We have already noted certain conveniences—personal use, portability, and so on. Portability is a great friend—you can easily take your simulations and displays on tour for demonstrations. Busy managers and others involved with the real system are much more ready to look at and play with moving pictures than be daunted by pages of tedious statistics. Their comments are very valuable; they know their system and you can easily adapt your model accordingly.

Cheapness

To develop the tank and tanker model of Sec. 4.5 cost on a mainframe machine (a CDC 7600) £1000; for the Apple II, for the equivalent model, £55. This compares very well with the cost of buying an Apple system: approximately £1500, for you to use for many years.

The microcomputer as a unit

We should emphasize the importance of the unity of a microcomputer. One can have colour graphics on a minicomputer or a mainframe; one can achieve interaction with some larger computers via analogue inputs; and terminals can be taken home and the computer operated remotely. But only a micro-computer such as an Apple II, a computer system in its own right, lets one have all these features together at a low price. Apple IIs are easily transported in a suitcase—very useful for demonstrating your latest model to potential customers, and persuading them with a colour presentation, especially if they are allowed to operate the keyboard and paddles.

The future

All the time, microcomputer equipment is becoming cheaper; and more widespread; the size of memories is increasing; compiler BASICs are becoming available; so, then, more and more people will turn to microcomputers for simulations.

Perhaps the biggest change is the development of 16-bit microcomputers which provide higher speed and support larger memories. This will also open the way for the implementation of simulation languages on microcomputers.

Simulators with many years' experience of traditional mainframe computers should have no hesitation in adopting a microcomputer. They already have considerable knowledge of computers, programming, and simulation, all of which is easily re-tuned to a microcomputer system. Then (in a very short time) they can build working models whose dynamic, colourful, and immediate impact far surpasses any attempts at conviction by waving tables of statistics at busy managers.

1.3   Limitations of microcomputers

We have so far painted a rosy picture of microcomputers—where are the thorns? We look at a few, not necessarily in order of importance, since a particular limitation may be critical for some applications and no problem for others.

Running speed

Slow running can be a problem especially with combined simulations. The major cause lies with interpretive BASIC. You can attempt to adjust your programs to improve running speed, but orders of magnitude increases require a compiler version of BASIC—interpreters allow quick debugging, compilers quick running.

The problem with speed is not so much with runs which you leave to their own devices (i.e., production runs which do not need any human intervention and can run for hours, if necessary), but with ones which require watching the screen, especially the combined simulations. Consider the tank and tanker model of Sec. 4.5. On first encountering the display, when it is still unfamiliar, the running speed is quite adequate. As experience is gained, one itches for greater speed but, alas, it is not easily available. In fact, an increase in running speed by as little as a factor of 5 would cure this itch, and would be easily achieved with a compiler BASIC. On the other hand if a model runs too fast it becomes impossible to interact with it sensibly, or follow the changes on the display. However, this is easily overcome by adding software delays.

Size of program/problem

Eventually, you will run out of core, if you have large numbers of entities, or your model requires a long program description and so on. This, however, has not been a restriction with any of the examples in this book. Nevertheless, following some sort of Parkinson's law, one always eventually overburdens whatever computer facilities are available. What can you do? There are ways of reducing storage—removing remarks, re-using array and variable storage, and so on. But these are not attractive techniques; they disrupt your programs and take organizational effort.

Before 16-bit CPUs became widespread, large models could be accommodated by using parallel processing on linked microcomputers or microprocessors. A large model may consist of several submodels, only some of which are directly involved in interaction with a user. Where interaction is required, the submodel could use one of the executives described here with links to other microprocessors or microcomputers simulating the other parts of the model. The Apple III already has 128K which would allow models or submodels about 16 times the size of our examples.

Languages

There are at present only very few simulation languages available for microcomputers. We have found references to only a couple (Bryant, 1981; Clementson, 1981) so any simulation you do on microcomputers will probably be back to basics—which is why this book is so useful!

Mainframe and micros

The comparison of more or less identical models on the CDC 7600 and Apple II showed that the CDC took 0.25 sec running time with no display (4.5 sec compilation) whilst its lesser brother occupied itself for 55 minutes! This is not an indictment of microcomputers, more a reflection of the huge power of large mainframe machines. From this arises a suggestion—when you cannot do it on a micro, or want a long run without displays or interaction, transfer to a mainframe.

Earlier we saw there are limitations on speed and size of models on microcomputers, but it may still be well worthwhile, for a large model, to produce a small, slow version on a micro first. You will gain considerably from the micro—you will have a working model (perhaps with restricted numbers of entities, etc.), thoroughly debugged, and this achieved in a very short time. If you have no direct link to the mainframe (via tapes, telephones, discs or whatever) you will have to retype the programs, but this is a minor task. Not only do you have a working model, you have more—you have gained experience of the system in building the model and running it as far as possible on the microcomputer. You may, for example, have found an approximation to an optimal solution, which the mainframe model can then quickly find, with the full complement of entities. To achieve this on the mainframe, would indeed have taken much more computer, programmer, and elapsed time along with their associated costs.

1.4 Graphics for simulation

We present, as an introduction, some of the facilities and effects available using static and dynamic displays (with and without colour). More details of how to generate them are given later in this chapter and descriptions of their use are found in the examples of Chapter 4.

Graphics, especially moving colour graphics, add so much to the appreciation of simulation models, that, once seen, you would never again rest content with the traditional forms of presentation of simulations and their results. Most simulation languages on mainframe machines produce various (paper) output reports, whose format is normally rigidly dictated by the particular language used. The reports include statistics of variables of the model—means, standard deviations, minimum and maximum values, number of observations, etc., in tabular form; and if requested, these also as histograms (see Sec. 1.6 for an example). They are usually final summaries, though printouts in the course of the simulation can sometimes be obtained. However, this can lead to pages and pages of data, if one is not careful. Hardly any languages (SLAM and GASP IV are exceptions—see Pritsker and Pegden, 1979; Pritsker, 1974) allow time-dependent graphical output. This of course, is produced on paper; it is therefore static and allows no interaction.

Television captivates

We have already noted the magnetic attraction of a colour television screen in generating interest in simulations. Television is a presentation medium which immediately captivates everyone, from laymen through programmer to manager. Suppose you are simulating a factory and you wish to check that your model performs in the same way as the people on the shop floor operate. How do you check? Do you go down there armed with masses of means and standard deviations; or would you prefer to show the operators a moving TV display of the factory? Take your microcomputer down there. This will soon attract other people from nearby—your efforts will be noised abroad. Quickly, gradually, others will creep up: colleagues, foremen, managers all

10

curious about the commotion. Soon you will be receiving all manner of useful data and comments, from those who know and appreciate how they and their part of the system work. Very useful experience for producing correct models, for finding mutually agreeable improvements; where is your pile of statistics now? Do these people know how your program works, do they know anything about BASIC; do they need to? No! The proof of your esoteric efforts they can readily appreciate by watching your display on the television screen.

Someone suggests an extra pair of hands at a particular stage of assembly might cut down delays. You can change your program there and then and re-run it. Did the suggestion improve things? Well, whether it did or not, you did not have to retire to the higher obscurity of your room and the mystique of a distant computer only to emerge days later; the changes can quickly be made and the results seen without delay.

Colours

Not all microcomputers provide multicolour displays. The advantages of those that do, once seen, are immediately apparent—the brain can very easily absorb information that can be emphasized or distinguished by colours. Without colour one has to resort to special symbols, which usually can only occupy certain positions on the screen—they make a low resolution picture (typically 40×24 symbols). With coloured dots, coloured shapes, symbols or drawings can be built up at any position in an area defined by 280×160 or 190 dots.

Static and dynamic displays

The layout of, say, a chemical plant or a warehouse are easily produced on the screen (see Figs 4.45 and 4.13) for describing and discussing the system being modelled.

As the model runs, you can display the effects of changes using this layout on the screen, or, if preferred, present the results as graphs, or combinations of these. Of course, if and when required, histograms and tables of numbers can also be displayed. However, as pointed out earlier, it is far easier for the eye to absorb information from a dynamic display (a summary of the information) than from endless reams of numbers.

The data displayed using histograms provide no time dependency. However, the same information presented as moving graphs reveals much more than this. We may see from a histogram that the length of a queue was 100 on 5 occasions—but from a graph we can see the build up of these queues and the consequences too. And, further (see next paragraph), we can interact with a model to control such queues and learn about the system thereby. The increase in knowledge and learning gained from such a display cannot be emphasized enough.

Paddles

We have adopted the games paddles provided with the Apple II, ostensibly as toys, for serious use. The paddles permit interactive simulations, and, in some cases, the results of these would be very difficult, if not impossible, to achieve on a mainframe computer. The paddles are connected to some chosen parameters of the model, and as the simulation runs, these can be constantly varied. This, combined with the visual displays, is a very useful tool. Microcomputers without paddles usually have input ports to which similar devices can be connected.

Aid in debugging

Many errors that may otherwise lie hidden for some time, become quickly and embarrassingly evident when a screen is used—curves cross axes, the wrong part of the picture changes and so on. The underlying cause may not be clear, but the result is; the screen is an extra aid in debugging.

Basics of drawing

We shall make use of the high resolution facility, for its greater detail and precision in drawing. However, low resolution (40×24 units) can be quite satisfactory for drawing some moving pictures as we shall see in Chapters 3 and 4. There we use symbols on the PET, and the Apple character generator.

In Applesoft high resolution graphics the instruction HPLOT allows you to connect two points by a 'straight' line in a specified colour (HCOLOR = 5, say, produces green). The line is as straight as the screen resolution permits —it is in fact a series of small stepped straight-line segments. Thus:

HCOLOR = 5
HPLOT 1,1 TO 50,51 TO 70,180 TO 1,1

will produce a green triangle, with vertices at the points given. The next section (1.5) shows how to develop complex drawings from this primitive beginning.

HGR, HGR2 Screens

There are two screens available with a 48K Apple called HGR and HGR2. If you have an Apple with less than 36K or one without Applesoft there are restrictions on the screens available to you, so do check your program manual. The screens each occupy 8K of your computer memory which might otherwise be used for other things so the HIMEM command may be needed to keep your program in bounds. POKE commands are also used in the Apple II executives (of Chapter 3) to make as large a space as possible available for program without interfering with the screen memory. While we do make use of this two-screen facility, we also show how an executive can be developed on a small machine with only one normal screen—e.g. a PET.

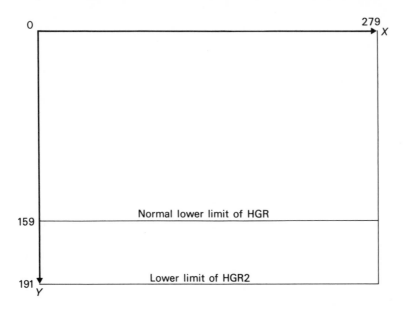

Fig. 1.4 Illustrating HGR, HGR2 graphics screens, and axes.

Apple screens are topsy-turvy for drawing graphs as shown in Fig. 1.4; the Y-axis is considered vertically DOWN! In both HGR and HGR2, the origin is at the top left, and the X-axis lies horizontally along the top—X increases left to right and the Y-axis is vertically down at the left-hand side. Again in both cases, X ranges from 0 to 279. However, HGR sets Y to range from 0 to 159, while HGR2 sets it from 0 to 191. This is because HGR allows four lines of normal text at the bottom of the screen. Only integer values for co-ordinates are allowed.

Shape table

A shape table is an Applesoft device allowing rapid drawings of repetitions of a given figure or shape. It is a permanent Apple memory record of some figures which can be manipulated via special commands (DRAW, XDRAW, ROT, SCALE, SHLOAD) to be drawn anywhere on the screen, at a specific orientation and size.

For example, specifying

ROT = 16
SCALE = 2
DRAW 5 AT 24,20

will draw shape 5 rotated through 90 degrees at double size starting at coordinates (24,20). Up to 255 shapes can be recorded in the shape table and used in one program.

13

Full details are to be found in the Applesoft manual (pages 92–7). Basically, one draws and records (in binary format) for each shape a number of vectors that outline the shape, as in Fig. 1.5.

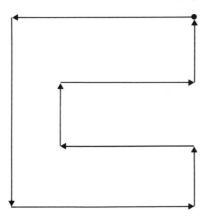

Fig. 1.5 Input vectors to shape table.

This procedure is a little tedious and has been automated to some extent (see *Practical Computing*, 1980). Nevertheless, it is very useful for a repetitious drawing such as appears in the warehouse problem (illustrated in Fig. 4.13 and described in Sec. 4.2.)

Character generator

Normally on the Apple the PRINT instruction functions only on the TEXT screen, and cannot be used to place script on the graphics screen (to annotate graphs, for example). It also has a restricted set of characters available, i.e., those on the keyboard. The Apple character generator allows text to be entered on the graphics screen without having to construct the characters in a shape table. It is a machine language program which has to be loaded by the BASIC program using it. Once loaded (after the command HGR or HGR2) two POKE commands

POKE 54,0 : POKE 55,12

extend the graphics area to the whole screen (for HGR) and allow characters anywhere on it.

These two commands will vary according to the position in the memory used to store the generator. The addresses given by the numbers 54 and 55 are the Apple location for printing characters. The numbers 0 and 12 direct the executive to the machine language program stored as in the picture and paddle executives of Secs 3.2 and 3.3 (Chapter 3). From this point on, all printing is done by the computer via the character generator; no normal text can be printed.

The extended set of characters can be positioned in the same way as any normal print statement on a TEXT screen using VTAB and HTAB. VTAB12 for instance moves the attention of the machine to line 12 (of the 24 lines available on the screen). The following PRINT command will then print on that line. The use of VTAB 24 may cause problems on a text screen because the text is automatically moved up when the last line is printed, but it can be used normally on the graphics screen. HTAB moves the printing position along the current line so HTAB 20 will cause the next PRINT statement to start in the middle of a line.

After the printing of graphics characters has been completed the screen can be restored to one allowing normal text on the last four lines by these statements:

```
POKE 54,189 : POKE 55,158
POKE -16301,0
```

Until normal screen text is desired the character generator can remain in force while the BASIC program runs. The discrete graph plotting described in Sec. 1.7 returns to normal text immediately after using the character generator to label its graph, while the continuous graph plotting of Sec. 1.8 has no normal text and leaves it in force.

1.5 Observing your system as it changes

In this section we show how you can build up moving pictures which are representations of your system, as it runs. A brief look at the picture in Fig. 4.41 will help you see what we mean. The left hand part is a still of the VDU moving display.

The following section 1.6, in contrast, deals with output, presented as moving graphs.

Semi-dynamic displays

Look at the left-hand part of Fig. 4.41, a 'still' from a model of a hydrogen reactor plant. What we mean by semi-dynamic is that, while the display changes with time, the parts of it do not move anywhere (cf. next example, where components move through the display). The only movement in the plant is the filling and subsequent emptying of reactors represented by rectangles. The display shows the amount remaining for process in the reactors, each of which is connected to a pressure vessel via pipes. Note the composition of the pictures:

1. Five static rectangles
2. Pipes—straight lines.
3. 'Filling' of reactors.

So all that is required is the ability to draw straight lines, join them into rectangles and carefully fill them (i.e., not over- or under-fill) with colour.

Before we look at this further we need a slight digression here on the colour idiosyncracies of the Apple graphics.

15

DRAW REACTOR LAYOUT

1. plot reactors
2. plot pressure vessel
3. draw pipes

4. fill each reactor with colour

---

1. PLOT REACTORS

choose lengths of sides
choose spacing of reactors
choose colour

FOR each reactor

determine starting corner
plot rectangle

---

2. PLOT PRESSURE VESSEL

choose lengths of side
choose position
choose colour
plot rectangle

---

3. DRAW PIPES

draw vertical pipe
connect it to pressure vessel
connect each reactor to pressure vessel

---

4. FILL REACTOR WITH COLOUR

select fill colour
fix start and top and bottom of reactor
draw vertical lines from left to right of reactor

Fig. 1.6 Description of program for drawing reactor layout.

The high resolution screen, though divided into 192 rows by 280 columns, is not sufficient to cover every possible location of the screen. To store the addresses of all positions with a number of colours for each, uses up far too much space in the computer—hence this compromise on storage by the designers of Apples. However, a consequence of this scheme is that, in order to ensure that correct colours are drawn, any non-horizontal line must be double plotted; that is, a ghost line is drawn immediately adjacent to the first. If this is not done some vertical lines may not appear at all, while others may be of the wrong colour. For example, the two instructions

HPLOT 5,5 to 5,100
HPLOT 6,5 to 6,100

should be used, instead of only the first, to draw the vertical line from $Y = 5$ to $Y = 100$ at $X = 5$ or 6.

Figure 1.6 gives the pseudocode for the reactor layout program. To fill each reactor with colour means the interior of each empty rectangle representing a reactor is filled with a colour different from the frame. To do this, vertical lines are drawn starting from the left, working right and being careful not to cross the upper and lower edges (Fig. 1.8). The BASIC code is given in Fig. 1.7. There, also, is found the subroutine for drawing a rectangle. To do this we start at its upper left corner at (X,Y) and draw the top (length A), right side (length B), bottom and left side, in that order.

```
51000   REM   FILL REACTORS WITH COLOUR
51005   REM   I9      = COLOUR PARAMETER OF CHOOSE COLOUR
        SUBROUTINE

51010   REM   IR      = REACTOR NUMBER
51015   REM   XJ      = X COORDINATE OF LINE DRAWN TO FILL REACTOR
51020   REM   XL      = X COORDINATE OF LHS OF REACTORS
51030   REM   YT(IR)  = Y COORDINATE OF TOP OF REACTOR IR
51040   REM   YB      = Y COORDINATE OF BOTTOM - 1
51050   REM   AR,BR   = LENGTHS OF SIDES OF REACTORS

51060   I9 = IR: GOSUB 26800: REM   CHOOSE COLOUR
51070   XJ = XL + 1:YT = YT(IR) + 1:YB = YT + BR - 2
51080   FOR J = 1 TO AR - 1
51090   HPLOT XJ,YT TO XJ,YB
51100   XJ = XJ + 1
51110   NEXT
51120   RETURN

51500   REM   PLOT RECTANGLE
51510   FOR J = 1 TO 2
51520   HPLOT X,Y TO X + A,Y TO X + A,Y + B TO X,Y + B TO X,Y
51530   X = X + 1:Y = Y + 1
51540   NEXT
51550   RETURN
```

Fig. 1.7 BASIC code for filling reactors and drawing a rectangle.

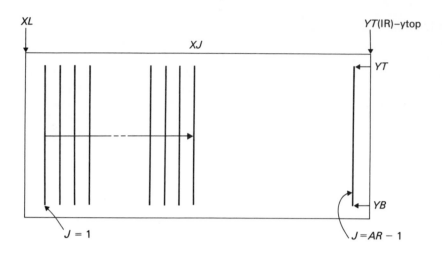

Fig. 1.8 Filling a rectangle with vertical lines.

Thus (X, Y, A, B) are parameters to the rectangle subroutine, which draws a double perimeter, the second line being displaced by one unit from the first. This is to ensure continuity of lines and colour as explained above.

What we have described so far is a very simple colourful layout which is very useful for explaining your system to your captivated audience. Now, how do you make it change? (the picture, that is). We wish to show the reactors reacting by blacking out (i.e., using the background colour) the interior of the corresponding rectangle, in proportion to the percentage of reaction completed. This is easy—calculate the change from the last update and draw, in black, the appropriate number of vertical lines, as used in filling.

Dynamic displays

Dynamic displays are ones in which entities are seen to move about the screen. The warehouse display of Sec. 4.2 is a fine example of this, for which a shape table was used. Figure 4.13 shows a still from it. Components move through a warehouse layout, so the direction of travel needs to be indicated. This is achieved by the shape in Fig. 1.5 where the direction of movement is easily shown by the orientation of the shape. States of the component can be represented by different colours: thus, blue indicates blocked, and yellow moving on. Two operators involved are also represented by the shape with black indicating normal operation and blue, again, not working. Shapes (that is, components) move from one station to the next as the simulation runs, so their paths through the warehouse are easily discerned. The shape does change slightly with different orientation and colours as shown in the figure. This is because of the colour idiosyncracies of the Apple mentioned above.

18

High or low resolution display?

Assuming you have a choice, when should you produce your own shapes in high resolution graphics and when should you use symbols provided on a keyboard or via a character generator? This is largely dependent on the layout of your model. The warehouse (Fig. 4.13) has a complex fixed physical layout and the moving components need to be related to the conveyor/lifting table they are currently occupying. High resolution graphics allows the drawing of lines and a coloured background to represent the warehouse machines with a moving coloured shape to represent components precisely placed on the screen. Careful use of the PET symbols would be required to produce a similar effect with the use of different symbols in place of colour to differentiate the states of components, cranes, and operators.

The trucks model (Sec. 4.3), on the other hand, has only to move trucks between queues and out on delivery. All of these locations can be easily fitted on the screen using a character generator or PET symbols. Repair gangs and loading bays remain fixed in the layout and are easily represented by symbols different from those used for the trucks.

The use of shapes and symbols is much quicker for discrete objects as they use only one BASIC instruction to move them, while it would take several instructions if HPLOT commands were used.

1.6 Moving records of the changing system

Very few simulation languages offer graph plotting, the usual display format for output being histograms. Because of their nature—a summary of statistical data gathered over a considerable time span—a good deal of information is lost in presentation, in particular how the quantities involved vary with time. Let us look at some examples to illustrate these points.

The first part of Fig. 1.9 shows a histogram—from which of the two time plots do you think the histogram arises? The sort of information you may learn from the histogram is that the range 80–100 was the most frequent, or that the value was less than 40 for 25 per cent of the time. From the graphs you can learn much more even from a cursory glance.

From the histogram can you say when the maxima occur? Can you indeed say whether there are several maxima? Both curves, in fact, give rise to the same histogram—the values are taken at the crosses indicated and are plotted from Table 1.1 which are derived from sines at 10° intervals. The first curve was plotted reading values across the rows; the sine curve from down the columns.

The case, you may claim, is somewhat contrived, but it does illustrate the points outlined above. More realistic perhaps is the following example extracted from the hospital model of Sec. 4.1.

Patients are seen first in an outpatient clinic at which a proportion are diagnosed as requiring inpatient treatment. They join a waiting list until beds are available for them. Figure 1.10 shows both histograms and graphs derived from this model. The second histogram gives the number of patients queueing for inpatient treatment (on the waiting list) but the first histogram of outpatients seen does not shed any light on this. When the two graphs are studied

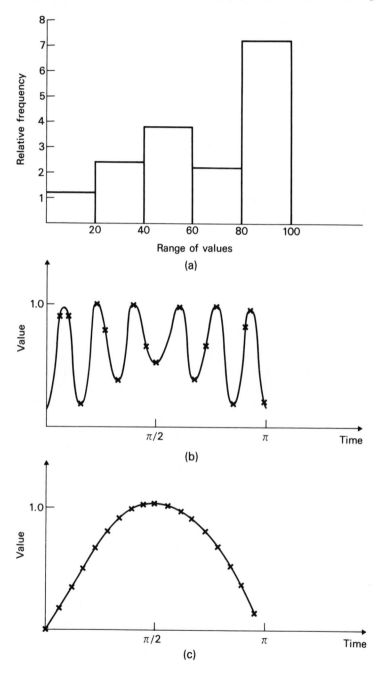

Fig. 1.9 Two time plots with same histogram.

it quickly becomes apparent that the inpatient waiting list only increases when the number of outpatients seen is high for several weeks. The demand for inpatient beds then can be controlled by restricting the number of patients seen at the outpatient clinic.

Table 1.1 Sines at 10° intervals

Time	Value	Time	Value	Time	Value
1	0	7	87	13	87
2	17	8	94	14	77
3	34	9	98	15	64
4	50	10	100	16	50
5	64	11	98	17	34
6	77	12	94	18	17

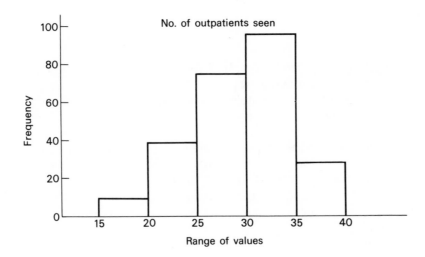

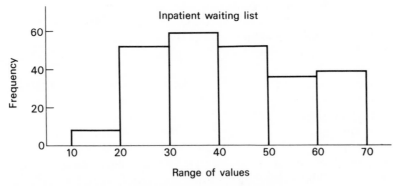

Fig. 1.10 (a) Histograms for hospital model (Sec. 4.1)

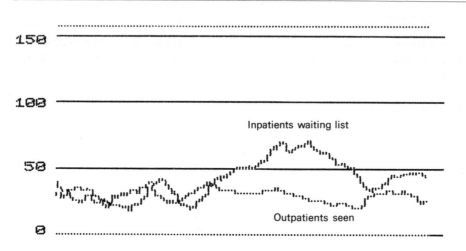

Fig. 1.10 (*cont.*) (b) graphs from the same model.

We turn now to drawing graphs of variables. Since simulations unfold with time, it is possible to display moving graphs of the simulation variables. As soon as the new values of these variables are found from the model, the graphs are extended along the X axis to the new points, using our old friend HPLOT. This procedure is in contrast to the static plotting available with mainframe computers where the graphs are drawn after all computation is finished (as on a Calcomp plotter for example). For this the entire range of data points has to be available at the time of plotting.

The appearance of the graphs in the discrete and combined cases are markedly different—the former are step functions, the latter are smoother—as can be seen from Figs 2.8 and 2.20.

Discrete simulations progress through time in uneven jumps (Sec. 2.1); since nothing happens between consecutive events, time is advanced directly from the old event to the next one and the values of all variables remain constant in this interval—hence the horizontal segments in Fig. 2.8. However, at event times, some, if not all, variables change values—hence the vertical segments. The variable values are on the Y axis and the time progresses along the X axis. Integer time units are used throughout the simulations.

Continuous graphs are smoother, since, in general, between the discrete events, many integration steps are taken and the graphs are updated at each of these times which may not be integer. See Fig. 2.20, upper curve.

In either case, the graphs eventually reach the right-hand edge of the screen. They can then be redrawn, part of the right-hand portion being moved to the left hand of the graph space and the remainder rubbed out; the plotting then continues. The redrawing machine language program is given in Appendix 2.

22

1.7 Discrete graph plotting

As we have already said, these graphs take the form of steps. At an event time, the plotting routine has first to draw a vertical line from the previous value of a variable (PV) to the new value of the variable (NV). This has to be a double line on the Apple because of the colour eccentricities. The graph then has to be extended by a horizontal line from the old time ($X1$) to the new time ($X2$). Thus:

```
HPLOT X1,PV  TO  X1,NV  TO  X2,NV
HPLOT X1+1,PV  TO  X1+1,NV
```

We then update the variables:

```
PV = NV
X1 = X2.
```

The new value for $X2$ is calculated by adding onto $X1$ the time between events after the next event has been found. The new value for NV will appear when the simulation activities have been carried out and changes to each variable are calculated.

Care needs to be taken because of the Y axis going down instead of up. In the discrete paddle executive of Sec. 3.3, PV(I), the previous value of a paddle variable I, is adjusted before plotting by the equation:

```
PV(I) = Y − PV(I) * SC(I)
```

Y is set in the initialization to 158 so the X axis is 158 points DOWN on the screen Y axis. SC(I) is the scaling factor required for paddle variable I to make the model values fit neatly on the screen. This is taken care of by the executive—all the modeller has to do is specify his scaling factors.

The value of $X1$ has also to be set in the initialization to start the graph at the correct point (28 points along the screen X axis) to allow room for the annotation of the variable axis. When the graph is redrawn (see Sec. 1.9) then the value of $X1$ is reset to continue the graph from the point reached by the redrawn graph. This point will vary from redrawing to redrawing. This is because each step of the graph is drawn only if it can be completed (i.e., without $X2$ crossing the right-hand edge of the screen) so the redrawing will occur at different values of $X1$. The reduction in the value of $X1$, however, is constant (168) as the same amount of graph is 'rubbed out' each time.

Both the time axis (integer time) and the variable axis can be annotated. The time axis is labelled in the text area of the HGR screen (which is also used for other information) while the variable axis labels use the character generator. Four labels are available, each with a horizontal line going across the screen, drawn in white using HPLOT.

Because the lines extend right across the screen they are not 'rubbed out' when the graph is redrawn (see Sec. 1.9).

The labels are model dependent so they are stored in an array SN$( ) and use the character generator to put them onto the screen in the following statements:

```
43070   POKE 54,0 : POKE 55,12: REM CHAR PRINT TO LABEL GRAPH
43080   FOR I = 1 TO 4:VTAB(6*I–4):PRINT SN$(I):NEXT
43090   POKE 54,189 : POKE 55,158:REM RESTORE NORMAL PRINT
43095   POKE–16301,0 : REM RESTORE TEXT LINES
```

1.8   Continuous graph plotting

The display for the chemical plant model (Sec. 4.4) includes both the plant layout and the graphs. To allow flexibility, the graph plotting routine allows the user to choose the size and position of axes and the scalings of the dependent and independent variables, and also the number of variables plotted. The graphs, however, must be to the right of any pictures or other information displayed on the screen. Again the horizontal axis represents time, the vertical axis the various variables involved. This is a plotting routine (i.e., not restricted to the world of simulation) and is described in detail here. It is also incorporated in the combined executive of Sec. 3.4.

We wish to plot our curves on normal cartesian axes drawn within a given window of the screen (Fig. 1.11), which we shall refer to as the $(T2,V2)$ space. $T2$ is (simulation) time (a real variable) and $V2$ (ICURVE) is the value of the Ith curve being drawn. The '2s' are appended to these variables to indicate that they are used within the plot routine and to distinguish them from other variables without the plot routine.

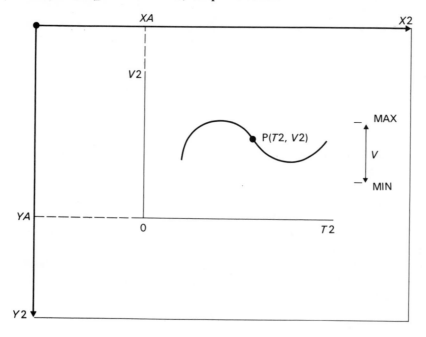

Fig. 1.11 Relation of screen and variable spaces.

Apple graphics, on the other hand, cover the entire screen using the upside-down axes described at the end of Sec. 1.4. We shall refer to this as the $(X2,Y2)$ space, $X2$ being the horizontal and $Y2$ the vertical coordinates respectively.

Choose to draw the origin of $(T2,V2)$ at 0, i.e. (XA,YA) referred to the screen coordinates. The subroutine which does the drawing needs some further information before it can function adequately. First, choose a time interval TL, such that the edge of the screen is reached after this time; for example, if your model is going to run for 5 hours, you may wish to plot graphs with a time axis of length 30 min, i.e., $TL = 30$. You need to supply the independent variables values $V2$ (ICURVE) and also information concerning their maxima and minima. In fact,

MAX(ICURVE) = a value > max obtained by ICURVE
MIN(ICURVE) = a value < min obtained by ICURVE

will allow you some leeway in shifting the vertical positions of the several curves as plotted. For example, suppose there is just one curve (CURVE = 1), $V2(1) = \mathrm{SIN}(T)$, say. Then $V2$ ranges between -1 and $+1$. By choosing $\mathrm{MAX}(1) = 1$ and $\mathrm{MIN}(1) = -3$ the graph will be plotted in the top half of the available space, as in Fig. 1.12.

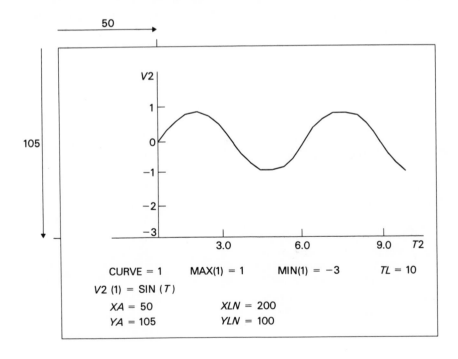

Fig. 1.12 Example of graph plotting.

The heart of the plot routine is the transformation from $(T2,V2)$ co-ordinates to $(X2,Y2)$ coordinates.

X2% = XO + XLN * (T2 − TZERO)/TL
Y2% = YA − YLN * (V2 (ICURVE) − MIN(ICURVE)/VR

These need some further explanation. First, $X2\%$ and $Y2\%$ must be integer values since the screen plotting allows integer only. Next, the transformation turns over the $(T2,V2)$ coordinates and scales them to fit the new axes and origin. Thus consider first the $Y2$ transform: YA is the origin, the length of the Y axis is YLN the − sign overturns and YLN/VR scales, VR is the range of the dependent variable given by ABS(MAX(ICURVE) − MIN(ICURVE)), and so the scale factor YLN/VR ensures a value in the range covered by the Y-axis. The $X2\%$ transformation is similar, but now TZERO is the time of the first point plotted on this particular screenful—it is updated whenever a new screen drawing is begun (see next subsection). $XO = XA + 8$ and ensures the plotting always starts clear of the Y-axis; $XLN + 8$ is the length of the X axis.

The plotting goes as follows. The user feeds his values of time and the variables into the subroutine via the parameters $T2$ and $V2(ICURVE)$: that is, $(T2,V2)$ is the next point to be plotted. These are converted to $(X2,Y2)$ coordinates and a straight line drawn from the old point $(X1,Y1)$, provided $X2$ is not beyond the right-hand edge of the screen. If it is, the picture is redrawn and then the plotting done. The pseudocode for the routine is in Fig. 1.13 while Fig. 1.14 shows the BASIC code and Table 1.2 gives the variable definitions.

(a)

PLOT A NUMBER OF GRAPHS

get variables to plot
1. find next X co-ordinate to which to plot
FOR each curve
  IF V is not in variable range THEN
    print data out of range : STOP
    transform from V to Y coordinates
  IF Y is not in screen range THEN
    print exceeded plot : STOP
2. plot curve
update X-coordinate

---

1. FIND NEXT *X* COORDINATE

---

transform from *T* to *X* coordinate
IF point is not beyond screen edge THEN RETURN

3. ELSE shift and redraw graph

---

2. PLOT A CURVE

---

select colour
draw double line from old to new point
update *Y* coordinate

---

3. SHIFT AND REDRAW GRAPH

---

adjust SH so new point will fit on screen
find K1 and K2
shift *X*-coordinates
shift time
shift graph
black out old portion

(b)

INITIALIZE PLOT

---

initialize X0, T0 and X1
provide safe values of XLN, YA, CS, if necessary
set up first points
plot axes

Fig. 1.13 Pseudocode for general graph plotting. (a) plotting the graphs;
(b) initialization.

```
26200   REM   PLOT A NUMBER OF GRAPHS
26202   GOSUB 900: REM   GET VARIABLES TO PLOT
26205   GOSUB 26500: REM   FIND X POSITION
26210   FOR IC = 1 TO CURVE
26215  VP = MAX(IC):VM = MIN(IC)
26220   IF V2(IC) > VP OR V2(IC) < VM THEN   PRINT "DATA OUT OF R
     ANGE"
26221   IF V2(IC) > VP OR V2(IC) < VM THEN   STOP
```

Fig. 1.14 BASIC code for continuous graph plotting (*continues*).

```
26225  VR =   ABS (VP - VM)
26230  Y2% = YA - (V2(IC) - VM) * YLN / VR
26235   IF Y2% > 180 OR Y2% < 0 THEN  PRINT "EXCEEDED PLOT": STOP
26245   GOSUB 26300: REM   PLOT
26250   NEXT
26255  X1 = X2%
26260   RETURN

26300   REM   PLOT A CURVE
26305  I9 = IC: GOSUB 26800: REM    SELECT COLOUR
26315   HPLOT X1,Y1(IC) TO X2%,Y2%
26320   HPLOT X1 + 1,Y1(IC) TO X2% + 1,Y2%
26325  Y1(IC) = Y2%
26330   RETURN

26500   REM   FIND X POS
26505  X2% = X0 + (T2 - TZERO) * XLN / TL
26510   IF X2% < X0 + XLN THEN  RETURN
26514   REM   SHIFT AND REDRAW
26515  SH = SC
26518   REM   ADJUST SH UNTIL POINT WILL FIT ON SCREEN
26520  TMP% = X2% - SH * 7
26525   IF TMP% >  = X0 + XLN THEN SH = SH + 2: GOTO 26520
26527   REM   FIND K1 AND K2
26530  K1 =   INT (X0 / 7) + SH:K2 =   INT (X1 / 7) + 1
26535   IF K2 <  = K1 THEN SH = SH - 2: GOTO 26530
26537   REM   SHIFT X-COORDINATES AND 'ZERO' TIME
26540  X2% = X2% - SH * 7:X1 = X1 - SH * 7
26545  TZERO = TZERO + SH * TL * 7 / XLN
26550   GOSUB 26600: REM   SHIFT PICTURE
26555   GOSUB 26700: REM   BLANK RH PART
26560   RETURN

26600   REM   TRANSFER
26605   POKE 37900,K1
26610   POKE 37902,K2
26615   POKE 37904,SH
26620   CALL 37906
26625   RETURN

26700   REM   BLANK OUT RH PART
26705   POKE 38128,(39 + SH - K2)
26710   CALL 38132
26715   RETURN

26800   REM    FIX COLOUR
26805   IF I9 = 1 THEN  HCOLOR= 1
26810   IF I9 = 2 THEN  HCOLOR= 2
26815   IF I9 = 3 THEN  HCOLOR= 5
26820   IF I9 = 4 THEN  HCOLOR= 6
26825   IF I9 = 5 THEN  HCOLOR= 3
26830   IF I9 = 999 THEN  HCOLOR= 0
26835   RETURN

43200   REM   INITIALISE PLOT
43210  X0 = XA + 8:TZERO = 0:X1 = X0
43220   REM   SAFEGUARDS
43230   IF XLN + XA > 270 THEN XLN = 270 - XA
43240   IF YA < YLN THEN YA = YLN + 2
43250   IF SC * 7 > X0 + XLN - 7 THEN SC =   INT ((X0 + XLN) / 7
       - 3)
43260   REM    SET UP FIRST POINT
43265   GOSUB 900: REM  GET FIRST PLOT VARIABLE
43270   FOR I3 = 1 TO CURVES
43280  VP = MAX(I3):VM = MIN(I3)
43290  VR =   ABS (VP - VM)
43300  Y1% = YA - (V2(I3) - VM) * YLN / VR
43310  Y1(I3) = Y1%
43320   NEXT

43330   REM   PLOT AXES
43340   HCOLOR= 3
43350   HPLOT XA,1 TO XA,YA + 3 TO 279,YA + 3
43360   RETURN
```

Fig. 1.14 (continued).

Table 1.2 Variables used in continuous plot routine

*CURVE	—number of curves to be plotted
$K1, K2$	—limits of part to be shifted
*MAX(ICURVE)	—> max value obtained by ICURVE
*MIN(ICURVE)	—< min value obtained by ICURVE
*SC	—shift constant (0–38 and even) selected by user
SH	—shift used by plotting routine (may change from SC)
*TL	—length of time axis
TMP%	—shifted $X2\%$ (temporary value)
*TR	—length of time axis in plotted time
TZERO	—time of first point plotted (changes when shift occurs)
T2	—time of next point to be plotted
*V2 (ICURVE)	—value of next point to be plotted on ICURVE th plot
VR	—range of variable = max–min
*XA	—X-coordinate of origin
*XLN	—length of X-axis (in dots)
X0	—X-coordinate of first point plotted = $XA + 8$
X1	—X-coordinate of present plot point
X2%	—X-coordinate of next point to be plotted
*YA	—Y-coordinate of origin
*YLN	—length of Y-axis (in dots)
Y1 (ICURVE)	—Y-coordinate of present plot point
Y2%	—Y-coordinate of next point to be plotted

* indicates supplied by modeller as parameter values to plot subroutine

Plot a number of curves (26200)

First the new values for plotting are input and from the new time $T2$ corresponding $X2\%$ is found—this may be complicated by picture redrawing. Then, each curve is extended in turn, provided the following safeguards are passed: (a) a user's variable lies within the supplied (MIN,MAX) range; and (b) the Y value lies within the range of the Apple screen. Finally, (26255) when all plotting is finished the X coordinate is updated in readiness for the next time plotting is done.

Find X-position (26500)

(26505) is the X coordinate transformation mentioned above. The shifting and redrawing (26514–26560) is described in the next section (Sec. 1.9).

Plot a curve (26300)

A double line (to ensure fidelity of colour) is drawn from $(X1, Y1)$ to $(X2\%, Y2\%)$ and then (26325) the Y coordinate remembered (for this particular variable) in readiness for the next time plotting is done.

Select a colour (26800)

This deals with the colour numbering idiosyncracies of the Apple so that black curves are not drawn.

Initialize plot (43200)

The $X0 = XA + 8$ (43210) ensures the curve plotting stays clear of the Y-axis. The safeguards arise as a result of oversights we committed in developing the plotting routine; there are, without doubt, many more that could be usefully built in. The reader is invited to insert his own.

1.9   Redrawing the graph

The discrete graph plotting uses the whole screen and integer time as used throughout discrete models. This makes the graph redrawing simpler than the continuous graph plotting which uses real time and has greater flexibility. Differences between the two types of plot are noted where appropriate, in this section. Consider Fig. 1.15 which shows the curve being drawn nearing the right-hand edge of the screen.

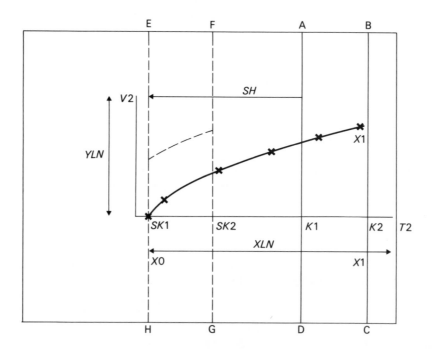

Fig. 1.15 Redrawing the last portion of a graph.

Suppose the next point to be plotted would lie off the right-hand side. Then the portion of screen between $K1$ and $K2$ is redrawn near the Y-axis by shifting it left a distance SH and the portion between $SK2$ and $K2$ is blacked out. This leaves the screen ready for continuing the graph plotting.

The value of shift, SH, must be even (to avoid a change of colour) and lie between 0 and 38. In the discrete executive it is set to 24; in the combined one the user chooses a constant SC which is used for SH provided it has an acceptable value. $K1$ and $K2$ are fixed in the discrete executive at 28 and 38. In the general graph plotting, $K1$ is automatically determined such that the shift takes the new graph just to the right of the Y-axis, $K2$ is selected to lie just to the right of where the last point was plotted, at $X1$.

The redrawing is straightforward; but complicated! The portion of the Apple's memory which contains the information needed to produce the graphics lying in ABCD is transferred to that part of memory which will produce the same graphics but now lying in EFGH; that's the straightforward bit. The complication lies in the way Apple stores the screen information; suffice it to say the BASIC program of Fig. 1.16 will do the job, but this takes one and a half minutes approximately of computer time, leaving you to twiddle your thumbs, or, better, to think of a quicker way of doing the job. The H,I,J, loops pertain to vertical position; K to horizontal.

```
100   FOR H = 0 TO 80 STEP 40
110   FOR I = I1 TO I2 STEP 128
120   FOR J = 0 TO 7168 STEP 1024
130   FOR K = K1 TO K2
140   AD = I + J + K + H
150   POKE AD - SH, PEEK (AD)
160   NEXT K: NEXT J: NEXT I: NEXT H
```

Fig. 1.16 BASIC code for moving an area of HGR or HGR2 screen.

The removal address is AD, while the destination one is AD-SH (shifted left). $I1$ and $I2$ are the start and finish addresses in core of the particular graphics screen used (HGR or HGR2).

In Appendix 2 we discuss a machine code version of this subroutine which runs in a twinkling of an eye.

The blacking out is just a repeated application of this subroutine, with SH increased by one each time until $SK2$ is reached. The 39th column is kept black for this purpose and consequently drawing there is not allowed. In fact, the X-axis and the horizontal lines used in the discrete plotting extend into the 39th column so that the blacking-out process does not obliterate them.

The general graph plotting routine of Figs 1.13 and 1.14 incorporates the redrawing (in lines 26514–26715). The reason the number 7 keeps appearing arises from the way the Apple stores the details of the picture screens—it does it in blocks of 7 spots and $7 \times 40 = 280$, corresponding to the 0–279 for the

X-coordinate. The 7 factor converts from one system to the other. (26520, 26525) selects a value for the shift (SH) so that the shifted $X2\%$ (TMP%) lies to the left of the end of the X-axis ($X0 + XLN$).

26530 fixes the values of $K1$ and $K2$—have a look at Fig. 1.15 to convince yourself. If it happens that $K1$ lies to the right of $X1$ (26535)—as it may if the time between plot points is relatively large—then SH is adjusted until a suitable value is found. This may of course conflict with the result of (26520, 26525); this implies the user has chosen parameters poorly for his graph plotting, in particular TL. These adjustments attempt to account for some of the problems we found in developing the shift routine. Of course, you may find others—for example, the step length is greater than the axis length!— now you know how the shift works, you can insert your own corrections. Once the shift and $K1$ and $K2$ are determined, shifted values for $X1, X2\%$ and $T0$ can be calculated.

Finally the shift of the picture and blacking-out of the right-hand part are done, by calling to the machine code programs described in Appendix 2. (26620, 26710).

References

Applesoft Basic Programming Reference Manual, published by Apple Computers Inc., 10260, Bardley Drive, Cupertino, California 95014 (1978).

BRYANT, R.M. (1981) 'Micro-Simpas: A microprocessor based simulation language', *14th Annual Sim. Symp.*, Tampa, Florida, March 81, 35–54.

CLEMENTSON, A. T. (1981) 'Fitting a gallon into a pint pot! or creating overlaid programs under CP/M', *J. Op. Res. Soc.*, **32**, April 1981, 319–327.

PIDD, M. (1983) *Computer Simulation in Management Science*, Wiley.
Practical Computing (1980) **31**, Issue 9, September, 98.

PRITSKER, A.A.B. (1974) *The GASP IV Simulation Language*, Wiley.

PRITSKER, A.A.B. and PEGDEN, C.D. (1979) *An Introduction to Simulation and SLAM*, Halstead Press.

SHANNON, R.E. (1975) *Systems Simulation—The Art and Science*, Prentice-Hall.

2. Simulation modelling

In the introductory chapter we looked briefly at simulation and graphics. We now embark on showing how you can develop software that helps you build and run simulation models.

This chapter introduces an approach popularly known as 'activity based' or 'A-B-C structure' with certain modifications for allowing displays and interactive use of paddles. The next chapter looks at the software that comprises the executive for this approach. Finally, Chapter 4 consolidates the information presented in these chapters with substantial examples of working programs of various models.

2.0 Types of simulation

There are available on mainframes a variety of simulation languages. These contain executives which look after various facets of simulation for you, chief amongst which are the timing control of the happenings in your model and the carrying out of these happenings as presented by you in your program. Other executive functions are coordinating initialization and finalization, providing results (graphs or tables of numbers, etc.), and so on. Simulation languages can be classified according to the nature of their time executive—event, activity or process based. The time executive is a piece of program, usually well hidden from the user, that controls the interplay of the entities involved in the simulation as time passes. Essentially, it arranges 'who' does 'what' and 'when'. In the end, we shall see that the 'event', 'activity', and 'process' approaches investigated below boil down to sifting these three pieces of information. However, because of the differing ways the approaches arrange this information the outward aspects of the languages can be very different. By presenting a very simple example, intended to be worked by hand, the distinction between the workings of the three types should be clear.

A simple launderette example

A launderette consists of one washer! When a customer arrives, he washes his clothes if the machine is free, otherwise, he waits until it is free. Then, after washing is complete, he removes the clothes and leaves. Let's assume washing takes fifteen minutes and that customers arrive at times (in minutes) 5, 25, 30, 35, 40, 75, ... Here is a narrative description of what happens. Notice that it's very easy to get lost quickly.

At minute 5, customer 1 (C1) arrives and washes till minute 20, while at 25, C2 arrives and he washes till 40, but C3 arriving at 30, has to queue to wash . . . and you soon realize the need for an executive to do all this for you. Notice all the time, it's a statement of who does what and when. Now to the various approaches.

Event-based approach

An event is a description of the steps that occur consequent to a change in the state of an entity—for example, when the washer (permanent entity) finishes (change of state), the machine is emptied (event) by the customer (temporary entity). The simulation consists of a number of such events. Which one occurs next? A list is kept of those scheduled to occur. When an event is due the executive enters the bit of program associated with the event and acts on the steps therein (which may include scheduling of further events) and then seeks the next event; and so on. For example, the event 'customer arrives' will schedule the next customer arrival. If the washer is empty, it is filled and set running for 15 minutes; if already busy, the customer is added to a queue. End of event.

At time = 0, everything is empty and idle, with the first scheduled arrival at 5—this is summarized in line one of Table 2.1. The arrival at 5 produces two further events (trace through event CA CUSTOMER ARRIVES): an arrival at 25, an end wash at 20. The washer is also set to busy. Thus, at time 5 the status and event list is as in the second row of the table. And so on. What will be the status and event list of minute 70?

Activity-based approach

A pure activity-based simulation contains a number of bits of program known as activities. An activity consists of two parts: a test head and a description of the steps that occur consequent to ALL tests in the test head being satisfied— for example, if there is a customer waiting to wash and if the washer is empty (satisfied tests), the washer can be set busy.

One way of keeping the time is to assume there is a master CLOCK which records simulated time, and associated with each entity is a 'time cell' which is the time the entity is due to finish its present activity. Thus TW = 20 means the washer will finish washing at time 20. If TW = 95 when the CLOCK = 100, this means the washer has been idle for 5 minutes. The time of the next happening is located by finding the minimum time cell on the list of time cells, which is greater than CLOCK time. When found CLOCK is advanced to this time. Then, the executive attempts every activity in turn, but enters the body of only those whose every test is satisfied. This is repeated until no activity is entered because some of these may update some time cells which could trigger another activity. At the end of the activities the whole cycle is repeated, starting with the search for the minimum time cell.

At time = 0, TW is set to minus infinity and TA to 5. (See Table 2.2 first row.) The minimum time of the time cells greater than CLOCK (= 0) is 5; thus CLOCK is advanced to 5. Now each activity is tried, in turn. Activity 1 can be entered (TA = 5) and this sets QW to 1, TA to 25 (next customer to arrive at 25). QW = 1 and TW = $-\infty$, so activity 2 is also entered, reducing the queue to 0. The entries for this time are given on the second row of the table, the arrow indicating the change of queue from 1 to 0 while the CLOCK is stopped.

Table 2.1 Event-based approach

EVENT CA: CUSTOMER ARRIVES	EVENT WF: WASHER FINISHES
schedule next arrival if washer busy add to queue else set washer busy for 15 min	if queue empty set washer free else remove customer from queue and set washer busy for 15 min

STATUS			EVENT LIST	
Present Time	W	Qw	Scheduled Time	Event
0	f	0	5	CA
5	b	0	20 25	WF CA
20	f	0	25	CA
25	b	0	30 40	CA WF
30	b	1	35 40	CA WF
35	b	2	40 40	WF CA
40	b	1 2	55 75	WF CA

f–free
b–busy
W–washer
Qw–queue for washer

Table 2.2 gives the activity-based approach up to time 40. What will be the status entry for time 70?

Process interaction approach

This approach combines the ideas of the previous two, and is characterized by phrases such as 'delay', 'wait until' and 'reactivation points'. A process is a collection of happenings detailing the history of an entity as it progresses through the simulation. For example, a customer arriving at the launderette will, if there is a queue, 'wait until' his turn arrives, when he will 'delay' for the duration of the wash. Otherwise, he 'delays' on entering. This describes the

Table 2.2 Activity-based approach

	ACTIVITY 1: ARRIVE	ACTIVITY 2: WASH
tests	If time for customer arrival $(T_A \leq \text{CLOCK})$	If queue not empty If washer not busy $(T_W \leq \text{CLOCK})$
body	schedule next arrival add to queue	remove customer from queue wash for 15 minutes

STATUS		TIME CELLS	
CLOCK (Present time)	Q_W	T_A	T_W
0	0	5	$-\infty$
5	$1 \rightarrow 0$	25	20
20	0	25	20
25	$1 \rightarrow 0$	30	40
30	1	35	40
35	2	40	40
40	$3 \rightarrow 2$	75	55

process for this particular customer (temporary entity); and of course it is true for all such entities, that is, while the description is the same, there is a distinct process for each customer. The interaction of these processes over time constitutes the simulation.

The unconditional delay is akin to the event-based approach; the conditional 'wait until' to the activity-based one. The executive seeks to take an entity through as much of the process as possible, until blocked by a 'delay' or 'wait until', and notes the point reached in the process. This is the reactivation point. When this particular entity's turn comes again (either the customer reaches the front of the queue, or the delay time elapses), the executive reactivates the entity at this point. Until this happens, of course, the executive deals with the processes associated with the other entities whose turn has come.

Table 2.3 gives the process approach up to time 40. What will be the entry for time 70?

Table 2.3 Process interaction approach

PROCESS: CUSTOMER

1: schedule next arrival
    if washer is busy then
        add customer to queue
2:    wait until washer is free for this customer
    remove from queue
    else washer set busy for 15 minutes
3: free washer
    end process

STATUS			SCHEDULE		
Present Time	W	Qw	Next Happening Time	Customer	Re-activation Point
0	f	0	5	C1	1
5	b	0	20	C1	3
			25	C2	1
20	f	0	25	C2	1
25	b	0	30	C3	1
			40	C2	3
30	b	C3	35	C3	2
				C4	1
			40	C2	3
35	b	C3:C4	40	C3:C4	2
				C5	1
			40	C2	3
40	b	C4:C5	55	C4:C5	2
				C3	3
			75	C6	1

37

Comparison of approaches

Many mainframe simulation languages assume one of these approaches or some combination of them. Debate over the purported advantages and disadvantages (we have never seen anything approaching a scientific appraisal) in the past has at times been acrimonious verging on pugilistic. We, in this book, have no axe to grind—we do indeed adopt a modification of the activity-based approach but for historical reasons rather than that we see a huge advantage in it. The advantages often cited are that logically complex systems are easily analysed and written in activity form, albeit to the detriment of computer run time—many useless tests possibly having to be performed. Indeed, with an interactive BASIC this may sometimes be a problem, but it is by no means catastrophic, especially with the modifications described below.

2.1   A-B-C structure

In this section we describe an activity-based approach which is an adaptation of the 'pure' one outlined above through the introduction of B-activities (see below). We investigate the building of simulation models from a modeller's point of view—what analysis should he perform, in what form should he present the problem for the computer's consumption? The models of Chapter 4 should provide abundant examples of the use of this approach but to illustrate its basis we look at the launderette of the previous section. See Fig. 2.1 which shows a pseudo-code version of the model and Fig. 2.2 which shows the working code with Table 2.4 giving the definition of the variable names used. These will now be explained in more detail.

B1 : ARRIVAL
schedule next arrival in 5 min add one to Q print entered B1, time, and Q

B2 : END WASH
set washer free print entered B2, time, and Q

```
C1 : START WASH

is there a customer in queue?
is washer free?
– – – – – – – – – – – – – – – – – – – – – – – – – –
remove customer from Q
set washer busy

schedule customer to end wash after 15 min
print entered C1, time, and Q
```

```
INITIALIZE

declare 1 arrival machine, 1 washing machine, 1 C-activity
set washer free; Q to empty
schedule first arrival at 3
```

Fig. 2.1 Pseudocode for simple launderette.

```
1000   REM   C1 START WASH
1010   IF Q <  = 0 THEN   RETURN
1020   IF WASHER = BUSY THEN   RETURN
1025   REM   ************************
1035 Q = Q - 1
1040 WASHER = BUSY
1050 EN = WM:BN = 2:ET = 15
1060   GOSUB 500: REM   SCHEDULE END WASH
1070   PRINT "ENTERED C1 START WASH AT TIME   ";TN;" WITH QUEUE =
   ";Q
1080   RETURN

11000   REM   B1 ARRIVAL
11010 BN = 1:ET = 5
11020   GOSUB 500: REM   SCHEDULE NEXT ARRIVAL
11030 Q = Q + 1
11040   PRINT "ENTERED B1 ARRIVAL AT TIME ";TN;" WITH QUEUE= ";
   Q
11050   RETURN

12000   REM   B2 END WASH
12010 WASHER = FR
12020   PRINT "ENTERED B2 END WASH AT TIME";TN;" WITH QUEUE = "
   ;Q
12030   RETURN

45000   REM   INITIALISATION-MODEL DATA
45010 ARR = 1:WM = 2: REM   ENTITY NUMBERS
45040 FR = 0:BUSY = 1
45050 NE = 2:NC = 1
45060   RETURN
```

Fig. 2.2 Simple launderette model (*continues*).

```
50000   REM   MODEL INIT
50010  WASHER = FR:Q = 0
50020  EN = ARR:BN = 1:ET = 3
50030   GOSUB 500: REM   SCHEDULE FIRST ARRIVAL
50040   PRINT "LEAVING INITIALISATION"
50050   RETURN
50080   RETURN

55000   END
```

Fig. 2.2 (*continued*)

The main difference from pure activities is the incorporation of B- (or bound) activities, which you may like to regard as 'events' in that they are scheduled for a particular entity. These are similar to C-activities except that since they do not depend on the cooperation of several entities they lack test heads and are entered automatically at certain scheduled times, when we know these activities are bound to happen. For example, the arrival mechanism in the launderette model has an 'arrival machine' (entity) with a B-activity which is rescheduled at each arrival time. When we schedule an event, a time is given along with a B-activity number to which the entity is bound at the scheduled time.

Figure 2.3 shows how the simplest executive functions.

Initialization

REPEAT

    Time Advance
    When end reached, finalization and stop
    B-phase
    C-phase

Fig. 2.3 Simple executive structure.

The modeller has to provide three or four segments of information—initialization, the B-activities, the C-activities, and possibly some finalization. In the initialization, he sets constants, initializes variables and presents sufficient detail to set the model going—the initial conditions. He does not have to keep track of the timing—the executive shoulders this responsibility. It seeks the next event(s) from a list of scheduled happenings, which it maintains as the model is run. Events are added to this list as a result of B- and C-activities and removed by the executive at their scheduled times. The C-activities are as described earlier, each consisting of a test head followed by the body (see Fig. 2.1), in which, for example, scheduling of further events, removing or adding entities to queues, collecting statistics, and so on may occur. The B-activities, in contrast, have no test heads and are often used as devices to schedule arrivals into the system, or to perform necessary actions when an entity ceases some activity. The B and C phases function as follows. Suppose the executive has just determined the next event time, i.e., it knows which entities are to have B-activities performed (there may be more than one). It directs the actions contained within these B-activities to be carried out for their respective entities. Then it tests all C-activities in turn and enters the bodies of all those whose every test is satisfied. This completes a cycle; if it is not the end of the simulation the whole operation is repeated, beginning again with the time-advance phase. This has been called the A-phase, presumably to allow the whole process to be known as the A-B-C structure approach!

We can illustrate these points by describing the building of a simple model.

Analysing and formulating the model

How does one start building a model using this approach? The aim is to engender some feeling for the activity approach, rather than to develop a super simulation. The launderette problem as stated is not at all difficult to understand; we are just interested in a queue length, and the correct scheduling of the events. We first decide on the entities needed (permanent and temporary), then look at the C-activities—these will presumably involve the cooperation of the entities. Then fix the B-activities—to arrange arrivals and terminate actions. And we finish with the initialization of the model and the finalization, if we need it.

What are the entities involved? They might be the washer and customers, but customers are ephemeral—once they work their way out of the system we do not need to worry about them so we treat them as temporary entities. They do, of course, keep on arriving so we need some permanent mechanism for this which we call, for historical reasons, an arrival machine! So, we have two permanent entities: a washer and an arrival machine.

Washing involves the cooperation of a customer and a washer so we write this as a C-activity START WASH. Nothing else seems to involve cooperation, so that's it!

No cooperation is needed for ending the wash; all this B-activity (B2: END WASH) does is set the washer free—the customer is lost to oblivion for ever in the present model. He is only a number in a queue.

Our arrival machine produces an endless stream of customers by rescheduling the B-activity: B1 ARRIVAL as soon as a customer arrives. In this simple model let us assume it produces one every 5 minutes.

Finally, in the initialization we define the number of machines and C-activities for the executive use; and set the initial state of the system—queue empty, first customer to arrive at time 3.

Figure 2.2 shows this model in BASIC, with a sample of the output (correct!) in Fig. 2.4. C1 starts at 1000. Note how the tests (in 1010, 1020) are inverted from the pseudo-code and end with RETURN to give control back to the executive.

```
HOW LONG DO YOU WANT TO RUN THIS SIMULATION?33

WHEN DO YOU WANT TO START COLLECTING STATISTICS?100
LEAVING INITIALISATION
ENTERED B1 ARRIVAL AT TIME 3 WITH QUEUE= 1
ENTERED C1 START WASH AT TIME  3 WITH QUEUE = 0
ENTERED B1 ARRIVAL AT TIME 8 WITH QUEUE= 1
ENTERED B1 ARRIVAL AT TIME 13 WITH QUEUE= 2
ENTERED B1 ARRIVAL AT TIME 18 WITH QUEUE= 3
ENTERED B2 END WASH AT TIME18 WITH QUEUE = 3
ENTERED C1 START WASH AT TIME  18 WITH QUEUE = 2
ENTERED B1 ARRIVAL AT TIME 23 WITH QUEUE= 3
ENTERED B1 ARRIVAL AT TIME 28 WITH QUEUE= 4
ENTERED B1 ARRIVAL AT TIME 33 WITH QUEUE= 5
ENTERED B2 END WASH AT TIME33 WITH QUEUE = 5
ENTERED C1 START WASH AT TIME  33 WITH QUEUE = 4
```

Fig. 2.4 Output from simple launderette model.

Line 1050 sets up the parameters for the subroutine SCHEDULE at line 500. This is where we tell the executive who does what and when: EN—ENtity, BN—B-activity Number, ET,—Entity Time. The call to the subroutine at 500 feeds this information to the executive for its use. END WASH is B2. So this is scheduled to take place for the washer in 15 minutes.

B1 ARRIVAL starts at 11000, it reschedules itself 5 minutes later by setting BN = 1,ET = 5, (11010) and adds one to the queue (11030). B2 END WASH starts at 12000 and just frees the washer (12010).

We have put simple print statements in each of our B- and C-activities— (1070, 11040, etc.) and in the initialization—this is a very useful device when writing any model to check the flow as the simulation runs (see below). In the present model this is in fact the only output. Both B- and C-activities contain RETURNs, as must any subroutine, to give control back to the executive.

Note we have used variable names for many of the constants used, e.g., BUSY = 1, FR = 0 for the states of the washing machine (1020, 1040, 12010); and ARR and WM for the entity numbers 1 and 2 of the arrival and washing machine, respectively. This is both for readability and efficiency. Unfortunately we cannot use FREE on the Apple—why not?—(try and see!). Needless to say, the output of Fig. 2.4 was not produced at the first attempt! On the first go the print statements showed the simulation entering B1 at time 6 (not 8): this was traced to 11010 where we had wrongly written 'BI = 5' for 'ET = 5'. The second shot showed the wash not ending at 18 as it should; this was eventually traced to an error in 1050: 'EN = WM' appeared as 'EN = WN'. Errors like this can be very hard to trace. We found the latter by inserting judicious print statements in the executive. So now we have a simple working model. More details of the ins and outs for coding B-activities, C-activities, etc., are given after the examples.

Table 2.4 Variable names used in simple launderette model

ARR	(=1) Entity number of arrival 'machine'
BN	B-activity number (for scheduling)
BUSY	(=1) State of washer when washing
EN	Entity number (in B-activities and for scheduling)
ET	Entity time (for scheduling)
FR	(=0) State of washer when free
NC	Number of C-activities in model (1)
NE	Number of entities in model (2)
Q	Number of customers queueing for washer
TN	Time Now (simulation time)
WASHER	State of washer (= FR or BUSY)
WM	(=2) Entity number of washing machine

Examples

1. Type in Figure 2.2 and get it working, using the executive of Sec. 3.1 (Chapter 3) in Figs 3.2, 3.4, 3.5, 3.7, 3.9, 3.10, and 3.11. You can omit line 41110 if you want to. Play with it:

   (a) What is the queue length at time 100 if the customers arrive every 10 minutes?

   (b) Further, what is its length if washing takes 20 minutes?

   (c) as (b), but customers arrive with a time uniformly distributed between 5 and 10.

2. Introduce a second washing machine into Fig. 2.2. Repeat example 1.

3. Repeat example 2 printing out at the end the average customer time in the system: run model for 500 and 1000 time units. Are the answers as you expected?

4. Introduce a drying phase: there are 3 driers each taking 30 minutes. When a customer finishes washing he queues if necessary for the driers. What is average utilization of washers and driers? Change the arrival rate to give a stable situation and repeat.

5. The customers each have between 1 and 3 loads to wash, uniformly distributed. A drier can take up to 3 loads from one customer. Customer interarrival time is exponentially distributed with mean 10 minutes. Washers take 20 minutes, driers 10. How many washers and driers are needed to reduce average time in the system for customers with two loads to 35 minutes? How much of the time would the extra washers and driers be utilized?

Summary: subroutines written by modeller

B-activities

B-activity n must begin at line number 1n000; no more than 9 are allowed. The total number of B-activities does not have to be stated. The number of the entity which instigated the activity is in the variable EN. End the activity with a RETURN.

C-activities

The set of C-activities is scanned in numerical order and the bodies of those whose every test is satisfied are entered. If not the next one is tried. If the C-activity has no tests, it will be carried out at every event—this can be useful for example, in printing out information at these times.

C-activity n must begin at line n000; no more than 9 are allowed. The total number of C-activities must be declared in the initialization section, (NC = 5, say). A C-activity will usually contain several RETURNs, to return to the executive; that is, one in each test and one to end the activity (but see C-activity 6 of Sec. 4.5 for instance).

Initialization

1. (45000-) must include the setting of NE (Number of Entities) and NC (Number of C-activities) for the executive's information and end with RETURN; and

2. (50000-) must initialize the model and set values of variables and starting conditions including possibly scheduling the first event using GOSUB 500. If no event is scheduled, the model may be activated by a C-activity's tests being satisfied. It must end with RETURN.

Finalization

Any statistics can be printed out and final calculations of averages, etc., can be done here. It is the final subroutine of the simulation run and must end in RETURN.

Schedule

This subroutine (at line 500) schedules an entity (number EN) to do some B-activity (number BN) after a time (ET) from now. For example:

EN = 5: BN = 2: ET = 50: GOSUB = 500

when issued at the time TN = 20 will cause activity B2 to be entered for entity 5 at time 70. Entity 5 is busy until then.

2.2 Adding a display phase

So now you have written and run your simulation model you want it to produce something more interesting while it is running. A list of activities completed may help you debug your model but will not convince any one else that the answers it produces are valid. Let us instead show a picture of the model as it runs. We do this by adding an update-screen module into the simple executive used in Sec. 2.1 to give the executive of Fig. 2.5 which also has modifications to the system parts of the initialization and B-phase as described in Sec. 3.2. The model initialization and B- and C-activities will also need additions to describe the picture to be displayed and the changes as they occur.

Initialization
REPEAT
   Time Advance
   When end reached, finalization and stop
   B-phase
   C-phase
   Update screen

Fig. 2.5 Picture executive structure.

The simple launderette model

For the initial launderette example of Fig. 2.2 we would like to see a representation of the washer showing when it is busy and when free. We also want to see how many customers are queuing for it. The picture of Fig. 2.6 gives us these things and also shows the current time. The washer is represented by ■ when busy and □ when free so it is busy in Fig. 2.6. Customers (each represented by *) are either immediately below the washer if they are using it or in a queue shown vertically to its left if they are waiting. The current time is given at the bottom of the picture in hours and minutes.

WASHER

TIME IS NOW 0 HOURS 23 MINUTES

Fig. 2.6 Picture display for simple launderette.

The initial picture

How do we produce this picture? The picture executive (Sec. 3.2) provides us with the additional subroutine GOSUB 600 and 700, which draw and erase the symbol representing entity EN. The symbols available include all those provided by the character generator described in Sec. 1.4. The additional variable names required for the launderette model are listed in Table 2.5 and the extra lines of code in Fig. 2.7.

Table 2.5 Additional variable names for picture model of simple launderette

HO	Hours part of simulation time
LX(EN)	Position of entity EN on screen X axis
LY(EN)	Position of entity EN on screen Y axis
MI	Minutes part of simulation time
RS(EN)	Representative symbol for entity EN

```
1026  REM  MOVE CUSTOMER FROM QUEUE TO WASHING
1028  VTAB Q + 3: HTAB 18: PRINT " "
1030  VTAB 4: HTAB 20: PRINT  CHR$ (42)
1070 RS(EN) = 127: GOSUB 600: REM  DRAW WASHER BUSY

11035  REM  DRAW NEW CUSTOMER
11040  VTAB Q + 3: HTAB 18: PRINT  CHR$ (42)

12020 RS(EN) = 4: REM  WASHER SYMBOL = FREE
12025  VTAB 4: HTAB 20: PRINT " "

20000  REM  MODEL INFORMATION TO UPDATE DISPLAY
20010 HO =  INT (TN / 60):MI = TN - HO * 60
20020  VTAB 24: HTAB 18: PRINT HO" HOURS "MI" MINS ";: HTAB 1:
   RETURN

50040 EN = WM:LX(EN) = 20:LY(EN) = 3:RS(EN) = 4
50050  GOSUB 600: REM  DRAW FREE WASHER TOP CENTRE
50060  VTAB 1: HTAB 18: PRINT "WASHER": REM  LABEL WASHER
50070  VTAB 24: HTAB 6: PRINT "TIME IS NOW 0 HOURS 0 MINS";:
   HTAB 1
```

Fig. 2.7 Additional code for picture model of simple launderette.

Before the model simulation starts, the model initialization section (50000 onwards) of our program uses GOSUB 600 to draw the washer. This is on screen line number three so the statement LY(EN) = 3 is required (50040). The position along this horizontal line is set by the statement LX(EN) = 20 to put the washer in the middle of the screen. The other piece of information needed by the executive is the number of the desired symbol. At the beginning the washer will be idle and represented by □ which has a symbol number of 4. This is achieved by the statement RS(EN) = 4.

The accompanying label for the washer is done by a normal print statement (50060). The executive allows for printing on the graphics screen by employing the character generator. VTAB and HTAB are used to position the label as necessary. In this example VTAB 1 is required to put the label on the top line and HTAB 18 to position it horizontally.

The time is entered in hours and minutes, initially at line 50070. It is updated as the simulation runs by calculating the values in a subroutine (20000–20020) from the executive's count of time units which is held in TN. The unit used in the launderette is one minute. The semicolon and HTAB 1 are required to prevent the screen scrolling after printing on the bottom line.

Changing the picture

The picture changes as alterations are made by the simulation activities. Each time the washer becomes busy (in activity C1: START WASH, 1000 onwards) its symbol is changed to ■ by the statement RS(EN) = 127 (after defining EN in 1050) and GOSUB 600 is used to draw the new entity (1070). No change of position is required so LY(EN) and LX(EN) do not need to be altered. There is no need to erase the previous symbol as the new one will overwrite it anyway.

When the washer becomes free (in B2 END WASH, 12000 onwards) the same procedure is applied except that RS(EN) is set to 4 to draw the 'free' symbol (12020). Here there is no need to define EN within the activity. Each B activity is entered having an associated entity EN whose previous symbol is already erased. GOSUB 600 is also called automatically by the executive for each entity linked to a B-activity performed. In B2 this entity is the washer. As the customers are not held as permanent entities in this simple version of the model, the above system cannot be used to display them on the screen or remove them. The customer using the washer is removed by line 12025 which prints a space at that position on the screen.

When a customer is added to the queue (in activity B1: ARRIVAL 11000 on) an additional customer symbol is required. Its position vertically will depend on the number in the queue. If the queue variable (Q) is updated first then this position will be $Q + 3$. Horizontally the queue is just before the washer at position number 18. The symbol number for * is 42 so line 11040 draws a new customer.

Customers are removed from the queue in activity C1 START WASH and this time it is simpler to remove them from the picture (1028) before taking them from the queue variable (Q) (1035). The customer symbol has to be redrawn in the position immediately below the washer symbol (1030).

Examples

Modify your program examples from Sec. 2.1 to add a display phase to each. The lines of Fig. 2.7 are all that are needed to modify the example of Fig. 2.2. Where the customer queue is extending indefinitely, you will have to decide how to display the customers who will not fit in the vertical queue of the initial

47

model or, alternatively, stop the simulation run. Use the picture executive of Sec. 3.2 with the character generator to run your new programs. This is the simple executive (Sec. 3.1) modified by Figs 3.12, 3.14–19, using the machine code programs of Fig. A2.4 and a character generator stored as in Appendix 2. Run your simulation (having saved it), using the program of Fig. 3.19. Press any key while the simulation runs to switch modes, from seeing each symbol drawn and erased separately to seeing each time beat shown at one instant. To see this more clearly, you can add a delay (FOR I = 1 TO 500: NEXT) before making the washer busy in C1 START WASH.

Summary: Subroutines written ⊦ modeller

B- and C-activities
As in Sec. 2.1 with the addition of the display changes, using RS(EN), LX(EN), and LY(EN). GOSUB 600 and 700 are needed for C-activities and any entity not linked to the relevant B-activity.

Initialization
1. (45000-) As in Sec. 2.1.
2. (50000-) As in Sec. 2.1 with picture initialization using RS(EN) etc. as above and GOSUB 600 and 700.

Finalization
As in Sec. 2.1.

Display, remove entity (GOSUB 600, 700)
The subroutine at line 600 *displays* entity EN symbol (or shape) number RS(EN) at horizontal position LX(EN) and vertical position LY(EN).

The subroutine at line 700 *removes* any symbol (or shape) at LX(EN), LY(EN).

Model information to update display (e.g., simulation time)
This subroutine starts at line 20000. It must specify both the information to be displayed and the lines at which it should be displayed. Calculations can also be included. For the executive with the character generator, information can be placed anywhere on the screen. Otherwise it must appear in lines 21–24. If line 24 is used the statement should end in ';:HTAB1' to prevent the text screen scrolling up one line. The subroutine must be included (and end with RETURN) even if no information is to be displayed.

Simulation with a display on a PET

The same lines of code are required to draw symbols using GOSUB 600 except for the use of RS(EN) to hold the symbol number. On the PET the symbols are available directly from the keyboard so no numbers are required and the statement RS$(EN) = " " will cause a filled square to be drawn. All the symbols can be entered directly in RS$ or used in normal PRINT statements.

The PET BASIC does not have VTAB and HTAB so the cursor movements for PRINT statements have to be programmed from the home position to the correct vertical position. Then TAB may be used to find the correct position horizontally. For example the washer label will be printed: PRINT "■": PRINT TAB(18); "WASHER".

The customers are placed and removed using the following POKE statements, as PRINT statements always appear on the visible screen (see subsection 3.2.1):

```
1028   POKE AD + 40* (Q + 3) + 18, 32
1038   POKE AD + 181, 42
11040   POKE AD + 40* (Q + 3) + 18,42
12025   POKE AD + 181, 32
```

The time initialization (50070) is reduced to 'TIME IS'; because of the different screen copying arrangements in the executive, which is the simple one of Sec. 3.1 (with no %) modified by Figs 3.12, 3.16, and 3.20–23.

2.3 Interacting with your simulation

From the picture of Sec. 2.2 you can see how your simulation changes as time moves forward. It is at this point that you may well think of variables you would like to play with to see the effect of different values on the behaviour of the system. This is achieved on the Apple II by associating particular variables with the games paddles provided. We have found from experience that a different type of display is required to make the most of this experimentation.

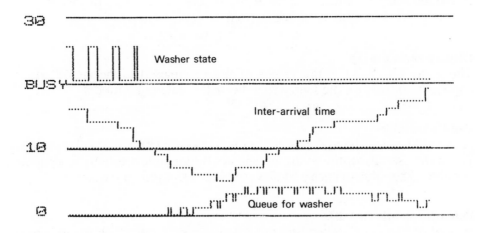

Fig. 2.8 Graphical display from simple launderette model.

Instead of a picture of the state of the whole model at only one instant of simulated time, graphs can be drawn showing the states of selected variables over a period of time (Fig. 2.8). These can be updated as the simulation runs so the changes introduced via the paddles can be based on the immediate history of the model. By this means trends can be more easily detected and the effect of the action taken (via the paddles) becomes clear.

These changes are achieved by adding two new modules into the simple executive used in Sec. 2.1, one to draw the graphs and the other to handle the interaction with the paddles. These are placed in the executive so the graphs (drawn up to the latest scheduled time) appear just before the interaction which will use their display information (Fig. 2.9).

Initialization

REPEAT

    Time Advance

    Plot graphs ⎱ end may be selected and lead
    Interaction ⎰ to finalization and stop

    B-phase

    C-phase

Fig. 2.9 Paddle/graph executive structure.

Before proceeding with this section we must clarify our use of four terms:

Model variables
A named variable which occurs in the model. This does not include any variable added for display or interaction.

Display variables (Q( ))
The array Q( ) holds the values of the variables that the model writer chooses to display on the screen to indicate the state of his model.

Paddle variables
A variable which the user has chosen to associate with a particular paddle. When the user discontinues the association the variable ceases to be a paddle variable. The value of each paddle variable is displayed on the screen.

Potential paddle variable
A pool of variables, defined by the model writer, from which the user may choose his paddle variables.

The launderette example

Returning to the simple launderette we can choose to alter both the inter-arrival and washing times, via the paddles. Then the most relevant variables for display are the number of customers in the washer queue and the state (busy or idle) of the washer. We thus have to decide how to display these four variables on the screen.

Initialization

We add statements to the initialization of Fig. 2.2 to give the subroutine of Fig. 2.10. The variable names used are listed in Table 2.6. We declare the number of display and potential paddle variables (NQ and VN). The corresponding model variables need to be initialized (45050, 45060). Other additional data required are the names of the potential paddle variables, their default values, and their scaling factors for display on the screen. The display variable scaling factors and graph labels are also needed and all these must be entered in the correct order in data statements (45100–45150).

```
45000   REM   INITIALISATION-MODEL DATA
45005   REM ********************************
45010 ARR = 1:WM = 2: REM   ENTITY NUMBERS
45040 FR = 127:BUSY = 102
45050 NE = 2:NC = 1:VN = 2:NQ = 2
45060 IT = 5:WT = 15

45100   DATA  "    INTER-ARRIVAL TIME"
45110   DATA  "    WASHING TIME"
45120   DATA  5,15: REM   DEFAULT VALUES
45130   DATA  5,5: REM   PADDLE VARIABLE SCALING
45140   DATA  5,1: REM   DISPLAY VARIABLE SCALING
45150   DATA  "30","BUSY","10": REM   GRAPH LABELS
45160   RETURN

50000   REM   MODEL INIT
50005   REM ************
50010 WASHER = FR:Q = 0
50020 EN = ARR:BN = 1:ET = 3
50030   GOSUB 500: REM   SCHEDULE FIRST ARRIVAL
50040 Q(1) = 0:Q(2) = FR
50080   RETURN
```

Fig. 2.10 Model initialization for paddle/graph version of simple launderette.

Preparing the layout for the graphical display

To provide these data we must decide how we wish to arrange the display on the screen. Since the potential paddle variables are both times, they are probably best displayed with a common vertical scale. We have to decide the maximum time we shall allow to be selected via the paddles and thus displayed on the screen. There are 159 positions available vertically above zero

Table 2.6 Additional variable names for paddle/graph model of simple launderette

FN F1(I)	Function giving value of variable on paddle one
FN F2(I)	Function giving value of variable on paddle two
HO	Hours part of simulation time
IP	Paddle Number
IT	Inter-arrival Time
MI	Minutes part of simulation time
NQ	Number of display variables (usually queues)
PDL(J)	Value returned from paddle J (J = 0,1)
Q(1)	Display variable 1—queue for washer
Q(2)	Display variable 2—washer state
V(IP)	Value of variable on paddle IP for use in model
VN	Number of potential paddle variables
VV(I)	Default value of potential paddle variable I
WT	Washing Time

for the display so a maximum time of 31 for washing or inter-arrival with a scaling factor of 5 would use most of the display space for each paddle variable. Each can have a default the same as its initial value.

The same maximum and scaling is also convenient for the first display variable—the number of customers in the queue. More than 31 customers waiting in a single-washer launderette would surely be unacceptable! The simulation user will have freedom to allow the queue to build up indefinitely by his choice of arrival and washing times so the queue displayed will have to be limited (see below).

The current state of the washer (second display variable) can only have two values—'free' or 'busy'—which are set conventionally in the initialization of Fig. 2.2 to 0 and 1. All the other variables can only take display values which are multiples of 5 (having a scaling of 5). We can therefore choose display values for these two states which do not coincide with the other variables, and label one of them for clarity. The executive provides three positions for graph labels so let us use the middle one for the label 'BUSY' (at $Y = 100$) and the other two for scale values for the other variables. Then 102 is a suitable display value for the state 'busy'. 'Free' can be set at 127, to give a clearly visible difference from 'busy' without interfering with the other graphs more than necessary. Both these states can be represented directly by these values, giving a scaling factor of 1 for the state of the washer. The display variables are held in the array Q( ) as they will be queues in most simulations. Q(1), the queue for the washer, is set to zero initially and Q(2), the washer state, to free (50040).

52

Producing the display—amendments to activities

Figure 2.11 shows the additions to the activities (of Fig. 2.2) required to produce the displays. Q(1) (1037, 11040) is not allowed to exceed 31, even if the queue (Q) does. In 1050, 11010, WT and IT are used instead of 15 and 5 as they correspond to potential paddle variables and so can be varied by the user.

```
1037   IF Q < 31 THEN Q(1) = Q(1) - 1
1045 Q(2) = BUSY
1050 EN = WM:BN = 2:ET = WT
1070   REM   REMOVE THIS LINE
11010 BN = 1:ET = IT
11040   IF Q < 32 THEN Q(1) = Q(1) + 1
12020 Q(2) = FR
```

Fig. 2.11 Modifications to code for activities of paddle/graph model of simple launderette.

You may find that there is no activity associated with a particular state change you want to display. For example you might wish to split the busy state of the washer into washing and spinning. This would need a new B activity, initiated by a GOSUB 500 in C1 START WASH to change the value of the display variable Q(2) to represent spinning.

Beneath the graphical display, four text lines are available. The executive uses the bottom two of these to tell the user which variables are currently associated with the paddles and what their values are (see below). The other two lines (numbers 21 and 22) are free for any model information which is entered at program line 20000. Figure 2.12 gives the coding for this. It differs slightly from the picture version as it is used both for initializing and updating the display.

```
20000   REM   MODEL INFORMATION FOR DISPLAY
20005   REM   ****************************
20010 HO =   INT (TN / 60):MI = TN - HO * 60
20020   VTAB 22: PRINT "TIME IS NOW "HO" HOURS "MI" MINS ":
   RETURN
```

Fig. 2.12 Subroutine to enter time on graphical display for simple launderette model.

Producing the paddle interaction

To carry out the paddle interaction as the simulation runs the executive needs the modeller to supply three other pieces of information, for each potential paddle variable:

1. The relationship between a paddle variable and the value read from the corresponding paddle (NEW VARIABLE ONTO PADDLE).

2. The model variable value (or state of the model) corresponding to any paddle variable value. This may seem unnecessary but see 'More complicated interaction' below (PADDLE VALUES INTO MODEL).

3. The value (constant) assumed by a model variable when it ceases to correspond to a paddle variable (OLD VARIABLE OFF PADDLE).

1. NEW VARIABLE ONTO PADDLE. Function F1 defines the relationship between the value of paddle variable 1 and PDL(1): and F2, between paddle variable 2 and PDL(0). We have relabelled paddle 0 as paddle 2 throughout the executive. PDL( ) gives an integer in the range 0–255; see Appendix 1.

For our simple launderette, Fig. 2.13 gives the two subroutines needed (beginning 40100 and 40200), one for each potential paddle variable. The model writer must define the same function for both paddles 1 and 2 (e.g., 40100 and 40110). This is because the user may associate any potential paddle variable with either one or the other paddle.

```
40000   REM   NEW VARIABLE ONTO PADDLE
40010   REM   ************************
40099   REM   INTER-ARRIVAL TIME
40100   IF IP = 1 THEN  DEF  FN F1(I) =  INT ( PDL (1) * 32 / 25
     6)
40101   IF IP = 1 THEN  RETURN : REM  PADDLE 1
40109   REM  PADDLE 2
40110   DEF  FN F2(I) =  INT ( PDL (0) * 32 / 256): RETURN

40199   REM  WASHING TIME
40200   IF IP = 1 THEN  DEF  FN F1(I) =  INT ( PDL (1) * 22 / 25
     6 + 10)
40201   IF IP = 1 THEN  RETURN : REM  PADDLE 1
40209   REM  PADDLE 2
40210   DEF  FN F2(I) =  INT ( PDL (0) * 22 / 256 + 10): RETURN
```

Fig. 2.13 Subroutines to put new variable on a paddle for simple launderette model.

IP is the number of the paddle. The I as the function parameter has no significance here (see Appendix 1).

We chose maxima for our paddle variables when deciding on the display. The minima assumed in Fig. 2.13 are 0 and 10 for inter-arrival and washing times respectively. The scalings (32/256, 22/256) are necessary to convert PDL( ) to numbers in the model variables range. Both variables are integers.

2. PADDLE VALUES INTO MODEL. The functions F1 and F2 produce paddle variable values (from paddles 1 and 2) which are changing in real time as the user turns the paddle knob. At every event in simulation time, before the activities are performed, these values must be entered into the model. The same values are to be displayed to the user later in real time so the executive uses V(IP), for the value of the paddle variable on paddle IP, to keep it unchanged for the two purposes.

In a simple interactive model like the launderette the values are entered into the model by a straightforward assignment of the corresponding model variables as in Fig. 2.14. Each potential paddle variable has its own sub-routine (at 25100, 25200 . . . .) which is entered when paddle IP is associated with that potential paddle variable.

```
25000   REM   PADDLE VALUES INTO MODEL
25010   REM   ************************
25100 IT = V(IP): RETURN : REM   INTER-ARRIVAL TIME
25200 WT = V(IP): RETURN : REM   WASHING TIME
```

Fig. 2.14 Subroutines to enter paddle values into simple launderette model.

3. OLD VARIABLE OFF PADDLE. When the user removes a variable from a paddle, the executive needs to have a 'default value' which the potential paddle variable will hold until it is again a paddle variable. This may be a constant value, as set in the initialization, or the modeller may wish it to depend on the final value just produced via the paddle.

In the launderette model we shall leave the inter-arrival time at the value last used, and indicate this to the executive by making it the new default, VV(1) (30100 of Fig 2.15). The washing time always reverts to the same default value supplied in the initialization (30200).

```
30000   REM   OLD VARIABLE OFF PADDLE
30010   REM   ***********************
30100 VV(1) = IT: RETURN : REM   INTER-ARRIVAL TIME
30200 WT = VV(2): RETURN : REM   WASHING TIME
```

Fig. 2.15 Subroutines to remove variable from paddle for simple launderette model.

More complicated interaction

Similar sets of subroutines are needed for any interactive simulation using the executive of Sec. 3.3. They do, however, become more complicated when you choose as a paddle variable a 'number of entities'. In a more sophisticated launderette simulation for instance, you might also wish to allow the number of washers and driers to be varied via the paddles without having any such model variables. This could be done by similar subroutines but the old variable coming off the paddle and the entering of paddle values into the model may need much more care by the modeller. Several questions will have to be answered. Do you allow a washer to be withdrawn via a paddle when it is in use? If you do what happens to the associated customer? When writing the interaction subroutines you must decide on answers to all such questions and establish rules for the introduction and withdrawal of entities. The executive does allow the modeller to prevent a user making any undesirable change and the trucks model of Sec. 4.3 give an example to show how this is done using a flag XX. (See summary below.)

55

Examples

Modify your program examples from Sec. 2.1 to add a graphical display with interaction. You will require Figs 2.10 to 2.15 for the example of Fig. 2.2. Make sure that you remove the print statements of lines 1070, 11040, and 12020 as they will interfere with the new display. Use the executive of Sec. 3.3 to run your new programs. This is the simple executive of Sec. 3.1 modified by Figs 3.25, 3.27, 3.28, 3.30 and 3.33 using the machine code programs of Figs A.2.2.(b), A.2.3.(b), and a character generator, stored as in Appendix 2. Use the program of Fig. 3.34 to run your simulation (after saving it).

Using your interactive simulation

There are three methods of interacting with your simulation, using

1. The paddle knob.
2. The paddle button.
3. The keyboard.

Paddle knob

Each paddle knob is linked to the value of its paddle variable (if any). The paddle is read twice each time step, and the value calculated, once for use in the activities (described above) and once at display time. Both these values are displayed, at each time step, below the graphs—the activities value preceding the other as it does in real time.

Paddle buttons

These are pressed to indicate to the executive a desire to change the identity of the associated variable.

The simulation stops and when the button is released the available potential paddle variables are listed on a scrolled display. The user presses the button again to accept a displayed variable. The executive then displays its value for the user to set by turning the paddle knob. He presses the button for a third time when he has the right value and the simulation proceeds.

The keyboard

Any key depressed when the simulation is running will cause the run to stop and up to three questions to be asked

1. Do you want to reset paddle 1? }
2. Do you want to reset paddle 2? } provided the paddle has an associated variable
3. Do you want to end this run?

The paddle is reset by its value being displayed for the user to change by turning the knob as above. He presses the button to indicate that his chosen value has been found so the simulation can continue.

If the user chooses to end the simulation run the modeller's chosen statistics are printed.

Summary: Subroutines written by the modeller

B- and C-activities
As in Sec. 2.1 with the addition of lines for display variables Q( ).

Initialization
1. (45000-) Includes paddle and display information, along with that of Sec. 2.1. VN and NQ must be set to the number of potential paddle and display variables (maximum 6 and 3 respectively). All model variables corresponding to potential paddle variables need to be initialized.

DATA statements are required (in the correct order) for:

(a) A label (in quotes) for each potential paddle variable—the first three characters in the quotes will appear on the screen on a separate line from the rest of the characters so these three should be left blank unless they form a complete word (e.g., NO). The length of each label should not exceed 26 characters.

(b) Potential paddle variable default values. These must be set to the initial values of the corresponding model variables (if any). If there is no corresponding model variable the default value will be the initial value of the potential paddle variable which must agree with the model initialization. For example, in a model which allows up to 6 washers, the default value could be 4 and thus 4 washers need to be set free or busy in the model initialization.

(c) Potential paddle variable scaling factors. Each paddle variable will be multiplied by its scaling factor to produce the value to be plotted which can be between 0 and 159.

(d) Display variable scaling factors—as for the paddle variables above.

(e) Graph labels for the lines drawn across the screen. There are three of these above the axis at $Y = 150, 100$, and 50. The labels are in order from the top down with up to four characters each—numbers and/or letters.

2. (50000-) As in Sec. 2.1 with the addition of the initialization of the display variables.

Finalization
As in Sec. 2.1 but with TEXT as the first statement.

Model information (e.g., simulation time)
This may be placed on the screen at lines 21 and 22. The subroutine begins at program line 20000 and is called every time step. It must be included and must end with RETURN even if no information is to be displayed.

New variable onto paddle
A subroutine is required for each potential paddle variable, beginning at line 40*n*00 where *n* is the potential paddle variable number. Each subroutine defines FN F1(I) if IP is one and FN F2(I) if IP is two where IP is the paddle number and I has no significance. These functions will define the relationship between the value returned directly by the paddle (PDL(1) or PDL(0)) and the value required for the potential paddle variable. PDL(1) and PDL(0) each return an integer value between 0 and 255. Each subroutine ends with RETURN.

Old variable off paddle
A subroutine is required for each potential paddle variable, beginning at line 30*n*00 where *n* is the potential paddle variable number. Each subroutine either:

(a) Sets the value of the corresponding model variable back to the default value previously specified (held in VV(*n*)); or

(b) Resets the default value of the corresponding model variable to the last value used in the model (as set by the user via a paddle). In this case the value of the model variable is left unchanged. The default will be used as a starting point for plotting if the model variable again corresponds to a paddle variable; or

(c) If the potential paddle variable is a 'number of entities' the subroutine must check that any change in the number (caused by reverting to a default value) is acceptable at that simulation time. Where the proposed change is unacceptable, XX is set to 1 and the subroutine RETURNs. Acceptable changes are implemented in the subroutine, adding or removing entities at appropriate points in the modelled system. Entities not currently in the model may be held in a 'waiting' array but the total number of entities in the model must never exceed the value of NE as set in the initialization.

Each subroutine ends with RETURN.

Paddle values into model
A subroutine is required for each potential paddle variable, beginning at line 25*n*00 where *n* is the paddle variable number. Each corresponding model variable is set to V(IP)—the value to be used in the activities at the next event. Where a 'number of entities' is the potential paddle variable, the value in

V(IP) may indicate a change in the 'number of entities' in the modelled system which will need to be tested and possibly implemented as in (c) above.

Each subroutine ends with RETURN.

2.4 Combined simulation

We met combined simulation briefly in Chapter 1. In this section we explore it in more detail by again looking at a simple example.

There are certain systems we model which have both a discrete aspect and a continuous one. The discrete part is already familiar, the continuous may be less so. The system may have quantities which are best modelled using continuous variables and indeed, these often are naturally represented in the form of differential equations. The counterpart of discrete events are known as 'state' events and they occur when some variable crosses a specified threshold value; for example the temperature in a room drops below 70 degrees, or the height of liquid pouring into a tank reaches the overflow level.

The method of solution of the differential equations is step-by-step, i.e., if we know all the solutions at the present time, we can determine them at a slightly later time, by making use of the differential equations formulae. We can then repeat this process, so that we arrive at the values of the variables at a much later time in a series of 'small' intermediary steps. The steps are usually necessarily small in order to maintain an accurate solution. The modeller specifies this accuracy but the executive chooses the step automatically.

Thus, the times of occurrence of state events are unpredictable at the outset of the integration, and so cannot be scheduled. The equations are step-wise integrated while the discrete clock is stopped, i.e., we know the potential time of the next discrete event (DE), but cannot advance simulation time to then until we have determined that no state event (SE) occurs before this time. If we find such an event, this may lead to the cancelling of the next discrete event, or even the scheduling of an earlier one. Of course it is possible that a number of thresholds are attained within one integration step; the state event is the earliest of them.

Combined C-activities

The C-activities of the previous sections have been extended to cater for these threshold tests. Thus, for example, consider water flowing from a tap into a tank, the changing level of which is governed by some differential equation, $\dot{y} = f(y,t)$. When the level y reaches a certain height (H) the tap is turned off. A C-activity to turn off the tap has a discrete test: IS TAP TURNED ON? and a threshold test: $Y > H$? Only when both these are satisfied is the action part entered to turn the tap off.

The C-activities with threshold tests have a dual role: first, in detecting the threshold crossings; and second, as normal C-activities to carry out the body when tests are satisfied. By detection, we mean that the presence of a relevant threshold crossing is reported to the executive. The actual time of crossing is yet to be found—the executive takes care of this. While in this detection phase the executive is prevented from going into the body of the activity by writing a statement:

IF EVNT = FALSE THEN RETURN

just before the activity body, where EVNT is a flag which is automatically set TRUE by the executive after a state event has been accurately located, or when a discrete event time has been reached.

Following the discrete and threshold tests, the modeller supplies statements for the executive to use in accurately locating the threshold time for the variables involved:

1. THRESH = TRUE, to indicate the existence of a threshold.

2. VN(ACTNUMBER,I) = VNUMBER. In any C-activity (number ACTNUMBER) there may be several threshold tests. For each of these, we must tell the executive which state variable is involved, by using a statement of the form given. Thus, for the Ith threshold test of activity ACTNUMBER, the number of the state equation is supplied through VNUMBER. For example, for activity number 5 which has two tests involving state variables 3 and 7 crossing thresholds of values 100 and 200 respectively, we must write

   VN(5,1) = 3
   VN(5,2) = 7

3. TV(VNUMBER) = the value of the threshold to be attained. For our example, these are:

   TV(3) = 100
   TV(7) = 200

Note that several continuous tests are allowed and that detection of thresholds in any particular C-activity takes place only when all its discrete tests are satisfied as only then is it relevant. This mechanism is a little ungainly but enforced by the strictures of BASIC.

The executive requires that all C-activities which involve threshold tests must be written before those which do not (in terms of line numbers, that is).

The Launderette model

Let us turn now to illustrating all this in practice with a simple example. We revert to the simplest launderette—one washer, no driers, but this time the washer malfunctions. It has an outlet filter which clogs up exponentially with time. This affects the performance of the machine by increasing its washing cycle time as the filter becomes clogged. Eventually, of course, it has to be cleaned. When this is best done is to be determined by experiment. While being cleaned (which takes 20 min) the washing machine cannot be used. Cleaning can only start when the machine finishes its cycle. The differential equation governing the clogging is given by

$$\dot{y} = A(R0 - y),$$

with $y = 0$, when the filter is clean.

This has the solution $y = R0[1 - \exp(-At)]$ so that we see the clogging approaches the level $R0$ with time, at a rate A. The filter is cleaned when the clogging exceeds a value $R1$, which is chosen at the outset by the user. The value for $R0(=5)$ is arbitrary and we choose $A = 0.01$ to give 50 per cent clogging after about 8 hours of washer use. While cleaning the filter, or the washer is idle, there is of course no clogging and the equation becomes $\dot{y} = 0$.

Equations section

Lines 100–120 of Fig. 2.16 show the BASIC code for this. Note that the derivative is represented by F(1)—a value used by the executive; and the state variable by YN(1). The variables used in the model are in Tables 2.7 and 2.8.

Table 2.7 Variables used by clogging-filter launderette model

A	clogging rate of filter
*BN	Number of B-activities to be scheduled
CLEANING	Switch indicating that cleaning is in progress
*EN	Number of Entities being scheduled
*ET	Elapsed Time before scheduled event
*EVNT	flag indicating a discrete or state event has occurred
*F(I)	derivative of Ith variable
FOULED	flag indicating filter is clogged
*N1	number of bleeps
*N2	pause between bleeps
*N3	duration of each bleep
R0	value at which filter is completely clogged
R1	value of clogging at which filter is cleaned
*THRESH	flag indicating threshold is reached
*TV(IV)	value of threshold to be obtained by state variable IV
*VN(ACT,I)	index of Ith state variable involved in activity ACT
*YN(1)	Value of state variable 1 (clogging of filter)

* values used by executive

```
100   REM   EQUATIONS
105   REM ***********************
110 F(1) = A * (RO - YN(1))
111   IF WASHER = FR OR CLEANING = TRUE THEN F(1) = 0
120   RETURN

900   REM   PLOTTING VARIABLES
950 V2(1) = Q:V2(2) = YN(1):T2 = T: RETURN

1000   REM   FILTER FOULED
1005   REM ********************
1008   IF FOULED = TRUE THEN   RETURN
1010   IF YN(1) < R1 THEN   RETURN
1020 THRESH = TRUE
1022 VN(1,1) = 1:TV(1) = R1
1025   IF EVNT = FALSE THEN   RETURN
1026   REM *******************
1030 FOULED = TRUE
1035   PRINT "FILTER FOULED"
1040 N1 = 1:N2 = 20:N3 = 20: GOSUB 300: REM     NOISES
1050   RETURN

2000   REM   C2 CLEAN FILTER
2001   REM *********************
2002   IF CLEANING = TRUE THEN   RETURN
2005   IF WASHER = BUSY THEN   RETURN
2010   IF FOULED = FALSE THEN   RETURN
2015   REM *********************
2016 CLEANING = TRUE
2020 EN = 2:BN = 3:ET = 20: GOSUB 500: REM  CLEAN FOR 20 MINS
2025   PRINT "CLEANING FILTER"
2030 N1 = 2:N2 = 20:N3 = 20: GOSUB 300: REM     NOISES
2040   RETURN

3000   REM   C1 START WASH
3005   REM ***********************
3010   IF Q <  = 0 THEN   RETURN
3020   IF WASHER = BUSY THEN   RETURN
3022   IF FOULED = TRUE THEN   RETURN
3025   REM ***********************
3035 Q = Q - 1
3040 WASHER = BUSY
3050 EN = WM:BN = 2:ET = 20 + 2 * YN(1)
3060   GOSUB 500: REM   SCHEULE END WASH
3070   PRINT "START WASH"
3080 N1 = 3:N2 = 20:N3 = 20: GOSUB 300: REM     NOISES
3090   RETURN

11000   REM   B1 ARRIVAL
11010 BN = 1:ET = 19 + 2 *  RND (1)
11020   GOSUB 500: REM    SCHEDULE NEXT ARRIVAL
11030 Q = Q + 1
11040   PRINT "ARRIVAL"
11045 N1 = 1:N2 = 10:N3 = 5: GOSUB 300: REM  NOISES
11050   RETURN

12000   REM   B2 END WASH
12010 WASHER = FR
12020   PRINT "END WASH"
12030 N1 = 2:N2 = 10:N3 = 5: GOSUB 300: REM     NOISES
12035   RETURN

13000   REM   B3 END CLEANING
13010 FOULED = FALSE:CLEANING = FALSE
13020 YN(1) = 0
13025   PRINT "END CLEANING"
13030 N1 = 3:N2 = 10:N3 = 5: GOSUB 300: REM  NOISES
13035   RETURN
```

Fig. 2.16 BASIC code for launderette model (combined).

62

Table 2.8 Additional variables used by combined executive—values to be set by modeller in model data initialization

CU	number of curves to be plotted
EPS(I)	user accuracy requirement for integration of state variable I
H	(initial) integration step
HM	maximum integration step allowed
MAX(I)	> maximum value obtained by Ith curve plotted
MIN(I)	< minimum value obtained by Ith curve plotted
NACTH	number of C-activities containing threshold tests
NS	number of state equations
SC	shift constant
TL	length of time axis in plotted time
XA	X-coordinate of origin of graph
XLN	length of X-axis in dots
YA	Y-coordinate of origin of graph
YLN	length of Y-axis in dots

Activities section

The C-activity START WASH has now become activity 3, since the new C1: FILTER FOULED contains a threshold test (1010) and must occur before the 'discrete' only activities. Otherwise, the B-activities ARRIVAL and END WASH and the C-activity START WASH are similar to the previous ones. We have changed the interarrival time to keep the queue in bounds and washing takes 20 min + an increasing amount as the filter fails (3050). An extra test is needed for the washer being fouled (3022). We have also introduced noises to help monitor the progress of the events when using graphics. There are two more C-activities. C1: FILTER FOULED and C2: CLEAN FILTER and an extra B, B3: END CLEANING. How did we arrive at these?

The filter is considered fouled when y becomes $> R1$. This must be written as a C-activity (C1). Can this same activity schedule the end of cleaning? No, because cleaning cannot commence until the washer is free: thus a second activity (C2) is needed with the two tests as in (2005,2010). Now, while the filter is fouled, there is no point in looking again for its becoming fouled; hence the test of (1008). All the body of C1 FILTER FOULED does is set FOULED true. All C2 CLEAN FILTER achieves is scheduling the end of cleaning (B3). This latter activity resets the switch FOULED and puts the value of the state variable to zero, in readiness for recommencing the integration.

The switch CLEANING is needed to prevent rescheduling of B3 END CLEANING (2020) if another customer arrives while cleaning is in progress. The filter remains fouled until cleaning ends and the washer free until the next START WASH, so 2005 and 2010 are both satisfied when a customer arrives.

63

Without 2002 this activity would be done again—incorrectly!

Note that the speaker is used by all the B and C activities to keep track of events as the model runs (1040, 2030, etc.). This is a valuable aid while debugging the model. N1, N2, and N3 are parameters to the noise routine (see Sec. 3.4) which, respectively, represent the number of bleeps, the pause between consecutive bleeps, and the duration of each. Note further lines 1020–1025; these are needed to pass the information to the executive for its use in finding the state events accurately.

While looking for thresholds EVNT is FALSE so the body of the activity is not entered; later, however, at a state or discrete event, EVNT will be TRUE, and the body will be entered if both tests 1008, 1010 are satisfied.

Initialization

To run the model we need to provide the executive with more data than those of the simple launderette. We need to provide information on the threshold C-activities; the differential or state equations; and the details of the graph plotting—size of axes, position of origin, scaling, and so on. Figure 2.17 shows the extra lines that achieve this. We chose accurately EPS = 0.001 (45060) somewhat arbitrarily—we do not require enormous precision for this illustrative example and the differential equation solver can easily achieve this accuracy with a large time step (H). We must specify an initial value for H and also for the maximum value we want the integration routine to use in our model. For the initial value of H, if we choose one relatively large, the routine will continually halve it until it can achieve an accuracy of EPS; on the other hand, if it is relatively small much more precision than required will be achieved—a waste of computing effort—and the routine will repeatedly double it until a reasonable value is found for H.

```
45055 NACTH = 1: REM   NUMBER OF THREHOLD CACTS
45059   REM   STATE EQUATION DATA
45060 NS = 1:EPS(1) = .001:YN(1) = 0:H = 10:HM = 10

45065   REM   GRAPH DATA
45070 XLN = 260:XA = 2:YLN = 130:YA = 150:TL = 550:SC = 24:CU
     = 2
45075 MAX(1) = 20:MAX(2) = 5:MIN(1) =   - 1:MIN(2) =   - 1
45080   RETURN
```

Fig. 2.17 Additional lines for model data initialization for clogging filter launderette.

For HM, the maximum step, a value must be chosen so that nothing of interest is possibly stepped over in the model.

The choice of both these values depends strongly on your system of state equations and may have to be decided from real life experience and running the model (i.e., by trial and error).

We also must specify the initial value for the state variables.

The choice of the graph parameters of 45070,5 was covered in Sec. 1.8. The executive draws the axes and prepares the graph for drawing (i.e., the first points), in the second system initialization.

The model initial conditions

The extra lines needed for the model initialization are to be found in Fig. 2.18 and merit little comment.

```
50050 CLEANING = FALSE:FOULED = FALSE
50060 RO = 5:A = .01
50065  INPUT "WHAT VALUE FOR CLEANING THRESHOLD?";R1
```

Fig. 2.18 Additional lines for model initial conditions for clogging filter launderette.

Paddle Code

As no paddles are used in this example, empty subroutines are used to return control to the executive as shown in Fig. 2.19.

```
27000   REM  PADDLE FOR DISCRETE VARS
27050   RETURN
27500   REM  PADDLE FOR CONT VARS
27510   REM *********************
27530   RETURN
```

Fig. 2.19 Paddles code—empty subroutines.

Display from the model

The results of running this simple model with $R1 = 2$ can be seen in Fig. 2.20, the upper curve being the clogging of the filter, the lower the length of queue. The cut off when the clogging reaches 2 is clearly seen, the horizontal section indicating the time it takes to clean the filter (20 min). The variables to be plotted are fed into parameters V2( ) and T2 (see Sec. 1.8) at line 950 for use by the executive.

Examples

1. Type in lines 45000—55000 of Fig. 2.2. and Figs 2.16–19 and the executive of Sec. 3.4 and get the clogging launderette working. See the effect of various values of $R1$–0, 1, 2, 3, 4, 5 say. What policy should you adopt for cleaning the filter?

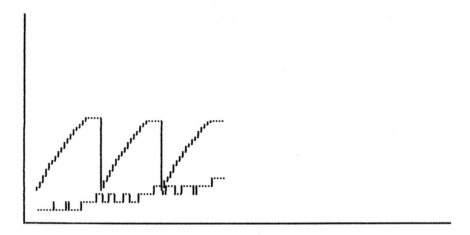

Fig. 2.20 Results of running clogging filter launderette.

2. Repeat 1, but with two washers, which clog at different rates (say $A = 0.01$ and 0.02).

Summary: Subroutines written by modeller

B-Activities
As before (Sec. 2.1).

C-Activities
These are now of two types; (a) as before; or (b) threshold. These contain tests involving continuous variables. After such tests the modeller must supply the following program statements to give the executive the information it requires in finding the time of the threshold accurately. (See above for more details.)

```
THRESH = TRUE
VN(ACTNUMBER,I) = VNUMBER
TV(VNUMBER) = value of threshold
IF EVNT = FALSE THEN RETURN
```

All the threshold activities must be placed before the discrete ones (i.e., the ones with no threshold tests).

Equations
Starting at line 100, the modeller supplies the differential equations for his state equations. YN(I) represents the Ith variable and F(I) its derivative.

Graphs (900–)
All that is required is to provide the parameters for the graph plotting routine

(see line 25000), i.e., the variables to be plotted are put in array V2( ) and the time T is put in T2.

Paddles code
1. (27000-) The linking of paddle(s) to model variables which do not effect the state equations.
2. (27500-) The linking of paddle(s) to model variables which do effect the state equations (see Sec. 4.5). Any change of paddle value must be detected and PADCH set TRUE.

Both subroutines must be included even if empty.

Initialization
In addition to these data for discrete model, the executive needs to know (a) the number of threshold activities (NACTH); (b) data on the state equations: their number, the initial values of the variables, the accuracy to within which they must be solved, the initial step length, and the maximum allowed for it; (c) data for displaying the moving graphs as detailed in Sec. 1.8.

Finalization
Any statistics can be printed out and final calculations of averages, etc., can be done here. It is the final subroutine of the simulation run and must end in RETURN.

3. Executives for running simulation programs

3.0 Introduction to the executives

In the last chapter we made a nodding acquaintance with various executives as we learned to use them for developing models. In this chapter we explore them in more detail, first learning their structure and then more intricate details of their BASIC code. Section 3.1. deals with the simple discrete executive for the APPLE (as illustrated in Sec. 2.1), the bare essentials to get you going. This is followed by the picture drawing version (Sec. 3.2), then the one with graphs and paddles (Sec. 3.3). Finally Sec. 3.4 presents details of the combined executive. We should perhaps reiterate that the modeller writes B and C-activities, some initialization, and all the finalization and that the executives are already written for him, to help him run his models.

3.1 The simple discrete executive (Fig. 3.1)

We first describe the simple executive which contains no provision for graphical or pictorial output, but which contains the bare essentials to make a simulation run. It includes a module to find the next event and also organize the calling of the B- and C-activities.

From this simple executive it is a straightforward operation to add in the different subroutines and statements to convert to either a picture version, or an interactive one with graphs. As in all our executives, there is a master subroutine which calls several subroutine modules: the four-part initialization, the time advance, and lastly the activities sections. The BASIC code is in Fig. 3.2, with a list of variables in Table 3.1.

Simple Executive

Initialization
REPEAT

    Time Advance
    When end reached, finalization and stop
    B-phase
    C-phase

Fig. 3.1 Simple discrete executive.

```
1   GOTO 60000
60000   REM   MASTER SUBROUTINE
60010   GOSUB 45000: REM   MODELLER'S DATA
60020   GOSUB 41000: REM   FIRST SYSTEM INIT
60030   GOSUB 50000: REM   MODEL INIT
60040   GOSUB 43000: REM   SECOND SYSTEM INIT
60050   GOSUB 28000: REM   TIME ADVANCE
60060   IF TN > DU GOTO 55000: REM   FINALISATION
60100   GOSUB 28200: REM   B-PHASE
60110   GOSUB 28300: REM   C-PHASE
60130   GOTO 60050
```

Fig. 3.2 Master subroutine for simple executive with its calling line (1).

Table 3.1 List of system variable names for simple executive

BN	B-activity number
DU	Duration of simulation
EN	Entity number
EN%( )	List of entities taking part at next event time
ET	Elapsed time before next event of entity
TE	Total number of entities with event at the next event time
IA	Counter of B- and C-activities
MX	Infinity (or maximum number allowed)
NB%(EN)	Number of B-activity at next event for entity EN
NC	Total number of C-activities
NE	Total number of entities
NT	Next event time
T%(EN)	Time of next event for entity EN
TN	Simulation time (Time Now)
TS	Time to start collecting statistics

Initialization (Fig. 3.3)

This is in four phases, two of which are provided by the model writer.

The first system phase (Fig. 3.4) sets up the integer arrays (41200) using NE (provided by the model writer in 45000), clears the screen for text (41090), and asks the user for the duration of the simulation and the time to start collecting statistics (41100–41110). Integer arrays (%) are used where possible to save space. 41220 sets all entities free and MX is effectively infinity (41300).

In his second stage the modeller provides (50000 onwards) the initial conditions or states for the particular system being modelled—for example, initial lengths of queues, which entity is doing what and so on. The second system phase (Fig. 3.5) caters for the model which has no events scheduled in its model initialization. It first tests for this state of affairs (43110–43120) and returns if it finds a scheduled event. If none is found the C-phase subroutine is called (43130) to initiate some scheduled events.

70

Modeller's data subroutine

First system phase

Input user data
Dimension arrays
Set entities idle
Initialize variable, set constants

Model initialization subroutine

Second system phase

Do C-activities if nothing scheduled

Fig. 3.3 Initialization.

```
41000   REM  FIRST SYSTEM INITIALISATION
41090   TEXT : CALL  - 936: REM  CLEAR TEXT SCREEN
41100   INPUT "HOW LONG DO YOU WANT TO RUN THIS SIMULATION?";DU
41109   PRINT
41110   INPUT "WHEN DO YOU WANT TO START COLLECTING STATISTICS?"
   ;TS
41200   DIM T%(NE),NB%(NE),EN%(NE)
41220   FOR EN = 1 TO NE:NB%(EN) =  - 1: NEXT : REM   SET ENTITI
   ES IDLE
41300 TN = 0:MX = 32767
42600   RETURN
```

Fig. 3.4 First system initialization subroutine for simple executive.

```
43000   REM   SECOND SYSTEM INITIALISATION
43100   REM   CHECK FOR SCHEDULED ENTITIES
43110   FOR EN = 1 TO NE: IF NB%(EN) > 0 THEN   RETURN
43120   NEXT
43130   GOSUB 28300: REM  C-ACTIVITIES
43140   RETURN
```

Fig. 3.5 Second system initialization for simple executive.

Time advance (Fig. 3.6)

This is carried out in two stages. The first finds the time of the next discrete event, which is the minimum time of all scheduled entities; and the second completes a list of all those entities with events scheduled for this same time.

The code for the subroutine is in Fig. 3.7. An entity is recognized as scheduled if it is associated with a particular B-activity, the number of which was stored in NB%(EN) by a previous call to the scheduling subroutine (Sec. 2.1). If it is not scheduled, NB%(EN) = −1 (see B-phase, below); by this device all past events are excluded from the present round.

71

Find next event time

Set simulation time to this next event time

Find entities with events scheduled at this time

Count them and store their entity numbers

Fig. 3.6 Time advance.

```
28000   REM   TIME ADVANCE
28010   REM   FIND NEXT EVENT TIME
28020 NT = MX:TE = 0
28029   FOR EN = 1 TO NE
28030   IF NB%(EN) > 0 AND T%(EN) < NT THEN NT = T%(EN)
28040   NEXT
28050 TN = NT
28060   REM   FIND ENTITES INVOLVED IN EVENTS AT THIS TIME
28070   FOR EN = 1 TO NE
28080   IF NB%(EN) < 0 THEN 28110: REM   ENTITY NOT SCHEDULED
28090   IF T%(EN) <  > NT THEN 28110: REM   NOT READY THIS TIME
28100 TE = TE + 1:EN%(TE) = EN
28110   NEXT
28120   RETURN
```

Fig. 3.7 Time advance subroutine.

The list of entities involved at the discrete event time is used by the B-phase to carry out the corresponding activities. The entities are stored from EN%(1) to EN%(TE).

B-phase (Fig. 3.8)

The executive subroutine (Fig. 3.9) carries out each B-activity (BN) corresponding to each entity which was placed on the list EN%( ) during the time advance, above. The entity is set free (NB%(EN) = -1) before going to the B-activity. This value may, of course, be changed at this event time by scheduling again in this activity or some subsequent C-activity. Note (28230) only nine B-acts are allowed and they must begin at the number 1n000.

For each entity stored by the last time advance

    Find its associated B-activity

    Cancel the association

    Do the selected B-activity

Fig. 3.8 B-phase.

C-phase (Fig. 3.10)

Every C-activity is tried in turn. Again note (28310) there is a maximum of nine, written at lines n000.

72

```
28200    REM    B-PHASE
28210    FOR IA = 1 TO TE:EN = EN%(IA):BN = NB%(EN):
         NB%(EN) =   - 1
28230    ON BN GOSUB 11000,12000,13000,14000,15000,16000,17000,
         18000,19000
28250    NEXT
28260    RETURN
```

Fig. 3.9 B-phase subroutine for simple executive.

```
28300    REM    C-PHASE
28309    FOR IA = 1 TO NC
28310    ON IA GOSUB 1000,2000,3000,4000,5000,6000,7000,8000,9000
28320    NEXT
28330    RETURN
```

Fig. 3.10 C-phase subroutine.

Schedule (Fig. 3.11)

This stores the scheduled B-activity number (BN) and the scheduled time (TN + ET) at the ENth position in their respective arrays.

```
500 NB%(EN) = BN:T%(EN) = TN + ET: RETURN
```

Fig. 3.11 Scheduling subroutine.

3.2   The picture executive

Recall from Sec. 2.2 that this executive produces a changing picture of the simulated system as the model runs—entities move their positions on the screen and may even change their representative shape or symbol to indicate an altered state. The warehouse (Sec. 4.2) and the trucks (Sec. 4.3) are model illustrations showing the event-by-event state of the systems.

We give in this section the extension of the simple executive of Sec. 3.1 to run such models. This extension allows:

1. The drawing of the picture, presented either at event times or as it is being built up;
2. Using shapes to draw it, or symbols/characters (via the character generator or the keyboard).

This display uses two 'screens', i.e., areas of memory reserved for the picture. One of these records the details as they happen of the changes of state between events, as directed by program activity statements; the other records the state of the simulation at the last event, and only changes in its entirety at each time step. Either of these 8K screens can be directed to the VDU on the Apple, so the simulation user can choose between the two. Screen 1 (HGR) has the picture which changes instantaneously with the option of 4 lines of text at the bottom. Thus, for example, the current time can be displayed even when the character generator is not in use (See Sec. 1.4.). Screen 2 (HGR 2) on the other hand does not have a text window and shows the picture as it changes.

```
1   GOTO 60000
60000    REM   MASTER SUBROUTINE
60010    GOSUB 45000: REM   MODELLER'S DATA
60020    GOSUB 41000: REM   FIRST SYSTEM INIT
60030    GOSUB 50000: REM    MODEL AND PICTURE INIT
60040    GOSUB 43000: REM   SECOND SYSTEM INIT
60050    GOSUB 28000: REM   TIME ADVANCE
60059    REM   FINALISATION
60060    IF TN > DU THEN   TEXT : POKE 54,189: POKE 55,158: GOTO 5
    5000
60100    GOSUB 28200: REM    B-ACTIVITIES
60110    GOSUB 28300: REM    C-ACTIVITIES
60120    GOSUB 24000: REM   UPDATE SCREEN
60130    GOTO 60050
```

Fig. 3.12 Master subroutine of picture executive with its calling line (1).

The amended master subroutine of the executive is in Fig. 3.12 and differs at this level, only by the inclusion of the 'update screen' module after the C-phase and the restoration of TEXT and normal printing at the end of a run. However, details of the initialization and B-phase have also changed and additional service subroutines have been added. Table 3.2 gives a list of the extra systems variables introduced.

Table 3.2   List of additional system variable names for picture executive

+RT(EN)	Rotation of shape EN
+SC(EN)	Scale of shape of entity EN
X	Position on X axis of LHS of colour block
Y	Position on Y axis of top of colour block

+ for use with shapes only

Initialization (Fig. 3.13)

Initialization has again to be in four phases, in the same order as before. Both system phases are extended to prepare for the picture display, and the modeller also has to initialize the picture.

Modeller's data subroutine

First system phase

Input user data

Dimension arrays

Set entities idle

Initialize variable, set constant

Load machine language programs

Set up screens

Model and picture initialization subroutine

Second system phase

Copy screen

Direct display (Apple) or drawing (PET)

IF no entity scheduled THEN do C-activities

Fig. 3.13 Initialization for picture executive.

The first system phase has additional lines to load machine language programs and prepare for the model-specific picture initialization on screen 2. The second phase copies the picture from screen 2 to screen 1 and displays screen 1, adding the text lines if there is no character generator.

First system phase (Fig. 3.14)

The lines marked * are to be included in the executive only if the character generator is being used; similarly with the + for the shape table.

```
41000   REM   FIRST SYSTEM INITIALISATION
41010   REM   **********************

41090   TEXT : CALL  - 936: REM   CLEAR TEXT SCREEN

41100   INPUT "HOW LONG DO YOU WANT TO RUN THIS SIMULATION?";DU
41109   PRINT
41110   INPUT "WHEN DO YOU WANT TO START COLLECTING      STATISTI
        CS?";TS
41200   DIM T%(NE),NB%(NE),EN%(NE),RS(NE),LX(NE),LY(NE)
+41210  DIM CL(NE),RT(NE),BG(NE),SC(NE)
41220   FOR EN = 1 TO NE:NB%(EN) =  - 1: NEXT : REM    SET ENTIT
        IES IDLE
41300   TN = O:MX = 32767
41500   HGR2 : HGR : REM   CLEAR GRAPHICS SCREENS

41520   REM   LOAD MACHINE CODE PROGRAMS
41530   D$ =   CHR$ (4)
*41540  PRINT D$;"BLOAD CHAR": REM   CHARACTER GENERATOR
+41550  PRINT D$;"BLOAD SHAPE": REM   SHAPE TABLE
41560   PRINT D$;"BLOAD COPYSC": REM   COPY SCREEN
+41570  POKE 232,112: POKE 233,148: REM   SHAPES ADDRESS
*41580  POKE 54,0: POKE 55,12: REM   SET UP CHARACTERS

41590   POKE  - 16299,0: POKE 230,64: POKE  - 16302,0: REM
        SCREEN 2

42600   RETURN
```

Fig. 3.14 First phase system of initialization (Apple picture version).

*lines for using character generator

+lines for using shape tables

Load and set machine code programs (41530–41580)

These are dependent on the size of the Apple being used and may need changing if it is smaller than 48K—see Appendix 2 for details. (Figures A.2.4 and A.2.5 give the machine code program COPYSC and the shape table used in the example of Sec. 4.2.) The accompanying POKE statements will also need modifying as they direct the machine to the appropriate address for the character and shape programs and the second screen (POKE 230,64). In each of these the second number after the POKE may need to be altered.

It may be useful to remind you that, for example, in POKE 232,112: POKE 233,148, the numbers are decimal and the effect is to store the hexadecimal number 9470 ($=148\times256+112$) in the consecutive addresses 232,233. This $9470 is the address 38000, the value of HIMEM required to run this executive (see below). After *41580 all subsequent printing is done by the character generator.

Statement 41590 sends all printing and drawing to screen 2. This is displayed with no text lines at the bottom, ready for the model's initial picture to be drawn as directed by the modeller in his next initialization phase.

Second System Phase (Fig. 3.15)

This phase is entered once the model has been initialized and the initial picture drawn. The result is that screen 2 is copied into screen 1 which is displayed (43020–43030). 38144 is the decimal address of COPYSC and will need changing if the program is moved to a smaller machine. When no character generator is in use the modeller's information will have to be printed at the bottom of the screen in normal text. In this case the bottom four lines are so designated (43040). If the character generator is used, then this information, of course, can be placed anywhere on the video screen.

```
43000     REM   SECOND SYSTEM INITIALISATION
43010     REM ***************************
43020     CALL 38144: REM   COPY SCREEN 2 TO 1
43030     POKE  - 16300,0: POKE  - 16304,0: REM   DISPLAY SCREEN 1

+ 43040   POKE  - 16301,0: REM   DISPLAY TEXT LINES

43100     REM   CHECK FOR SCHEDULED ENTITIES
43110     FOR EN = 1 TO NE: IF NB%(EN) > 0 THEN   RETURN
43120     NEXT
43130     GOSUB 28300: REM  C-ACTIVITIES
43140     RETURN
```

Fig. 3.15 Second system phase of initialization (Apple picture version).
+lines with no character generator

B-phase (Fig. 3.16)

The time advance remains the same as before so the next additions occur in the B-phase subroutine. There are only two extra lines which remove (28220) and draw (28240) the character or shape representing the entity. Because each entity involved is known to the executive and each B-activity will include a change of state of the entity this process has been made part of the system and done automatically. The C-activities do not have entities directly associated with them so nothing similar can be included in the C-phase (Fig. 3.10). The subroutine, GOSUB 600 and 700 are among the system routines described below.

```
28200   REM   B-PHASE
28210   FOR IA = 1 TO TE:EN = EN%(IA):BN = NB%(EN):NB%(EN) = - 1
28220   GOSUB 700: REM   REMOVE CHARACTER/SHAPE
28230   ON BN GOSUB 11000,12000,13000,14000,15000,16000,17000,
        18000,19000
28240   GOSUB 600: REM   DRAW CHARACTER/SHAPE
28250   NEXT
28260   RETURN
```

Fig. 3.16 B-phase (picture version).

Update screen (Fig. 3.17)

This prepares and presents the display of the simulation (see Sec. 2.2). The two POKES (24010) are required to reset COPYSC ready for use. The user has a choice: he can change from the display of screen 1 (state of simulation at last event) to screen 2 (the details as they happen of the changes of state between events) or vice versa by depressing any keyboard key. The executive always copies screen 2 to screen 1 at event times so both screens are kept up to date.

Change from screen1/screen 2 (24020–24060)

If a key is pressed (24020), a change is made. P9 is a flip-flop remembering which screen is being displayed (for screen 1, P9=0; for screen 2, P9=1). 24040 changes back to screen 2; 24050 to screen 1. If the character generator is used 24060 must NOT be included—it restores the 4 lines of text at the bottom of the screen.

```
24000   REM   UPDATE SCREENS
24002   REM   ***************
24005   GOSUB 20000: REM   DISPLAY MODELLER'S INFORMATION

24008   REM   COPY SCREEN
24010   POKE 38153,64: POKE 38156,32: CALL 38144

24015   REM   CHANGE SCREEN DISPLAYED
24020   IF  PEEK ( - 16384) < 128 THEN  RETURN : REM   NO KEY PRE
        SS
24030   POKE  - 16368,0: REM   KEYBOARD USED
24039   REM   CHANGE TO SCREEN 2
24040   IF P9 = 0 THEN  POKE  - 16299,0: POKE  - 16302,0:P9 = 1:
        RETURN
24050   POKE  - 16300,0:P9 = 0: REM CHANGE TO SCREEN 1

+ 24060 POKE  - 16301,0: REM   RESTORE TEXT
  24100 RETURN
```

Fig. 3.17 Subroutine to display information, copy screen, and change mode for Apple picture version.

+line with no character generator

System routines for modeller's use (Fig. 3.18)

The modeller uses a number of system routines, like the scheduling subroutine of the simple executive, which display characters, remove shapes, etc.

```
* 600   REM   DISPLAY CHARACTER
* 605   IF LY(EN) = 0 OR LX(EN) = 0 THEN  RETURN
* 610   VTAB LY(EN): HTAB LX(EN): PRINT  CHR$ (RS(EN)): RETURN

* 700   REM   REMOVE CHARACTER
* 705   IF LY(EN) = 0 OR LX(EN) = 0 THEN  RETURN
* 710   VTAB LY(EN): HTAB LX(EN): PRINT " ": RETURN

+ 600   REM   DISPLAY SHAPE
+ 610   IF SC(EN) = 0 THEN  RETURN : REM   NO DRAWING
+ 620   HCOLOR= CL(EN): ROT= RT(EN): SCALE= SC(EN)
+ 630   DRAW RS(EN) AT LX(EN),LY(EN): RETURN

+ 700   REM   REMOVE SHAPE
+ 710   IF SC(EN) = 0 THEN  RETURN
+ 720   HCOLOR= BG(EN): ROT= RT(EN): SCALE= SC(EN)
+ 730   DRAW RS(EN) AT LX(EN),LY(EN): RETURN

  800   REM   DRAW BLOCK
  810   FOR II = Y TO Y + B: HPLOT X,II TO X + A,II: NEXT : RETURN
```

Fig. 3.18 Additional system subroutines for Apple picture version.

*lines required using characters for entity states

+lines required using shapes for entity states

Display character (*600)

This uses the character's ASCII number, stored in RS(EN), and its co-ordinates stored in LX(EN) and LY(EN).

Display shape (+600)

The five parameters for the DRAW command are found in the arrays CL( ), RT( ), SC( ), LX( ) and LY( ). Their values have been placed there as a result of B or C-activities or in the initialization.

Remove character, shape (700)

A space is used to remove characters; and the colour is set to that of the background to remove shapes.

Running picture simulation on the Apple II (Fig. 3.19)

The storage addresses of the machine language programs have already been mentioned. To allow the model to use as much space as possible, the start address of the program coding has also been adjusted. This cannot, of course, be done within the actual program so a separate program must run the executive the first time the machine is switched on or after reset. Subsequent runs can be done normally as the address will remain set. The opportunity is also taken to set HIMEM, to prevent the program overwriting the machine code programs.

```
5   REM  PROGRAM TO RUN PICTURE SIMULATIONS
10    TEXT
20    HIMEM: 38000
30    POKE 24575,0: POKE 103,0: POKE 104,96
40    INPUT "WHAT IS THE NAME OF YOUR PROGRAM?";A$
50    PRINT  CHR$ (4);"RUN";A$
60    END
```

Fig. 3.19 Program to run picture simulations.

3.2.1   PET picture executive (Fig. 3.12)

The simple executive of Sec. 3.1 and the picture one above with some modifications, also run on a PET. The graph/paddle alternative, of course, cannot since our PET has neither paddles nor high-resolution graphics. We shall not repeat the simple executive as such but include it in the description of the picture one, from which one can extract it, if desired, keeping an eye on the above for guidance. The master subroutine is the same except for the omission of the TEXT and POKE commands of 60060.

The modifications from Apple to PET are fairly minor as both have the 6502 microprocessor, but the two 1K screens are used differently. On the PET only screen 1 (the visible screen) can be displayed, though drawing can be directed to either screen 1 or screen 2. The printing, on the other hand, will always go to the visible screen (as on the Apple with no character generator). The drawing is directed to one screen or the other by use of the parameter AD. The drawing then may be seen as it appears if directed to the visible screen or at each time beat when the invisible screen picture is copied onto the visible one. PETs already have a good range of symbols so neither the shapes nor the character generator machine code programs are needed. % denoting INTEGERS on the Apple are not required on the PET and so are simply omitted. Thus the time advance, and B and C phase routines, for example, are the same as on the Apple but with the % signs removed.

The system variable names used are almost the same as those on the Apple. All those of the **simple** executive are included with the single omission of %. The additions for the PET picture drawing are given in Table 3.3. RS$( ) is used instead of RS( ) because the symbol can be entered directly from the keyboard instead of having to find the correct ASCII number for RS( ).

Table 3.3 Additional variables for PET picture version

A	Length of horizontal side of colour block
B	Length of vertical side of colour block
+BG(EN)	Background colour entity EN
+CL(EN)	Colour of shape of entity EN
LX(EN)	X-coordinate of entity EN
LY(EN)	Y-coordinate of entity EN
P9	Mode switch for picture
	= 0—display picture at each event only
	= 1—display picture as it is being drawn
RS(EN)	Number of representative symbol or shape for entity EN
AD	Address immediately below memory area being used for drawing picture
C$	Character from keyboard to change mode of operation
LX(EN)	Position on X axis for symbol of entity EN
LY(EN)	Position on Y axis for symbol of entity EN
RS$(EN)	Representative symbol for entity EN

First system initialization (Fig. 3.20)
We use a PET with cassettes instead of discs so the machine code program for the screen swapping is simply POKEd into place, using DATA statements (41510–41530). This is the only machine code program required and is virtually the same as COPYSC.

AD (41540)
The address AD is set to that immediately below the visible screen, ready for the system subroutines GOSUB 600, GOSUB 700 which draw and remove the symbols. This allows the picture to be initialized on the visible screen as before.

80

```
41000 REM SYSTEM INIT 1
41005 REM **************

41100 INPUT":HOW LONG DO YOU WANT TO RUN THIS        SIMUL
ATION";DU
41110 PRINT:INPUT"WHEN DO YOU WANT TO START COLLECTING    S
TATISTICS";TS
41120 DIM T(NE),NB(NE),EN(NE),RS$(NE),LX(NE),LY(NE)

41130 FOR I=1TO NE:NB(EN)=-1:NEXT:REM SET ALL ENTITIES IDLE

41300 TN=0:MX=999999:PRINT":"

41500 REM LOAD SCREEN SWAP MACHINE CODE PROGRAM
41510 DATA 169,52,141,17,232,162,4,160,0,185,0,128,153,0,50
200,208,247,238,69
41520 DATA 3,238,72,3,202,208,236,169,60,141,17,232,96
41530 FOR I=826TO858:READ J:POKE I,J:NEXT

41540 AD=32767: REM DIRECT DRAWING TO VISIBLE SCREEN
42600 RETURN
```

Fig. 3.20 First system phase of initialization (PET picture version).

Second system initialization (Fig. 3.21)

The screen copying is carried out, this time to the invisible screen. Instead of changing the screen displayed, as on the Apple, the destination of the drawing is changed via AD. This has the same effect, as on the Apple, of displaying a screen which will not change during a time beat. The address used for AD may need to be altered to take advantage of a large machine. The associated parameter N is the 50 in the data statement of 41510 (Fig. 3.20). With AD at $2799, the second screen memory starts at 12800 (which is 50 × 256), and goes to $3823. The relationship between the value (N) in the data statement (now 50) and AD is thus:

$$AD = N \times 256 - 1$$

AD and N can be changed to hold the second screen memory in any 1K of memory otherwise unused. N occurs at two other places in the executive, lines 24005 and 24060 in Fig. 3.22. AD occurs in lines 43020 (Fig. 3.21) and 24000–24050.

```
43000 REM SYSTEM INIT 2
43005 REM **************
43010 SYS(826):REM COPY TO INVISIBLE SCREEN
43020 AD=12799:REM DIRECT DRAWING TO INVISIBLE SCREEN
43100 REM CHECK FOR SCHEDULED ENTITIES
43110 FOR EN=1 TO NE:IF NB(EN)>0 THEN RETURN
43120 NEXT
43130 GOSUB 28300:REM C-ACTIVITIES
43140 RETURN
```

Fig. 3.21 Second system phase of initialization (PET picture version).

B- and C-activities and time advance (Figs 3.7, 3.10, 3.16)

These are the same as the Apple picture version (without the %) but the B-activity phase does use different subroutines, described below.

Update screens (Fig. 3.22)

In this version, screen 2 (always invisible) is only kept up to date when drawing is directed there. Initially screen 1 (visible) is updated if necessary and the modeller's printed information is added (24005, 24010). 24020–24050 check for any keypress and change the drawing address (AD) if one is detected. If the invisible screen is to receive the new drawing, it must first be updated (24060).

```
24000 REM UPDATE SCREEN.12799=SCREEN2;32767=SCREEN1
24002 REM ***************************************
24003 REM COPY SCREEN IF NOT ALREADY VISIBLE
24005 IF AD=12799 THEN POKE 837,50:POKE 840,128:SYS(826)

24010 GOSUB 20000:REM DISPLAY INFORMATION

24015 REM SWITCH SCREENS
24020 GET C$:IF C$="" THEN RETURN:REM NO KEYPRESS
24040 IF AD=12799 THEN AD=32767:RETURN
24050 AD=12799:REM CHANGE TO INVISIBLE SCREEN

24055 REM UPDATE INVISIBLE SCREEN
24060 POKE 837,128:POKE 840,50:SYS(826)
24100 RETURN
```

Fig. 3.22 Subroutine to copy screen display information and change mode for PET picture version.

System routines for modeller's use (Figs 3.23, 3.11)

These again are similar to those of the Apple with one routine (GOSUB 600) to draw a symbol and another (GOSUB 700) to remove it. (The scheduling subroutine is the same as before.)

```
600 REM DISPLAY SYMBOL
605 IF RS$(EN)="" THEN RETURN
610 RS=ASC(RS$(EN)):IF RS<193 THEN RS=RS+64
620 IF RS<128 THEN RS=RS+64
630 POKE AD+40*(LY(EN)-1)+LX(EN),RS-128:RETURN
700 REM REMOVE SYMBOL
710 POKE AD+40*(LY(EN)-1)+LX(EN),32:RETURN
```

Fig. 3.23 Additional system subroutines for PET picture version.

With no high-resolution graphics there is no block drawing routine. The symbol drawing subroutine is complicated by the relationship between the ASCII numbers produced by the ASC function and the number required for the POKE to draw a particular symbol. Some of the symbols do not have unique numbers from ASC and so the manipulations of 610 and 620 are necessary. The address for each symbol will depend on the current screen for drawing, indicated by AD, and its coordinate in LX( ) and LY( ). The symbol removal is achieved by drawing a space (number 32) in 710.

Running simulations on the PET

No special program is required to run the executive but the second screen is not protected from overwriting. A satisfactory screen address (AD) for one model may have to be changed for a larger one.

3.3   Paddle/graph executive (Fig. 3.24)

In Sec. 2.3 we saw how this executive presents the state of the simulation as a graphical display of selected variables which unfolds as simulated time elapses. This gives much more information than can be remembered accurately from a picture display. Further, by 'connecting' variables to the paddles, a selection of the important ones can be altered during a simulation run so the effects can be observed directly. The hospital model (Sec. 4.1) used a simplified paddle/graph version of the executive, while the trucks (Sec. 4.3) illustrates the full one.

Initialization

REPEAT

   Time advance

   Plot graphs ⎱ Include opportunities for user
   Interaction ⎰ to decide to have finalization

   B-phase

   C-phase

Fig. 3.24 Paddle/graph executive.

In this section, we again extend the simple executive of Sec. 3.1 to run such models. The extension permits:

1. The association of a variable with a paddle so its value may be altered.

2. The choice of variable associated with a paddle (subject to any model restrictions).

3. The graphical display of the values of variables currently associated with paddles.

4. The graphical display of selected indicators of the state of the simulation, often queues.

```
1   GOTO 60000
60000   REM   MASTER SUBROUTINE
60010   GOSUB 45000: REM   MODELLER'S DATA
60020   GOSUB 41000: REM   FIRST SYSTEM INIT
60030   GOSUB 50000: REM   MODEL INIT
60040   GOSUB 43000: REM   SECOND SYSTEM INIT
60050   GOSUB 28000: REM   TIME ADVANCE
60060   GOSUB 26000: REM   UPDATE GRAPHICAL DISPLAY
60070   GOSUB 27000: REM   INTERACTION
60100   GOSUB 28200: REM    B-ACTIVITIES
60110   GOSUB 28300: REM    C-ACTIVITIES
60130   GOTO 60050
```

Fig. 3.25 Master subroutine for paddle/graph executive with its calling line (1).

Table 3.4 Additional system variable names for paddle/graph executive

A$	Number of paddle variable supplied by user
FNF1	Function to give value of variable on paddle 1
FNF2	Function to give value of variable on paddle 2
IP	Paddle number
K1	Starting point of redrawn graphs—28
K2	End point of redrawn graphs—38
NQ	Total number of queues for display
PP(IP)	Number of variable on paddle IP
PV(IP)	Previous value of variable on paddle IP
Q(I)	Length of queue I
SC(J)	Display scale factor for potential paddle variable J
SH	Shift factor for redrawing graphs—24
SN%(I)	Graph label I
SQ(I)	Display scale factor for queue I
SV	Number of variable selected for paddle
TI	Previous event time
V(IP)	Present value of variable on paddle IP
VN	Total number of potential paddle variables
VV(J)	Default value for potential paddle variable J
V$(J)	Name of potential paddle variable J
XE	Limit on screen for plotting along X-axis
XX	Indicator ($XX=1$) that variable cannot be removed from paddle
X1	Old plotting position on X-axis
X2	New plotting position on X-axis
Y	Length of Y-axis
Y(I)	Last position on Y-axis of queue I
YQ	Present position on Y-axis of queue
YV	Present position on Y-axis of paddle variable
YY	Position on Y-axis of scaling lines
Y$	'Y' or 'N' supplied by user in answer to question

The amended master subroutine is in Fig. 3.25 and differs, at this level, only by the inclusion of two extra modules (plot graphs and interaction) placed after the time advance and before the B- and C-activities, and the altered triggering of the finalization. However, again, details of the initialization have also changed. Plot graphs is called by GOSUB 26000 and paddle interaction by GOSUB 27000 in the main executive. Table 3.4 gives a list of the system variables introduced, additional to those of the simple executive. The variable DU of that executive is no longer required as the user has control of the run as it proceeds.

Initialization (Fig. 3.26)

As in the picture executive, this is again in four phases.

Modeller's data subroutine
(including initial values for paddle variables)

First system phase

Load machine language programs
Input user dat
Dimension arrays
Set entities idle
Initialize variables and set constants
Enter and display paddle variable names
Choose initial paddle variables
Define paddle functions and set values
Enter paddle default values and scaling
Queue scaling and graph labels
Paddle values initialize plot positions
Clear screen

Model initialization subroutine

Second system phase

Initialize plot positions for queues
Put paddle values into model
Graphics screen with clear text (4 lines)
Draw axes and label with character generator
Restore normal print and screen
Do C-Activities if nothing scheduled

Fig. 3.26 Initialization for paddle/graph executive.

First executive phase (Fig. 3.27)

```
41000    REM   FIRST SYSTEM INITIALISATION
41010    REM   *************************
41020    HGR
41021    REM
41025    REM    LOAD MACHINE CODE PROGRAMS
41030 D$ =   CHR$ (4)
41040    PRINT D$;"BLOAD CHAR"
41050    PRINT D$;"BLOAD RAPID"
41051    REM
41090    TEXT : CALL  - 936: REM   CLEAR TEXT SCREEN
41091    REM
41110    PRINT
41111    INPUT "WHEN DO YOU WANT TO START COLLECTING    STATISTICS?";TS
41200    DIM T%(NE),NB%(NE),EN%(NE),Q(NQ),V$(VN),VV(VN),SC(VN)
41201    DIM SN$(4),PV(2),V(2),PP(2),SQ(NQ),Y(NQ)
41203    REM
41220    FOR EN = 1 TO NE:NB%(EN) =  - 1: NEXT : REM    SET ENTITIES IDLE
41221    REM
41300 TN = 0:MX = 32767:Y = 158:X1 = 28:XE = 270:K1 = 28:K2 = 38:SH = 24
41301    REM
41900    REM   PADDLE INFORMATION
42000 V$(0) = "     NOTHING      "
42010    FOR J = 1 TO VN: READ V$(J): NEXT : REM   NAMES
42011    REM
42020    CALL  - 936
42021    PRINT "WHICH VARIABLES DO YOU WISH TO CONTROL?";
42022    PRINT "PLEASE GIVE THE TWO NUMBERS"
42030    FOR J = 0 TO VN: PRINT : PRINT J;"-";V$(J): NEXT : PRINT
42040    FOR IP = 1 TO 2: VTAB 17 + IP: CALL  - 958
42050    GET A$: IF  VAL (A$) > VN THEN 42050
42060 PP(IP) =  VAL (A$)
42070    PRINT "PADDLE NO.";IP;" CHANGES ";V$(PP(IP))
42080    GOSUB 27220: REM   PADDLE FUNCTION DEFINED
42090    IF PP(IP) > 0 THEN  VTAB 22: GOSUB 27170
42091    REM   USER CHOOSES PADDLE VALUE
42110    NEXT IP
42111    REM
42120    FOR I = 1 TO 1000: NEXT : REM   DELAY
42121    REM
42200    FOR J = 1 TO VN: READ VV(J): NEXT : REM    DEFAULT VALUES
42210    FOR J = 1 TO VN: READ SC(J): NEXT : REM    PADDLE SCALING
42220    FOR I = 1 TO NQ: READ SQ(I): NEXT : REM    QUEUE SCALING
42230    FOR I = 1 TO 3: READ SN$(I): NEXT : REM    GRAPH LABELS
42231    REM
42240    REM   GRAPH ZERO AND SCALE FOR PADDLE VARIABLE 'NOTHING'
42250 SN$(4) = " 0":SC(0) = 1
42290    REM   PUT PADDLE VARIABLE VALUES INTO GRAPHICAL DISPLAY
42300    IF PP(1) > 0 THEN PV(1) =  FN F1(I)
42310    IF PP(2) > 0 THEN PV(2) =  FN F2(I)
42311    REM
42500    CALL  - 936: REM   CLEAR TEXT SCREEN
42501    REM
42600    RETURN
```

Fig. 3.27 First system phase of initialization (paddle/graph version).

Machine language programs (41030–41050)

CHAR (41040) provides characters to label the graphs. RAPID (41050) redraws the graph when it reaches the edge of the screen. (See Appendix 2 for details.)

Graph parameters (41300)

Y and X1 set the positions of the axes on the screen. XE limits the graph drawing so it does not run off the right-hand side of the screen. K1, K2, and SH determine the portion of the screen to be redrawn when required.

Paddle variable names (42010)

The modeller, in the first phase of the initialization, gave the number of his potential paddle variables (VN) and their names, in a DATA statement (Sec. 2.3). The executive now reads them.

Choosing initial variable names (42020–42070)

The user is presented with a list of potential paddle variable names from which he chooses the ones he wants to associate with the paddles, if any.

Paddle functions (42080)

These are used to define the relationship between the actual paddle value and that required for the chosen paddle variable.

Paddle/graph data (42200–42240)

The modeller again provided DATA statements for these in the first phase (Sec. 2.3) except for the zero graph label and the scaling factor for the null paddle variable.

Initial display values for paddle variables (42300, 42310)

The values of many paddle variables will not affect the model initialization (as in Sec. 2.3) but the trucks model (Sec. 4.3) gives an example where there is an interaction. The executive sets the graphs to show the user's initial values in this first phase so the model writer can cancel this if he wishes to, for particular variables, in the next phase.

Second executive phase (Fig. 3.28)

The second phase is entered after the initial conditions of the model have been set up. The details of the initial queue sizes are stored for plotting. The paddle plotting variables are set for any graph drawing prior to the first interaction. The graph axes are drawn. Paddle values are entered into the model ready for the C-activities when no entities are scheduled.

```
43000   REM   SECOND SYSTEM INITIALISATION
43005   REM   ***********************
43010   REM   QUEUE SIZES FOR PLOTTING
43015   FOR I = 1 TO NQ:Y(I) = Y - SQ(I) * Q(I): NEXT

43020   REM   PADDLE VARIABLE PLOTTING
43025   V(1) = PV(1):V(2) = PV(2)

43030   HGR : CALL  - 936: REM   CLEAR SCREEN

43035   REM   PLOT SCALING LINES
43040   HCOLOR= 3: REM   WHITE
43050   FOR I = 0 TO 3:YY = 50 * I + 9
43060   HPLOT X1,YY TO 279,YY: NEXT

43070   POKE 54,0: POKE 55,12: REM   CHAR PRINT TO LABEL GRAPH
43080   FOR I = 1 TO 4: VTAB (6 * I - 4): PRINT SN$(I): NEXT

43090   POKE 54,189: POKE 55,158: REM   RESTORE NORMAL PRINT
43095   POKE  - 16301,0: REM   RESTORE TEXT LINES

43100   REM   CHECK FOR SCHEDULED ENTITIES
43110   FOR EN = 1 TO NE: IF NB%(EN) > 0 THEN   RETURN
43120   NEXT
43125   GOSUB 27410: REM   PADDLE VALUES INTO MODEL
43130   GOSUB 28300: REM   C-ACTIVITIES

43140   RETURN
```

Fig. 3.28 Second system phase of initialization (paddle/graph version).

Plot graphs (Figs 3.29, 3.30)

The plotting and printing is normally updated unless the next plot would overstep the screen. In this case, the user is asked if he wishes to continue and, if so, the graph is shifted and redrawn (Sec. 1.6); otherwise the simulation run ends. The model writer's finalization statistics are displayed with a reminder to the user how to recover the graphical display.

```
IF end of screen reached
      IF end of run reached THEN finalize
      ELSE shift screen and redraw

Plot graphs of queues
Plot graphs of paddle variables
Display modeller information
Display paddle details
```

Fig. 3.29 Plot graphs.

Recall that the graphs are drawn in straight line segments using HPLOT, and are drawn double vertically to avoid problems with colour (Sec. 1.7). The vertical segments display the changes produced by the last B- and C-activities, while the horizontal parts reflect the unchanging values of the variables between the events. The variables as calculated in the model must be scaled appropriately to fit the screen coordinates. Where a displayed queue can extend indefinitely, it may be necessary to have two variables in the model. Q( ) will hold the value for display while another variable holds the true value which may be greater than Q( ), as in the hospital model (Sec. 4.1).

```
26000   REM   UPDATE GRAPHICAL DISPLAY
26005   REM *************************
26010   IF X1 + TN - TI < XE THEN 26500: REM   SCREEN NOT FULL

26015   REM   SCREEN FULL
26020   VTAB 24: INPUT "DO YOU WISH TO CONTINUE(YES/NO)?    ";Y$
        : VTAB 23
26030   IF Y$ <  > "YES" AND Y$ <  > "NO" THEN 26020
26040   IF Y$ = "NO" THEN   TEXT : GOSUB 55000: PRINT "TYPE POKE
        -16304,0  TO REGAIN GRAPHS": END : REM   FINAL OUTPUT
26050   REM   REDRAW AND CLEAR TEXT
26060   POKE 37900,K1: POKE 37902,K2: POKE 37904,SH
26070   X1 = X1 - 168: CALL 37906: CALL 38132: CALL  - 936

26490   REM   DRAW GRAPHS
26500   X2 = X1 + TN - TI: REM   NEW POINT

26505   REM   PLOT STATE INDICATORS(QUEUES)
26510   FOR I = 1 TO NQ: HCOLOR= I
26520   YQ = Y - Q(I) * SQ(I): REM   SCALE VARIABLES
26530   HPLOT X1,Y(I) TO X1,YQ TO X2,YQ
26540   HPLOT X1 + 1,Y(I) TO X1 + 1,YQ
26550   Y(I) = YQ: REM   SAVE NEW VALUES FOR NEXT PLOT
26560   NEXT

26565   REM   PLOT PADDLE VARIABLES
26570   FOR IP = 1 TO 2: HCOLOR= 4 + IP
26580 PV(IP) = Y - PV(IP) * SC(PP(IP)):YV = Y - V(IP) * SC(PP(
        IP))
26590   HPLOT X1,PV(IP) TO X1,YV TO X2,YV
26600   HPLOT X1 + 1,PV(IP) TO X1 + 1,YV
26610 PV(IP) = V(IP): REM   SAVE NEW VALUES FOR NEXT PLOT
26620   NEXT

26630   X1 = X2:TI = TN: REM   SAVE VALUES FOR NEXT PLOT

26640   VTAB 21: GOSUB 20000: REM   PRINT MODEL INFO

26645   REM   PRINT PADDLE DETAILS,NAME OF VARIABLE AND VALUES

26650   VTAB 23
26651   IF PP(1)  > 0 THEN   PRINT V$(PP(1));"=";V(1);"...."; FN
        F1(I);"  ";
26660   IF PP(2)  > 0 THEN   PRINT V$(PP(2));"=";V(2);"...."; FN
        F2(I);"  "
26661   IF PP(2)  > 0 THEN   HTAB 1
26700   RETURN
```

Fig. 3.30 Subroutine to update graphical display.

End of screen reached (26010)

The last point was plotted at X1. The new one will be (TN–TI) units along from this at X1 + (TN − TI). If this is greater than XE, the graph must be redrawn if the run is to continue.

Redrawing (26050–26070)

Redrawing is done via the machine code described in Appendix 2 which replaces the right-hand portion of the graph at the left-hand side, and blacks out the rest of the screen (CALL 7906 and CALL 38132, respectively). The POKEs of 26060 are required to reset the machine code program. X1 is reset for the graph plotting to carry on. The width of graph redrawn will vary slightly from time to time as the redrawing will be at an event time, and these have unpredictable positions on the X axis.

Plot to new event time (26500–26620)

Each plot consists of a vertical line then a horizontal line, starting at the previous point (Sec. 1.7). Each variable has to be scaled and have its position on the Y axis determined. The past values of each variable indicating the state of the system (Q( )) is used only for plotting so the old position on the Y axis is retained rather than the actual value (26550). The old value of the paddle variable, however, is also used for interaction purposes so the actual value is retained, not the plotting position (26610).

Model information (26640)

Unlike the picture executive the modeller is restricted in the information which can be displayed. The normal allowance is only two lines as the executive uses the other two text lines for paddle information. If, in a particular model, not all the graphical area is used for plotting, the modeller could call the character generator to place information elsewhere provided normal print and the text lines were restored afterwards.

Paddle details (26650–26660)

Two values are given for each paddle variable so that the user knows both the value used at the event time just plotted and the current value. These will be different if the paddle knob has been turned between the model activities and the plotting of their effects. The semicolon and HTAB1 are needed at the end of line 26660 in case text line 24 is used. Without them both, all the text moves up one line or the next print is not at the left-hand side of the screen.

Interaction (Figs 3.31, 3.32)

From the tree of Fig. 3.31, you can see the interdependence of the interaction subroutines. These were mentioned in the introduction to this section and the modeller's subroutines were described in detail in Sec. 2.3. Apart from entering the paddle values into the model, which is always done, the user determines what else, if anything, is done in this module. The user may have pressed one or both paddle buttons or a key on the keyboard. The former leads to the exchange of variables (if possible) on the paddle concerned. The

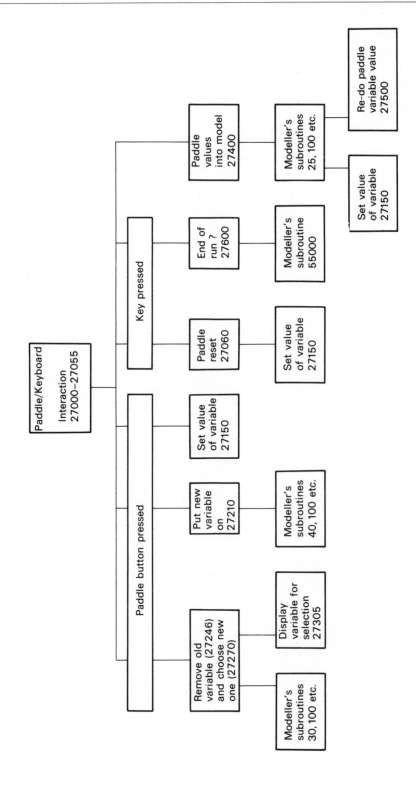

Fig. 3.31 Subroutine tree for interaction.
N.B. Subroutines 27210, 27150 are also called by the first system initialization.

latter stops the simulation for the user to be asked three questions: 'Do you want to reset paddle 1?', the same for paddle 2, and 'Do you want to finish this run?' The executive continues according to the answers received. The sub-routines' code is in Fig. 3.33.

Paddle/Keyboard Interaction

IF button pressed THEN   Exchange variables, if possible.

                                            Try to remove old variable

                                            IF successful THEN put new variable on and set its value

IF key pressed THEN   set value of paddle variable(s)

                                            AND/OR go for finalization

Enter paddle values into model

Fig. 3.32 Interaction outline.

```
27000   REM   INTERACTION VIA PADDLES AND KEYBOARD
27005   REM  ***************************************
27008   REM   IF BUTTON PRESSED, EXCHANGE VARIABLES IF POSSIBLE
27010   FOR IP = 1 TO 2
27012   IF  PEEK ( - 16285 - IP) < 128 THEN 27022: REM   BUTTON
        NOT PRESSED
27014   GOSUB 27240: REM  OLD VARIABLE OFF IF POSSIBLE
27016   IF  PEEK ( - 16285 - IP) > 127 THEN 27016: REM   WAIT FOR
        BUTTON RELEASE
27018   IF XX = 0 THEN  GOSUB 27210: GOSUB 27160: REM   NEW ONE O
        N AND SET VALUE
27020   CALL  - 936
27022   NEXT

27025   REM  IF KEY PRESSED, USER MAY RESET PADDLE VALUE OR STOP
27030   IF  PEEK ( - 16384) > 127 THEN  POKE  - 16368,0: GOSUB 2
        7060: GOSUB 27600
27040   FOR I = 1 TO 200: NEXT
27050   GOSUB 27400: REM   ENTER PADDLE VALUES
27055   RETURN

27060   REM   KEYBOARD INTERACTION:USER RESETS PADDLE VALUE
27065   REM  *********************************************
27070   FOR IP = 1 TO 2: VTAB 22
27080   IF PP(IP) = 0 THEN 27130: REM  NO VARIABLE ON PADDLE
27090   PRINT "DO YOU WANT TO RESET PADDLE ";IP;"(Y/N)?    ";
27100   GET Y$: IF Y$ <  > "Y" AND Y$ <  > "N" THEN 27100
27110   IF Y$ = "Y" THEN  HTAB 1: GOSUB 27150: REM   SET PADDLE
        VALUE
27120   CALL  - 936
27130   NEXT
27140   RETURN

27150   REM   SET VALUE OF PADDLE VARIABLE
27155   REM  *********************************
27160   VTAB 24: IF PP(IP) = 0 THEN  RETURN : REM    NO VARIABLE
        ON PADDLE

27170   PRINT "PLEASE PRESS THE PADDLE BUTTON WHEN THE VALUE IS
        RIGHT"
27180   IF IP = 1 THEN  PRINT V$(PP(1));" = " FN F1(I)" "
27185   IF IP = 2 THEN  PRINT V$(PP(2));" = " FN F2(I)" "
27190   IF  PEEK ( - 16285 - IP) > 127 THEN  RETURN : REM   BUTT
        ON PRESSED

27200   VTAB 23: GOTO 27180: REM   NO BUTTON PRESS
```

```
27210    REM    NEW VARIABLE ONTO PADDLE
27215    REM  **************************
27220    IF PP(IP) > 0 THEN  ON PP(IP) GOSUB 40100,40200,40300,40
    400,40500,40600: RETURN
27230 V(IP) = 0: RETURN : REM   NOTHING ON PADDLE

27240    REM   OLD VARIABLE OFF PADDLE
27245    REM  ***********************
27250 XX = 0
27260    IF PP(IP) > 0 THEN   ON PP(IP) GOSUB 30100,30200,30300,3
    400,30500,30600
27265  IF XX = 1 THEN  RETURN : REM   CAN'T TAKE VARIABLE OFF

27270    REM    CHOOSE NEW PADDLE VARIABLE
27275    REM  ****************************
27280    IF   PEEK ( - 16285 - IP) > 127 THEN 27280: REM    WAIT FOR
    BUTTON RELEASE
27285 SV = MX
27290    FOR J = 0 TO VN: IF J = 0 OR (PP(1) <  > J AND PP(2) <
    > J) THEN GOSUB 27310: IF SV = J THEN   CALL - 936: RETURN :
    REM   NEW VARIABLE SELECTED
27295    NEXT
27300    GOTO 27290

27305    REM   DISPLAY VARIABLE FOR POSSIBLE SELECTION

27307    REM  *********************************************
27310    PRINT : PRINT "PRESS NO.";IP;" PADDLE BUTTON IF YOU WAN
    T ";V$(J);" ON THIS PADDLE"
27320    FOR I = 1 TO 500
27321    IF   PEEK ( - 16285 - IP) > 127 THEN SV = J:PV(IP) = VV(
    J):PP(IP) = J: RETURN
27322    REM   VARIABLE SELECTED
27330    NEXT
27340    RETURN : REM VARIABLE NOT SELECTED

27400    REM    PADDLE VARIABLE VALUES INTO MODEL
27405    REM  ********************************
27410    IF PP(1) > 0 THEN V(1) =   FN F1(I)
27420    IF PP(2) > 0 THEN V(2) =   FN F2(I)
27430    FOR IP = 1 TO 2: IF PP(IP) > 0 THEN   ON PP(IP) GOSUB 25
    100,25200,25300,25400,25500,25600
27440    NEXT
27450    RETURN

27500    REM    REDO PADDLE VARIABLE VALUES FOR MODEL
27505    REM  **************************************
27510    IF IP = 1 THEN V(IP) =   FN F1(I)
27520    IF IP = 2 THEN V(IP) =   FN F2(I)
27530    RETURN

27600    REM    OPTION TO END THE RUN
27605    REM  *********************
27610    VTAB 22: PRINT "DO YOU WISH TO FINISH THIS RUN (YES/NO)"
27620    INPUT Y$: IF Y$ <  > "YES" AND Y$ <  > "NO" THEN 27620
27630    IF Y$ = "YES" THEN   TEXT : GOSUB 55000: PRINT "TYPE POKE
    -16304,0 TO REGAIN GRAPHS": END : REM        FINALISATION
27640    CALL  - 936: RETURN : REM     RUN CONTINUES
```

Fig. 3.33 Systems subroutines for interaction of user with paddle/graph simulation.

Exchange variables if possible (27008–27020, 27240–27265)

The paddle buttons are checked by PEEK (-16286) and PEEK (-16287). If one (or both) is pressed, the modeller's subroutine for that paddle variable (if any) is called to remove the variable if possible (27260). The modeller may forbid a change of variable under certain conditions, as demonstrated in the trucks model (Sec. 4.3). If this is so the indicator XX will be set to 1 and no further action is taken with that paddle. Otherwise a new paddle variable must be selected.

New variable selection (27270–27300), (27210–27230)

The executive waits for the user to release the paddle button as this is required again for the variable selection (27280). The variables not already on the paddle are displayed one at a time until the user presses the button to indicate his choice of the one currently displayed. This is noted by setting SV (previously MX, 27285) to the variable number. The text can then be cleared (27290) and the selected variable (if any) associated with the paddle via the modeller's subroutine (27220). When the user chooses to associate no variable, V(IP) is set to zero for plotting (27230).

Display of variable for possible selection (27305–27340)

The user is presented with the name of the variable and the request to press the paddle button if he wishes to select it (27310). The paddle button is checked repeatedly (27320, 27330) and if it is pressed, SV and the paddle variable number (PP(IP)) are set to the variable number (J) and the previous value for plotting purposes (PV(IP)) is set to the new variable default value (VV(I)). Control is then returned. If the button is not pressed control is eventually returned so the next variable can be tried (27340).

Set variable value (27150–27200)

By turning the paddle knob, the value of the variable displayed will change accordingly. When the user sees the correct value displayed, he presses the paddle button to confirm his choice.

Questions with simulation stopped (27060–27130), (27600–27630)

The two paddle value questions are asked in the loop 27070–27130. The option to end the run is given in 27610 and if accepted leads to the modeller's finalization (GOSUB 55000) with the reminder that the graphs can be regained by the POKE-16304,0 command.

Paddle values into model (27400–27450), (27500–27530)

The values for the graph are derived from the modeller's defined functions (F1 and F2). These values are then used by the modeller to update his model state according to the current values of the paddle variables (27430). Often this will be a simple assignment (Sec. 2.3) but numbers of entities can be changed on paddles which will require more model alteration (Sec. 4.3). Where the user has the power to choose unacceptable values for paddle variables, the modeller may need to ask for the paddle value to be reset (GOSUB 27150). In this case V(IP) must also be reset (27510–27520) so the new value can be tried as before.

Running graph/paddle simulation (Fig. 3.34)

The B- and C-activity phases and the time advance are the same as for the simple executive, but as for the picture one a program is required to run the simulation. This executive will run with the same memory available as in the picture version but larger models can be accommodated with the program of Fig. 3.34 as only one screen is needed, saving 8K of memory.

```
5   REM  PROGRAM TO RUN PADDLE/GRAPH SIMULATION
10   TEXT
20   HIMEM: 36000
30   POKE 16384,0: POKE 103,1: POKE 104,64
40   INPUT "WHAT IS THE NAME OF YOUR PROGRAM?";A$
50   PRINT  CHR$ (4);"RUN";A$
60   END
```

Fig. 3.34 Program to load and run paddle/graph simulation on the Apple II.

3.4 The combined executive

The combined executive, as mentioned in Sec. 2.4, is an extension of the simple executive, but the time advance is much more involved. Figure 3.35 shows the pseudocode of the commanding structure, and Fig. 3.36 its subroutine tree. The subroutines for plotting are given in Figs A.2.2b, and A.2.3b, the rest are in this chapter.

Initialize

    REPEAT UNTIL end reached
    Find next discrete event (DE) time
    Plot graphs for changes at events

        REPEAT UNTIL event reached
        Check continuous paddle
        Integrate one step
        Update graphs

    Check discrete paddle
    IF DE THEN do B-activities
    Do C-activities

Finalize

Fig. 3.35 Combined executive.

The time advance has been split—first the next discrete event (DE) time is found but simulation time is not advanced directly to then. Time is advanced by integrating all the variables step-by-step until an event (the next state or discrete event whichever is earlier) is reached. Recall that for combined simulation all times are real. The vertical bits of the graphs are plotted, arising from changes at events; the rest of the graphs (changes in continuous variables and horizontal portions for discrete variables) are drawn immediately after integrating one step. The paddle checking is also done in two parts: for

95

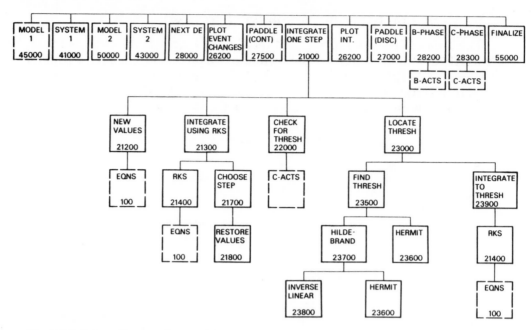

Fig. 3.36 Subroutine tree for combined executive.

discrete variables after the time advance, as before; for continuous ones, just before integrating one step. The B-activities are done only at a DE. Figure 3.37 gives the BASIC code for the master program of this executive and Table 3.5 contains a list of names used.

```
60000    REM    COMBINED EXECUTIVE
60010    REM ******************
60020    GOSUB 45000:  REM    MODELLER'S DATA
60025    GOSUB 41000:  REM    SYSTEM INIT 1
60030    GOSUB 50000:  REM    MODEL INIT
60035    GOSUB 43000:  REM    SYSTEM INIT 2

60050    GOSUB 28000:  REM    FIND NEXT DE
60060    GOSUB 26200:  REM    PLOT EVENT CHANGES

60070    GOSUB 27500:  REM    CONTINUOUS PADDLE
60080    GOSUB 21000:  REM    INTEGRATE ONE STEP
60090    GOSUB 26200:  REM    PLOT INTEGRATION CHANGES
60100    IF EVNT = FALSE THEN    GOTO 60070

60110    GOSUB 27000:  REM    DISCRETE PADDLE
60120    IF SE = FALSE THEN    GOSUB 28200:  REM    BPHASE
60130    GOSUB 28300:  REM    CPHASE
60140    IF T < DU THEN    GOTO 60050:  REM    END NOT REACHED

60150    GOSUB 55000:  REM    FINALISE
```

Fig. 3.37 Combined executive.

Table 3.5 BASIC variables used in combined executive

ACC	Accuracy requirement for integration = ½ that supplied by user
BIGDF	Flag indicating rapidly changing derivative

C1, 3, 4, 9	Integration constants
CROSS	Flag indicating threshold has been crossed
D0,D1	Inverse derivatives at left and right sides of interval—parameters to Hermite subroutine
DM	Derivative of left side of interval
DP	Derivative of right side of interval
DU	Duration of simulation
EN%(EN)	Number of entities
EPS(I)	User accuracy requirement for integration
ER(I)	Error in integration
EVNT	Flag indicating event (discrete or state) has occurred
FALSE	=0, indicates flag is false
F1(I)	Derivative of Ith state variable
H	Integration step
H1–H4	Fractional step lengths
HA–HD	Integration constants
HERM	Flag indicating Hermite method to be used
HM	Maximum step length
IN	Flag indicating integration is inaccurate
IV	Number of variable involved in threshold test
K1(I)–K4(I)	Derivatives used in integration
M0T,M1T	Temporary variable in Hermite interpolation
MAXD	Maximum of (DM,DP)
MN	Smallest number recognized by Apple
MX	Largest number representable on Apple
N	C-activity number
NACTH	Number of C-activities containing threshold tests
NB%(EN)	Number of B-activities
NC	Total number of C-activities
NE	Number of entities
NRYM	Flag indicating threshold is nearer YM than YP
NS	Number of state variables
NV	Threshold variable number
PADCHNGE	Flag indicating paddle value has just changed
SE	Flag indicating state event has occurred
SMALL	Flag indicating derivatives are small
T	Integration time
T0,T1	Time parameters of left- and right-hand sides of interval for Hermite and inverse interpolation subroutines
TA	Interpolation time
T(EN)	Time of next event for entity EN
THRESH	Flag indicating threshold has occurred
TINV	Inverse of time interval
TM	Time of last integration point (T-minus)
TN	Time of next discrete event
TNV	Inverse of time interval
TP	Time of next integration point (T-plus, of Figs 3.57, 3.60)

Table 3.5 Continued

	Number of equations too precise in Fig. 3.48
TRUE	=1; indicates flag is true
TT	Threshold time
TV(IV)	Value of threshold to be obtained for state variable IV
U0,U1 } V0,V1 }	Temporary variables used in Hermite interpolation
VCLOSE	Flag indicating YM is very close to YP
VN(ACT,I)	Index of the Ith variable involved in activity number ACT
Y	Interpolated value in Hermite interpolation Approximation to YT in Hildebrand method
Y0,Y1	Dependent variable values of left and right sides of interval—parameters to Hermite and Hildebrand routines
Y3	Third-order solution to Y for integration
YM	Dependent variable value at left side of interval—parameter to Find Threshold routine
YN(I)	Dependent variable value at time TP (new state variable)
YO(I)	Dependent variable value at time TM (old state variable)
YP	Dependent variable value at right side of interval—parameter in Find Threshold routine
YT	Dependent variable threshold value

First system initialization (Fig. 3.38)

Constants used by the executive are defined (41020). MN is the smallest number recognized by the particular computer being used. EVNT is set TRUE (see below) and TT to 'infinity' (41030) ready for use in 'integrate-one-step' and 'find-threshold-time', respectively—see below. 41245 defines constants used by the integration routine RKS.

```
41000  REM  FIRST SYSTEM INITIALISATION
41020 TRUE = 1:FALSE = 0:MX = 32767:MN = 1E - 38
41022 EVNT = TRUE
41030 TN = 0:TT = MX
41050  PRINT  CHR$ (4);"BLOAD RAPID"
41090  TEXT : HOME
41100  INPUT "HOW LONG DO YOU WANT TO RUN THIS SIMULATION?";DU
41200  DIM T(NE),NB%(NE),EN%(NE)
41220  FOR EN = 1 TO NE:NB%(EN) =  - 1: NEXT : REM   SET ENTITI
     TIES IDLE
41240  REM  INTEGRATION CONSTANTS
41245 HA = 32:HB = 8:HC = 3:HD = 1.5:C1 = 15:C3 = 3:C4 = 4:C9 =
     9
41350  RETURN
```

Fig. 3.38 First system initialization for combined executive.

Second system initialization (Fig. 3.39)

This is straightforward. The high resolution screen is switched on and the graph plotted initialized (axes drawn, first values plotted) as described in Sec. 1.8. Then the accuracy requirement supplied by the user is halved as explained in 'find-threshold-time'. The 'new' state variables are transferred to the 'old' ones in readiness for the first step of the integration, below.

```
43000   REM    SECOND SYSTEM INITIALISATION
43010   HGR
43015   GOSUB 43200: REM   GET GRAPH PLOTTING READY
43020   FOR I = 1 TO NS:EPS(I) = .5 * EPS(I):YO(I) = YN(I): NEXT
43030   RETURN
```

Fig. 3.39 Second system initialization for combined executive.

Find next DE

This is almost the same as the 'time-advance' of the simple executive (Fig. 3.7) with some small but important differences. Since all times are real the % is dropped from all mentions of T% (28030, 28090); and this is true throughout the combined executive (41200). Secondly 28090 is replaced by

28090 IF ABS(T(EN)-NT)>MN THEN 28110

where MN is smallest number representable on the microcomputer.

Plot event changes

This is simply a call of the continuous plotting subroutine (Sec. 1.8) for drawing any changes in the graphs that have occurred due to consequences of events. Time has not advanced since the last plotting (integration changes) so this simply draws vertical segments to keep the user up to date for any interaction.

Continuous paddle

This is a subroutine supplied by the modeller at 27500. The continuous paddle may effect changes in the model from one integration step to the next. This continuous executive does not contain the mechanism to change the identity of paddle variables provided by the discrete executive of Sec. 3.3. Instead it allows the modeller to supply values of the variables he has associated with the paddles and indicate if there has been any change in their values to the executive in this one subroutine. We illustrate this in Sec. 4.5. The flag PADCHNGE must be set TRUE if there has been a change, for use in 'integrate-one-step' below.

Integrate one step (Figs 3.40, 3.41)

This subroutine calls several subroutines whose functions are described later. At event times it is quite possible that the state equations enter a new regime—thus the derivatives found at the end of the previous step (which would normally be used for the next one—see below) may be unreliable; similarly, after a paddle change. After the integration, the executive tries

IF event has occurred
OR paddle value has changed THEN find new derivatives and state variable
    values
Reset event and paddle flags
Integrate using RKS
Check for threshold
IF threshold detected THEN locate earliest accurately
IF SE or DE is found THEN set EVNT flag
Update times and value

Fig. 3.40 Integrate one step.

```
21000   REM   INTEGRATE ONE STEP
21010   REM ********************
21030   IF EVNT = TRUE OR PADCHNGE = TRUE THEN   GOSUB 21200: REM
             GET NEW VALUES OF Y AND F1
21035 EVNT = FALSE:PAD = FALSE:SE = FALSE
21040   GOSUB 21300: REM   INTEGRATE USING RKS
21045   GOSUB 22000: REM   CHECK FOR THRESH
21050   IF TH = TRUE THEN   GOSUB 23000: REM   LOCATE THRESH
21052   IF SE = TRUE OR  ABS (T - TN) < MN THEN EVNT = TRUE
21055   REM  UPDATE TIME AND VALUES
21060 TM = T: FOR I = 1 TO NS:YO(I) = YN(I): NEXT
21065   RETURN
```

Fig. 3.41 Integrate one step.

every C-activity in turn (21045) to look for evidence of any threshold cross-ings (i.e., some of the relevant threshold conditions in the test heads of C-activities are satisfied). In this case THRESH is set true in the C-activity. If at least one is detected, then the time of the earliest is found accurately (21050).

21052 sets EVNT true when either a state event or a discrete event is reached. SE is set in 'locate threshold' at 23020, when any threshold crossing is found. T is the integration time which is advanced in 'RKS', the integration routine. When nearing a discrete event, a step is chosen to take T to the event time (21322 in 'integrate using RKS').

Plot integration changes

This again is simply a call of the continuous plotting subroutine, but this time to update the graphs for any changes in the variables that have been integrated one step.

Discrete paddle

Discrete paddle is supplied by the modeller at 27000. The discrete paddle may effect changes in the model from one discrete event to the next and is the equivalent of the paddle mechanism of Sec. 3.3. PADCHNGE must not be used.

B-phase and C-phase

These are the same as for the simple executive.

Get new values (Fig. 3.42)

New derivatives are found and the new values of the state variables stored in the old ones for use in starting the integration afresh. The modeller supplies the subroutine at 100 and it gives the equations for the derivatives.

```
21200   REM  GET NEW VALUES
21205   REM **************
21210   GOSUB 100: REM  NEW DERIVATIVES
21220   FOR I = 1 TO NS:YO(I) = YN(I): NEXT
21225   RETURN
```

Fig. 3.42 Get new values.

Integrate using RKS (Figs 3.43, 3.44)

Near DE means the present time plus the step length will give a time greater than the next discrete event time.

The integration advances the solution of the state equations from the old time to the new one. If the solution is inaccurate, the integration is re-done from the old time with the step length halved; otherwise the new values and times are used. Thus, the next step selected will be the present one, half of it, or double it depending on whether the solution is accurate, inaccurate or too precise.

IF near DE set step to reach it

    REPEAT UNTIL solution is accurate enough
    Integrate all equations and determine error
    Select next step

Fig. 3.43 Integrate using RKS.

```
21300   REM  INTEGRATE USING RKS
21310   REM *********************
21322   IF T + H - MN >  = TN THEN H = TN - T
21325   GOSUB 21400: REM  RKS
21340   GOSUB 21700: REM  CHOOSE NEXT STEP
21345   IF IN = TRUE GOTO 21325
21350   RETURN
```

Fig. 3.44 Integrate using RKS.

RKS (Figs 3.45, 3.46)

The integration scheme used is a Runge–Kutta–Shampine (Ellison, 1981), shown in Fig. 3.45 for a single equation $\dot{y} = f(t,y)$. Assume we have just obtained an acceptable approximation y_n to the solution at time t_n and we now proceed to find one at t_{n+1}, where $h = t_{n-1} - t_n$. The third-order integration formula gives a solution y_{n+1}. The fourth-order equation is to allow an estimate of the error to be made so that the step length (h) can be altered to produce the desired accuracy. One can then use this error estimate to improve the third-order solution: i.e., a better solution is

$$\hat{y}_{n+1} + \text{error estimate}$$
$$= \hat{y}_{n+1} + (y_{n+1} - \hat{y}_{n+1})$$
$$= y_{n+1}$$

The pair of formulae is so chosen that the function evaluations (the ks) are the same in each formula, thereby reducing the amount of computation. There are thus only four function evaluations per step, the last one also being the first of the next step (k_1 is the same as the k_5 of the previous step).

The last point is also important for the method of accurately determining the time of threshold crossings; as soon as a step is finished we have available four pieces of information for this: two values y_n, y_{n+1} and two derivatives $\dot{y}_n$, $\dot{y}_{n+1}$ (i.e., k_1, k_5). This is a little different from the usual scheme of integrations, when the derivative, $f(t_{n+1}, y_{n+1})$, becomes available only at the start of the next step, i.e., in calculating y_{n+2}. y_{n+1} is then also available for use in threshold tests if required. We, of course, integrate simultaneously all the equations supplied by the modeller.

$$y_{n+1} = y_n + \frac{h}{8}(k_1 + 3(k_2 + k_3) + k_4) \qquad \text{4th order}$$

$$\hat{y}_{n+1} = y_n + \frac{h}{32}(3k_1 + 15k_2 + 9k_3 + k_4 + 4k_5) \qquad \text{3rd order}$$

with

$$k_1 = f(t_n, y_n)$$

$$k_2 = f\left(t_n + \frac{h}{3}, y_n + \frac{h}{3}k_1\right)$$

$$k_3 = f\left(t_n + \frac{2h}{3}, y_n + \frac{h}{3}(-k_1 + 3k_2)\right)$$

$$k_4 = f(t_n + h, y_n + h(k_1 - k_2 + k_3))$$

$$k_5 = f\left(t_n + h, y_n + \frac{h}{8}(k_1 + 3k_2 + 3k_3 + k_4)\right)$$

error estimate $= y_{n+1} - \hat{y}_{n+1}$

Fig. 3.45 Runge–Kutta–Shampine integration.

102

```
21400  REM  RKS
21405  REM  *******************
21410  REM   H1=H/32: H2=H/8: H3=H/3: H4=2H/3
21415  REM   C1=15: C3=3: C4=4: C9=9
21420  REM  *******************
21425  IF H = 0 THEN  PRINT "H=0 IN RKS": STOP
21430  H1 = H / HA:H2 = H / HB:H3 = H / HC:H4 = H / HD
21435  REM  K1,K2
21440  T = TM + H3
21445  FOR I = 1 TO NS
21450  K1(I) = F(I)
21455  YN(I) = YO(I) + H3 * K1(I)
21460  NEXT
21465  GOSUB 100: REM  EQNS FOR K2
21470  REM  K2,K3
21475  T = TM + H4
21480  FOR I = 1 TO NS
21485  K2(I) = F(I)
21490  YN(I) = YO(I) + H3 * ( - K1(I) + C3 * K2(I))
21495  NEXT
21500  GOSUB 100: REM  EQNS FOR K3
21505  REM  K3,K4
21510  T = TM + H
21515  FOR I = 1 TO NS
21520  K3(I) = F(I)
21525  YN(I) = YO(I) + H * (K1(I) - K2(I) + K3(I))
21530  NEXT
21535  GOSUB 100: REM  EQNS FOR K4
21540  REM  K4,K5
21545  FOR I = 1 TO NS
21550  K4(I) = F(I)
21555  YN(I) = YO(I) + H2 * (K1(I) + C3 * (K2(I) + K3(I)) + K4(
       I))
21560  NEXT
21565  GOSUB 100: REM   EQNS FOR K5 (=K1 FOR NEXT STEP)
21570  REM  FIND 3RD ORDER Y AT NEW TIME AND ERRORS
21575  FOR I = 1 TO NS
21580  Y3 = (C3 * K1(I) + C1 * K2(I) + C9 * K3(I) + K4(I) + C4
       * F(I))
21581  LET Y3 = Y3 * H1 + YO(I)
21585  ER(I) =  ABS (Y3 - YN(I))
21590  NEXT
21595  RETURN
```

Fig. 3.46 Runge–Kutta–Shampine integration.

Select next step (Figs 3.47, 3.48)

Once the integration step is complete, the next step must be found. Each of the error estimates found is compared with the accuracy criteria which are one-half of those supplied by the modeller (Sec. 2.4). They will be either satisfactory, inaccurate, or too precise. In the first case there is no change. In the second, the step is halved and the integration redone, after resetting the old values (at t_n). In the last alternative, too much work may be being done, so the step is doubled only if all equations are too accurate. At the same time, the system is not allowed to increase the step beyond the maximum value supplied by the modeller.

Reset solution inaccurate flag and too precise counter

FOR all variables

    IF solution is inaccurate THEN set flag, halve *h*, restore integration values and RETURN

    IF solution is too precise THEN add to counter

IF all equations too precise THEN step = min (double step, maximum step)

Fig. 3.47 Select next step.

```
21700   REM   CHOOSE NEXT STEP
21710   REM ****************
21730 IN = FALSE:TP = 0
21735   FOR I = 1 TO NS
21740   IF ER(I) > EPS(I) THEN IN = TRUE:H = H / 2: GOSUB 21800:
    RETURN
21741   REM   SOLUTION INACCURATE
21745   IF ER(I) < EPS(I) / 40 THEN TP = TP + 1: REM   TOO ACCURA
    TE
21750   NEXT
21754   REM   IF EQUATIONS TOO PRECISE, STEP = MIN(DOUBLE STEP,MA
    XSTEP)
21755   IF TP = NS THEN H = 2 * H: IF H > HM THEN H = HM
21770   RETURN
```

Fig. 3.48 Select next step.

Restore values (Fig. 3.49)

Whenever the step is halved because the solution is inaccurate, the values of the derivatives at the start of the step (t_n) need to be restored. The values of the state variables have not yet been updated from t_n to t_{n+1} so they remain the same.

```
21800   REM   RESTORE VALUES
21805   REM *************
21815 T = TM
21820   FOR I = 1 TO NS:F(I) = K1(I): NEXT
21825   RETURN
```

Fig. 3.49 Restore values.

```
22000   REM   CHECK FOR THRESH
22005   REM ****************
22015 TH = FALSE
22016   FOR N = 1 TO NACTH
22017   FOR NV = 1 TO NS
22018 VN(N,NV) = 0: NEXT : NEXT
22020   FOR I = 1 TO NACTH
22021   ON I GOSUB 1000,2000,3000,4000,5000,6000,7000,8000,9000:
    NEXT
22025   RETURN
```

Fig. 3.50 Check for threshold.

Check for threshold (Fig. 3.50)

TH is set FALSE, the array VN set to zero (see next section), and each C-activity containing a threshold test is entered in turn. If any threshold test succeeds, TH is set TRUE—see Sec. 2.4 for the way one writes them. Only the first NACTH C-activities contain threshold tests.

Locate threshold accurately (Fig. 3.51, 3.52)

Once a threshold is detected, all thresholds occurring in the present step must be found accurately and the earliest one chosen as the state event. The time of each crossing is found in general by inverse Hermite interpolation (Shampine, 1978); or, in cases when this proves inaccurate (i.e., when the derivative is small or rapidly changing), an iterative method is employed (Hildebrand, 1956). Both methods require no further integration and are thus inexpensive compared to other methods that have been employed in the past (see Ellison (1981) for details).

```
Set threshold time to infinity
    FOR each continuous activity
        FOR each threshold variable in activity
        IF variable has just crossed threshold THEN find threshold
        Reset threshold variable indicator
IF SE found THEN integrate to threshold
```

Fig. 3.51 Locate threshold accurately.

```
23000   REM   LOCATE THRESHOLD
23005   REM   ****************
23011 TT = MX
23012   FOR N = 1 TO NACTH
23017   FOR NV = 1 TO NS
23019 IV = VN(N,NV): IF IV = 0 THEN   GOTO 23032: REM   NO THRESH
    OLD
23020   IF (YO(IV) - TV(IV)) * (YN(IV) - TV(IV)) < 0 THEN SE = T
    RUE: GOSUB 23500: REM  FIND THRESH
23027 VN(N,NV) = 0
23032   NEXT
23034   NEXT
23200   IF SE = TRUE THEN   GOSUB 23900: REM INTEGRATE TO THRESHO
    LD
23220   RETURN
```

Fig. 3.52 Locate threshold accurately.

First let us explain the outline of the scheme for locating the thresholds accurately. Suppose that the threshold test is simply '$y>Y$' in a certain C-activity, and that the executive, while searching for possible thresholds, has indeed found this condition to be true (it may, of course, have found others true in other C-activities). We test that it has just become true in this time step—y crossed from less than to greater than Y (23020 in Fig. 3.52). (It may have been true for some time, in which case there is no threshold crossing to be located associated with this particular test.) Now, we know the values of y and its derivatives at t_n and t_{n+1}, so we can use these to interpolate to the time of the crossing (Fig. 3.53).

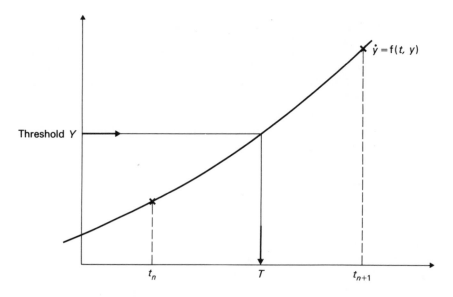

Fig. 3.53 Interpolating to find threshold time T, given y, $\dot{y}$ at times t_n, t_{n+1}.

Shampine has shown that this Hermite Interpolation is as accurate as the solution of the differential equation at the mesh points (t_n etc.). Hermite interpolation means no more than that one makes use of the derivative values as well as those of the variable itself in constructing a polynomial approximation to the curve through the known points. In our case we have only two points and thus can construct a cubic approximation as given in Fig. 3.54.

$Y = u_n y_n + u_{n+1} y_{n+1} + v_n \dot{y}_n + v_{n+1} \dot{y}_{n+1}$

where $\quad u_n \quad = [1 + 2 (T - t_n)/h]((T - t_{n+1})/h)^2$

$\qquad\quad u_{n+1} = [1 - 2 (T - t_{n+1})/h]((T - t_n)/h)^2$

$\qquad\quad v_n \quad = (T - t_n) ((T - t_{n+1})/h)^2$

$\qquad\quad v_{n+1} = (T - t_{n+1}) ((T - t_n)/h)^2$

$\qquad\quad h \quad = t_{n+1} - t_n$

Fig. 3.54 Second-order Hermite interpolation formula to find Y given T.

106

Thus, given T we can find the corresponding Y, using $y, \dot{y}$ at t_n and t_{n+1}. This, of course, is just the reverse of our problem; given Y we want to find T! So we use Inverse Hermite interpolation; that is, Hermite's formula is used with the roles of y and t interchanged, and thus with $\dot{y}$ replaced by $1/\dot{y}$. Therein lies a danger—if $\dot{y}$ is small. For this case, and also when $\dot{y}$ is changing rapidly, we switch to an iterative method, to maintain accuracy (Hildebrand (1956), p. 52). This uses inverse linear interpolation to find an approximation to T, $\bar{T}$ say. Then direct Hermite interpolation based on y_n, y_{n+1} determines $y(\bar{T})$. Then again the linear form is used but now based on $y(\bar{T})$ and y_n or y_{n+1} (whichever is the other side of Y). The cycle is repeated until the threshold is found as accurately as the user has specified.

The time found for the threshold crossing by these methods is of course subject to error and the executive must ensure that this is consistent with the accuracy demanded by the modeller and, further, that this threshold time is later than the 'precise' time of the event.

Let ϵ be the dependent variable integration accuracy sought by the modeller (Sec. 2.4); then all the executive knows is that the solution lies somewhere in the range $Y-\epsilon$, $Y+\epsilon$ and the threshold time found by the above method will be in the corresponding range T^- to T^+. Suppose it is located at $\tilde{T}$ in Fig. 3.55. Then, when the C-activities are carried out for the state event at time $\tilde{T}$, $y < Y!$, i.e., no event. The executive will of course try again and possibly and probably locate the event. However, it is conceivable (and has occurred in practice) that it finds itself in an elaborate infinite loop. To avoid this, the executive replaces the threshold value Y by $Y+\epsilon/2$ in determining the time of the crossing $y > Y$ (and by $Y-\epsilon/2$, for a threshold condition $y < Y$) and further, all integration is done to $\epsilon/2$ accuracy.

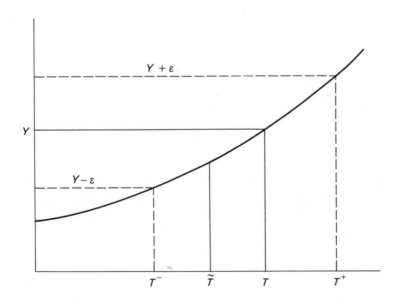

Fig. 3.55 Illustrating accuracy in determining threshold time of $y > Y$.

Returning to the BASIC of Fig. 3.52, the first NACTH C-activities contain threshold tests (23012). 23017 and 23019 sort out which threshold variables occur in each activity; and 23020 finds the threshold, if there is a crossing. TV(IV) and VN(N,NV) are given values by the modeller in the C-activity number N for state variable number IV (see Sec. 2.4). 23027 resets the array VN for future use.

Find threshold time (Figs 3.56, 3.57)

Different state variables will be involved from time to time in finding thresholds, so their values are first transferred into parameter lists for the subsequent subroutines (23512). We have adopted the convention M (for Minus) for OLD and P (for Plus) for NEW; thus, for example, YM is the parameter for YOLD. If the value of y_{n+1} (YP) is already close to the value of the threshold YT then it is assumed to be sufficiently accurately found. The rest of the subroutine follows the description of the last section.

Transfer values into parameter list
IF solution already accurate THEN RETURN
Correct threshold value to ensure crossing
IF derivative is small OR rapidly changing
    THEN use Hildebrand method
    ELSE use Hermite method
Reset Threshold time if earlier time found

Fig. 3.56 Find threshold time.

```
23500   REM FIND THRESHOLD
23505   REM **************
23506   REM    YM=YOLD: YP=YNEW: YT=THRESHOLD VALUE: DM=OLD DERI
        (VATIVE
23507   REM   DP = NEW DERIVATIVE
23512 ACC = EPS(IV):YT = TV(IV):YP = YN(IV):YM = YO(IV):DP = F
      IV)
23513 DM = K1(IV):TP = T
23515   REM   IF ALREADY ACCURATE RETURN
23520   IF ( ABS (YT - YP) < ACC) THEN TT = .5 * (TM + TP): RET
        URN
23525   REM   FOR + AND - CROSSINGS CORRECT YT TO ENSURE
23526   REM   THRESH IS PAST VT TIME
23530   IF YT >  = YM THEN YT = YT + ACC
23535   IF YT < YM THEN YT = YT - ACC
23538 SMALL = FALSE:BIGDF = FALSE
23540   IF ( ABS (DM) < 1 OR  ABS (DP) < 1) THEN SMALL = TRUE
23545 MAXD =  ABS (DM): IF  ABS (DP) > MAXD THEN MAXD = DP
23550   IF ( ABS (DP - DM) / MAXD) > .1 THEN BIGDF = TRUE
23555   IF (SMALL = TRUE OR BIGDF = TRUE) THEN  GOSUB 23700:
        REM  HILDEBRAND
23558   IF (SMALL = FALSE AND BIGDF = FALSE) THEN HERM = TRUE
23560   IF HERM = TRUE THEN DO = 1 / DM:D1 = 1 / DP:YO = TM:TO
        = YM
23561   IF HERM = TRUE THEN Y1 = TP:T1 = YP:TA = YT: GOSUB 2360
        O
23572   IF Y < TT THEN TT = Y
23575   RETURN
```

Fig. 3.57 Find threshold time.

Hermite interpolation (Figs. 3.54, 3.58)

This subroutine is written for direct interpolation, not inverse, since it is also used by the Hildebrand method. Subscripts n and $n+1$ have been represented by 0 and 1 in the BASIC code to avoid name conflicts. Similarly, we represented T of Fig. 3.54 by TA.

```
23600  REM   HERMITE INTERPOLATION
23610  REM ************************
23622 TINV = 1 / (T1 - T0)
23637 MOT = (TA - T1) * TINV:M1T = (TA - T0) * TINV
23647 U0 = (1 + 2 * TINV * (TA - T0)) * MOT * MOT
23652 U1 = (1 - 2 * TINV * (TA - T1)) * M1T * M1T
23657 V0 = (TA - T0) * MOT * MOT
23662 V1 = (TA - T1) * M1T * M1T
23667 Y = U0 * Y0 + U1 * Y1 + V0 * D0 + V1 * D1
23672  RETURN
```

Fig. 3.58 Hermite interpolation.

Hildebrand's method (Figs 3.59, 3.60)

The method is described above. The inverse linear subroutine uses parameters Y0, Y1, T0, T1 since the values fed in change from iteration to iteration. It must also be protected against very small differences in y values—if this occurs the mid-point value of time is assumed (23725). In 23730 the parameters for the Hermite interpolation are set up. (Note that Y0, for example, is also used as a parameter name in inverse linear interpolation.) NRYM is used to denote that the left-hand value of the interval should be used in the next iteration.

```
Transfer values to parameter list
REPEAT
    Perform inverse linear interpolation
    IF solution already accurate THEN record threshold time and RETURN
    Count iteration number
    Perform Hermite iteration
    IF solution accurate THEN record threshold time and RETURN
    Set up new parameter list
```

Fig. 3.59 Hildebrand method for finding threshold time.

109

```
23700   REM HILDEBRAND ITERATION
23705   REM *****************
23710 VCLOSE = FALSE:NRYM = FALSE
23712 I = 0:YO = YM:Y1 = YP:TO = TM:T1 = TP
23715   GOSUB 23800: REM   INVERSE LINEAR
23720 I = I + 1
23725   IF VCLOSE = TRUE THEN Y = (TO + T1) * .5: RETURN
23730 YO = YM:TO = TM:DO = DM:Y1 = YP:T1 = TP:D1 = DP: GOSUB 2
      3600
23731   REM   HERMITE
23735   IF  ABS (YT - Y) < ACC THEN Y = TA: RETURN : REM   SOLUT
      ION FOUND
23740   IF ( ABS (YT - YO) <  ABS (Y - YO)) THEN NRYM = TRUE
23745   IF NRYM = TRUE THEN YO = YM:TO = TM:Y1 = Y:T1 = TA
23750   IF NRYM = FALSE THEN YO = Y:TO = TA:Y1 = YP:T1 = TP
23755   GOTO 23715: REM   REPEAT ITERATION
```

Fig. 3.60 Hildebrand's method.

Inverse linear interpolation (Fig. 3.61)

```
23800   REM   INVERSE LINEAR INTERPOLATION
23805   REM *************************
23815   IF ( ABS (YO - Y1)) < MN THEN VCLOSE = TRUE: RETURN
23820 TA = TO + (YT - YO) * (T1 - TO) / (Y1 - YO)
23825   RETURN
```

Fig. 3.61 Inverse linear interpolation.

Integrate to threshold (Fig. 3.62)

Once the earliest threshold time (= state event) is found accurately, all variables must be re-integrated to this time, using the appropriate step length. Of course, the derivatives have to be restored before this is done.

```
23900   REM   INTEGRATE TO THESHOLD
23910   REM *********************
23915   REM   SET STEP TO REACH THRESHOLD AND RESTORE DERIATIVE
23920 H = TT - TM
23930   FOR I = 1 TO NS:F(I) = K1(I): NEXT
23940   GOSUB 21400: REM   INTEGRATE
23950 T = TT
23960   RETURN
```

Fig. 3.62 Re-integrate to threshold time.

Noises

We saw in Sec. 2.4 how accompanying activities with coded bleeps can help to keep track of a simulation while debugging. The subroutine to achieve this is in Fig. 3.63 and requires three input parameters: N1, N2, and N3. N1 is the number of bleeps to be emitted, the one separated from the next by a pause of N2. The duration of the bleep is N3. The PEEK of 320 by itself produces one bleep. 330 is an optional delay to separate events.

```
300  REM  NOISES
305  REM  ******************
310  FOR K1 = 1 TO N1
315  FOR K3 = 1 TO N3
320  SO =  PEEK ( - 16336)
325  NEXT
330  FOR K2 = 1 TO N2: NEXT K2
335  NEXT
340  FOR K2 = 1 TO 500: NEXT
345  RETURN
```

Fig. 3.63 Bleep producing routine.

Scheduling subroutine (Fig. 3.64)

This has the same function as in the simple executive (Fig. 3.11). But it has to be modified by changing TN to T as scheduling may take place at a state event and TN is a discrete event time only.

Running the executive

The executive and model for a combined simulation are run using the starter module of Fig. 3.34.

```
500 NB%(EN) = BN:T(EN) = T + ET: RETURN
```

Fig. 3.64 Scheduling subroutine.

References

ELLISON, D. (1981) 'Efficient Automatic Integration of Ordinary Differential Equations with Discontinuities', *Mathematics and Computers in Simulation*, **XXIII**, 12–20.

HILDEBRAND, F.B. (1956) *Introduction to Numerical Analysis*, McGraw-Hill, New York.

SHAMPINE, L.F. (1978) 'Solving Ordinary Differential Equations for Simulations', *Mathematics and Computers in Simulation*, **XX**, 204–207.

4. Examples of simulation models

4.1 Hospital model

Features included

Graphical display built up as the simulation runs.
Interaction with the simulation via the paddles.
A choice of variables for the paddles.

Introduction

This is a very simple model as can be seen from the flow diagram of Fig. 4.1. It is concerned solely with the flow of non-emergency patients through an outpatient clinic and (sometimes) an inpatient ward, as commonly found in British hospitals. The two measures of interest are the queues of patients

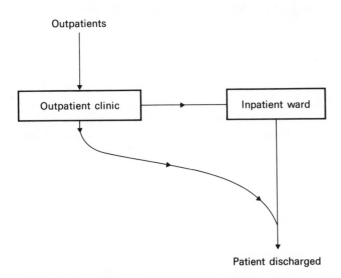

Fig. 4.1 Flow diagram of the hospital model.

which form for the outpatient clinic and for the inpatient ward. These queues are usually known as the 'waiting lists' of patients needing examination or treatment. The sizes of these lists are important because they are often used as measures of demand for any particular medical service. The aim of this simple model is to act as a learning device showing how the lists change under the varying circumstances which may occur in real life.

113

Model structure

This model does not include the standard A-B-C phases of the executive as described in Chapters 2 and 3 because it has a constant time step. An outpatient clinic is held each week and batches of patients are transferred to and from waiting lists and into the inpatient ward every week. (The changes are listed below.) This representation has proved quite adequate and the inclusion of day-to-day fluctuations would only confuse the longer-term trends.

The weekly changes, which replace the B- and C-activities of the normal executive, are given by equations adding patients to and subtracting them from the two waiting lists. The outpatient waiting list is increased by the number of outpatients seeking appointments at the clinic and decreased by the number seen. This number seen will either be the number of appointments available at the outpatient clinic or the number previously waiting if that is less. The inpatient waiting list will gain a percentage of those seen at the clinic and lose the number transferred to inpatient beds.

Allowance has to be made for the waiting lists becoming too large to be shown adequately on the graphical display. Small changes need to be seen to allow close control of the waiting lists. The display cannot therefore cope with the queues becoming very large, as they may do when the model is unstable. This problem is solved by displaying the queue at its maximum screen value (158) when the real queue exceeds this value, as in Sec. 2.3.

Coding of model changes with time

Lines 1000 and 1010 of Fig. 4.2 allow Q(1) and Q(2) to be converted from their graphical to their real values if these were too large to be represented accurately on the graph. Line 1020 calculates the number of patients (IA) to be admitted to inpatient beds. Provided there is an adequate waiting list this will be $0.14 \times$ the number of available bed-days (for example 10 beds in a

```
1000 Q(1) = Q(1) + W1
1010 Q(2) = Q(2) + W2

1020 IA = IB * 0.14: IF IA > Q(2) THEN IA = Q(2)
1030 AC = OC: IF Q(1) < OC THEN AC = Q(1)

1040 Q(1) = Q(1) + FN RN(AP) - AC:Q(2) = Q(2) + INT ( FN RN(
     AD) * AC / 100 - IA)

1050 W1 = O: IF Q(1) > 158 THEN W1 = Q(1) - 158:Q(1) = 158
1060 W2 = O: IF Q(2) > 158 THEN W2 = Q(2) - 158:Q(2) = 158
1070  RETURN
```

Fig. 4.2 Subroutine replacing the activities section for the hospital model.

Table 4.1 List of variables in simple hospital model

AC	Actual number of Appointments at outpatients Clinic
AD	Average percentage of outpatients for ADmission as inpatients
AP	Average number of Applications for outpatient appointments
FN RN(I)	Function producing Random Number between 0 and 2*I
IA	Number of Inpatients to be Admitted
IB	Number of Inpatient Bed days available per week
*NQ	Number of queues to be displayed
OC	Number of appointments available at each Outpatient Clinic
*Q(1)	First queue to be displayed—waiting list for outpatient clinic
*Q(2)	Second queue to be displayed—waiting list for inpatient beds
*VN	Number of paddle variables
W1	Excess of Waiting list 1 over displayed Q(1)
W2	Excess of Waiting list 2 over displayed Q(2)
WE	Weeks part of simulation time
YE	Year part of simulation time

* Variables used by the executive

5-day week = 50 bed-days). The multiplication by 0.14 gives a realistic figure for the weekly admissions for those bed-days. When there are insufficient patients waiting, all of them (in Q(2)) will be admitted.

Line 1030 calculates the number of patients seen at the outpatient clinic (AC) in a similar manner to line 1020; the usual number will be the number of appointments available (OC), but when there are few enough on the waiting list (Q(1)), all will be seen.

Line 1040 carries out the additions and subtractions on the waiting lists, with Q(1) gaining the number of new applications (FN RN(AP)) and losing those seen at the clinic (AC). Q(2) gains the percentage (FN RN (AD)) of AC and loses those admitted (IA).

Lines 1050 and 1060 reset Q(1) and Q(2) to values suitable for plotting (if necessary) by storing any excess in W1 and W2.

The two uses of the single function RN, viz. FN RN(AP) (Outpatient Applications) and FN RN(AD) (percentage for Admission), introduce the random change built into the model. FN RN takes the current average (number of outpatient applications (AP) or percentage of outpatients requiring inpatient admission (AD)) and multiplies it by the scaled sum of three random numbers to give realistic weekly changes. This function is defined in the initialization section, where the other variables are also given values (see Fig. 4.5).

The simulation time unit is one week and the time is displayed in years and weeks leading to the subroutine of Fig. 4.3.

115

```
20000   REM   MODEL INFORMATION
20010   REM ******************
20020   YE = 1 +   INT (TN / 52):WE = TN - 52 * (YE - 1) + 1
20030   VTAB 22: PRINT " IT IS NOW YEAR ";YE;" WEEK ";WE;" "
20040   RETURN
```

Fig. 4.3 Subroutine to display the simulation time.

The paddle variables

These are shown in Fig. 4.4. Variable 1 (AP) is used when the function call FN RN (AP) is made as described above and variable 2 (AD) is similarly used for FN RN(AD). Variables 3 (OC) and 4 (IB) appear directly in the equations.

0. Nothing.

1. The average number of new outpatient applications each week.

2. The number of outpatient appointments at the clinic each week.

3. The percentage of outpatients who require inpatient treatment.

4. The number of inpatient bed-days available each week.

Fig. 4.4 Potential paddle variables for the hospital simulation.

Initialization

The data, dimensions, and initial conditions for this model are in Fig. 4.5. The number of paddle variables is set to 4 and of queues (display variables) to 2. The names of the variables are entered as data statements to be read by the first system phase of the initialization. A further data statement gives the four default values for the paddle variables which are 15, 15, 24, and 22 respectively, each about half the maximum value allowed. The next two data statements in the first initialization include scaling factors for the display of the four paddle variables and the queues with the final one the labels for the graphs. Line 45110 initializes all the paddle variables, while 45120 defines the function FN RN discussed above. The model initialization simply gives starting values for the two waiting lists.

Interactive section of executive

As described in Secs 2.3 and 3.3 there are three sets of subroutines in this section which are specific to the model and its particular selection of paddle variables.

The array V(IP) holds the current value of paddle IP when the subroutines are called to enter the paddle values into the model variables. This gives the

116

```
45000   REM   MODEL DIMENSIONS AND DATA
45010   REM   **************************
45020   VN = 4:NQ = 2
45030   DATA  "   O/P APPLICATIONS"
45040   DATA  " % O/P FOR ADMISSION"
45050   DATA  "   O/P CLINIC SLOTS"
45060   DATA  "   INPATIENT BED DAYS"
45070   DATA  15,24,15,22: REM  DEFAULT VALUES
45080   DATA  2,2,2,2: REM  PADDLE VARIABLE SCALING
45090   DATA  1,1: REM  QUEUE SCALING
45100   DATA  "150","100","50": REM  GRAPH LABELS
45110   AP = 15:AD = 24:OC = 15:IB = 22
45120   DEF  FN RN(AP) =  INT (AP * ( RND (1) +  RND (1) +  RND
    (1)) * 0.667)
45130   RETURN

50000   REM   MODEL INIT
50005   REM   **********
50010   Q(1) = 50:Q(2) = 60
50020   RETURN

55000   RETURN
```

Fig. 4.5 Model specific initialization subroutines and finalization.

```
25000   REM   PADDLE VALUES INTO MODEL
25010   REM   *************************
25100   AP = V(IP):  RETURN
25200   AD = V(IP):  RETURN
25300   OC = V(IP):  RETURN
25400   IB = V(IP):  RETURN
```

Fig. 4.6 Subroutines for putting paddle values into model variables.

first set of four subroutines of Fig. 4.6. The executive goes to 25100 for variable 1, to 25200 for 2 and so on; IP is the number of the paddle concerned.

The subroutines for putting new variables onto the paddles are given in Fig. 4.7. (The parameter, I, is not used.)

When a variable is removed from a paddle, its value is kept the same as the final paddle value and this becomes the new default, leading to the subroutines of Fig. 4.8.

```
40000   REM   NEW VARIABLE ONTO PADDLE
40010   REM ***************************
40100   IF IP = 1 THEN   DEF   FN F1(I) =   INT ( PDL (1) * 32 / 2
    56): RETURN

40110   DEF   FN F2(I) =   INT ( PDL (0) * 32 / 256): RETURN
40200   IF IP = 1 THEN   DEF   FN F1(I) =   INT ( PDL (1) * 49 / 2
    56): RETURN

40210   DEF   FN F2(I) =   INT ( PDL (0) * 49 / 256): RETURN
40300   IF IP = 1 THEN   DEF   FN F1(I) =   INT ( PDL (1) * 31 / 2
    56): RETURN

40310   DEF   FN F2(I) =   INT ( PDL (0) * 31 / 256): RETURN
40400   IF IP = 1 THEN   DEF   FN F1(I) =   INT ( PDL (1) * 46 / 2
    56): RETURN

40410   DEF   FN F2(I) =   INT ( PDL (0) * 46 / 256): RETURN
```

Fig. 4.7 Subroutines for putting a new variable onto a paddle.

```
30000   REM   OLD VARIABLE OFF PADDLE
30010   REM *************************
30100 VV(1) = AP: RETURN
30200 VV(2) = AD: RETURN
30300 VV(3) = OC: RETURN
30400 VV(4) = IB: RETURN
```

Fig. 4.8 Subroutines to remove variable from paddle.

Running the model

The modifications to the executive of Sec. 3.3 are given in Fig. 4.9. They replace the time advance by a simple unit increment (28010) and allow the lines of Fig. 4.2 to replace both B- and C-activities. The question about statistics (41110) is also removed as there are none, the finalization subroutine at 55000 is empty (Fig. 4.5).

```
28010   TN = TN + 1 : RETURN
28020–28300   DELETED
41110   DELETED
41220   DELETED
43100–43130   DELETED
60100   GOSUB 1000
60110   DELETED
```

Fig. 4.9 Changes to executive of Sec. 3.3 needed to run hospital model.

Using the graphical display

The four graphs displayed on the screen are the waiting lists for the outpatient clinic, for the inpatient ward, and the two paddle variables which are selected from those listed in Fig. 4.4.

The model when stable with no use of the paddles produces graphs like those of Fig. 4.10. When you consider that each point on the graph represents one week (the whole X axis is 250 weeks) you can easily see how random changes can be interpreted as a long-term trend. Suppose for instance the model was at simulation time T, so that only the graphs to the left of T (representing 152 weeks), were on the screen. It would be very easy to assume that the outpatient waiting list was going to rise indefinitely from that point onwards. Unnecessary action could be taken which would appear to solve the problem as in real life. Users of the model are encouraged first to watch the simulation running without using the paddles so they can become familiar with these random variations.

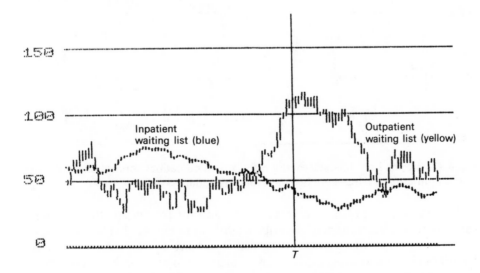

Fig. 4.10 Graphs from hospital model with no use of paddles.

As mentioned earlier the waiting lists can quickly become very large when the demand for treatment overburdens the resources available (Fig. 4.11). As the model is designed for teaching, the user is allowed to let the model become unstable by altering variables on the paddles. In 5 seconds (real time) the model can cover up to 10 time steps, so the user has to react quickly to remain in control.

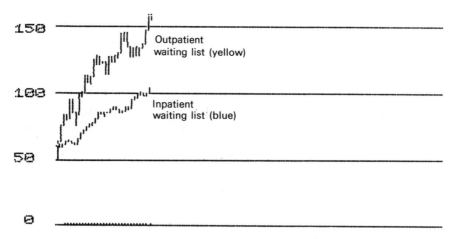

Fig. 4.11 Graphs from hospital model with demand exceeding supply.

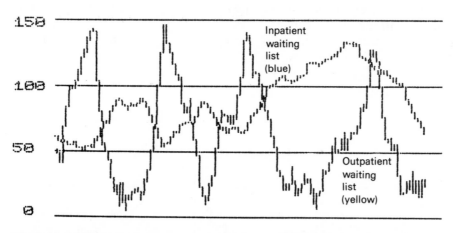

Fig. 4.12 Graphs from hospital model with varying outpatient applications, outpatient appointments, and inpatient bed days (display variables only).

To simulate response to change in demand for treatment, the number of outpatient applications can be varied slightly as in Fig. 4.12. The user is given the task of controlling the waiting lists by changing two other variables—length of clinics and available bed-days—in an acceptable manner. The temptation is to make changes too late and too large for stability to show in the figure. Only the waiting lists are displayed as the paddle variable display

120

confuses the black and white picture. Lines 26590, 26600 were deleted from the executive of Sec. 3.3 to remove the paddle variable graph.

When the screen becomes filled with the graphs, the user can choose whether to abandon that run or continue. No statistics are included in this model as the aim is simply to control the waiting lists and the success in doing this is immediately obvious to the user from the graphical display as the model runs.

4.2 Warehouse model

Features included

Use of shape table in high-resolution picture.
Use of two screens to show changes at an instant of time.
Coloured blocks to enhance picture.

Introduction

This model is more complicated than the others of this chapter so the description provides only an outline understanding of the model. The pseudocode is given for all the activities, with the BASIC subroutines for the B activities. The initialization is described with particular attention being paid to the picture but it is not detailed in either pseudocode or BASIC as it is long and repetitive. Statistics were not collected so there was no finalization. It uses the executive of Sec. 3.2 with a shape and no character generator.

The model was written for a firm investing in a new warehouse for temporary storage of components between their delivery and assembly in an adjacent factory. There are two cranes and a succession of lifting tables/conveyors to move components in and out of the warehouse. On inspecting the proposed operating system for this equipment, it was suspected that it could not handle the specified flow rates of components into and out of the warehouse. By modelling it with a picture display (illustrated in Fig. 4.13) you can watch the warehouse operating and see the system slowly seize up as the input path becomes permanently blocked by the flow of components out of storage into the factory.

In the diagrammatic layout of Fig. 4.14 the components enter the system as input for storage, at the top right-hand side. If they are faulty they go out again to the bottom right as rejects. Otherwise they are labelled for one of the two cranes and move left until they reach the appropriate crane input junction. The cranes move from one end of their tracks to the other to load a component and take it into storage, or to bring an item out from storage. An item from storage goes via the crane output path (below left of the crane track) to the main path at the bottom of the diagram. This is followed left into the factory at the left-hand side of the picture.

There are 33 entities in the model, each of which has its own place in the physical warehouse and most of which are pieces of fixed equipment for

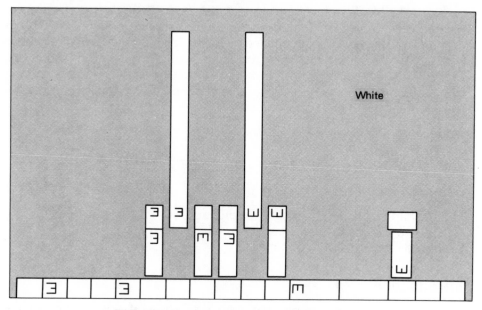

TIME NOW IS 209 MIN 28 SEC AFTER START

Fig. 4.13 Picture display from warehouse model.
　Warehouse cranes and lifting tables to move components in and out of warehouse
Ⅎ Component being moved (rotation indicates path to be followed).
Storage area is at the top of the picture, input is from the right and output to the left at the bottom.

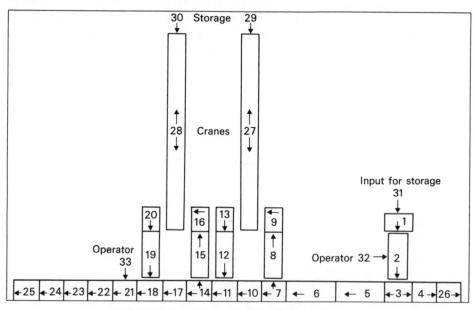

TIME NOW IS 209 MIN 28 SEC AFTER START

Fig. 4.14 Diagrammatic layout of warehouse model with entity numbers.

122

moving components around the warehouse. The locations of these entities are shown in Fig. 4.14, with each entity represented by its number.

Entities numbered 1 to 26 are lifting tables each of which can take one component at a time and pass it on in the direction of the arrow on the diagram. Numbers 27 and 28 are cranes which again take components one at a time, from 9 and 16 into storage and out of storage to entities 13 and 20. To do this they must load, move, and unload, each of which takes time. Entities 29 to 31 are 'arrival machines' which produce components at scheduled times: 29 and 30 provide items for the cranes to take out of storage and 31 delivers them as input to the warehouse. No account is required of the components' stay in storage in this model so the 'arrival machines' just produce unidentified components. Entities 32 and 33 are operators required to inspect components at 2 and 21. They may be either 'permissive' or 'obstructive', i.e., components may pass easily or may be held at that position for a period. Components leave the system as rejects at entity 26 or go into the factory for assembly at 25. They are given a 'destination label' as they arrive so when an item reaches a junction point it can be directed according to its label. Components need directing as they leave entities 3, 7, and 14.

The picture (Fig. 4.13) produced by the simulation has the same layout as Fig. 4.14. It has a white background with blocks of black representing the lifting tables and crane tracks. Each crane is represented by a shape (Fig. 1.5) which both changes colour and moves from one end of the track to the other to indicate what the crane is doing. Each component is also represented by a shape which moves from block to block as it is passed between entities. The shape rotation indicates the component's 'destination label' and its colour tells whether it is moving or has stopped because its path is blocked. Further shapes represent the operators with the colour changing to show their 'permissive' or 'obstructive' state. The shape is drawn automatically for entities associated with B-activities (Sec. 2.2).

Model structure

The model has nine B-activities and three C-activities, one of which (C1) is necessarily extremely long and complicated as it handles the start of all component movements off lifting tables (entities 1–26) except where this requires a crane. The model detects the state of each table from the colour of the component on it. The remaining two C-activities start up a crane (i.e., start loading or start a move to pick up) (C2) and start loading entity 1 from input (C3). Their pseudocode is in Fig. 4.15(a).

The only function of B-activities B5–B7 is to contribute to the display. The B-activities of the crane are thus separated into four parts instead of being written as one single activity. These are: a crane finishes moving to pick-up (B5), finishes loading (B6), and finishes moving loaded (B7). These activities follow one another automatically and always end with the crane being unloaded (B4), ready for the next activity. It is only when unloaded that the crane becomes unscheduled without being rescheduled immediately as in

123

C1 MOVING OFF LIFTING TABLES

IF there are any stationary components (recorded in B2)

FOR each lifting table from 26 downwards excluding 9 and 16

IF	(i)	it contains a stationary component
AND	(ii)	its next destination is free (this may involve up to 3 other tables)
AND	(iii)	(given there is an operator) he is permissive
THEN	(i)	schedule table to finish clearing (B3)
	(ii)	display table clearing (yellow shape)
	(iii)	schedule receiving table to finish loading (if any) (B2)
	(iv)	transfer destination label to next table (if any)
	(v)	subtract one from stationary component count
	(vi)	If there are any more stationary components try next table.

C2 START CRANE (see Fig. 4.15b)

FOR each free crane

IF crane is at storage end, out table is free and there is a component in storage:

THEN	(i)	schedule finish loading (B6)
	(ii)	display crane loading (purple)
	(iii)	subtract one from queue in storage
	(iv)	try next crane

ELSE IF there is a component for storage:

THEN EITHER (crane not at storage end)

(i)	schedule finish of loading (B6)
(ii)	display loading (purple)
(iii)	schedule end of clearing of 9 or 16 (B3)
(iv)	display 9 or 16 clearing (yellow shape)
(v)	try next crane

OR (crane at storage end)

(i)	schedule crane to finish moving to pick-up (B5)
(ii)	display crane moving to pick-up (purple)
(iii)	try next crane

ELSE IF out table is free and there is a component in storage:

THEN	(i)	schedule crane to finish moving to pick-up (B5)
	(ii)	display crane moving to pick-up (purple)
	(iii)	subtract one from queue in storage
	(iv)	try next crane

C3 LOAD TABLE ONE

IF table one is free and a component is waiting

    (i)   remove component from input queue

    (ii) schedule table to finish loading (B2)

    (iii) choose destination label.

Fig. 4.15(a) C-activities of warehouse model.

IF crane at storage end THEN take component out of storage if possible

ELSE IF there is a component for storage THEN put it in.

ELSE (crane at warehouse end) go to fetch any component from storage

Fig. 4.15(b) Summary of pseudocode for activity C2.

B5–B7, so B4 is the only crane B-activity needed for the actual running of the model.

The first B-activity (B1) is responsible for scheduling arrivals by entities 29–31. The next two concern entities 1–26 and finish loading them with a component (B2) and clearing them again (B3). The last two B-activities are to change the state of the operators—B8 makes them permissive and B9 obstructive. These B-activities are summarized in Fig. 4.16, and their BASIC code is given in Fig. 4.17 using the variables listed in Table 4.2. Remember that each entity EN involved in a B-activity automatically has its shape redrawn by the executive of Sec. 3.2. The B-activity just has to change the position (using LX(EN) and LY(EN)), the colour (using CL(EN)), and the rotation (using RT(EN)) if required. If EN is altered in an activity, as it is in B5, the shape will be drawn automatically for the new EN.

B1 A NEW ARRIVAL FROM STORAGE OR FOR INPUT

    (i)   schedule next arrival (B1)

    (ii) add one to queue

B2 A LIFTING TABLE FINISHES LOADING

    (i)   display as loading (blue shape)

    (ii) add one to count of stationary components (for C1)

Fig. 4.16 B-activities of warehouse model (*continues*).

B3 A LIFTING TABLE FINISHES CLEARING

(i)   display as clear (no shape inside)

B4 A CRANE FINISHES UNLOADING

(i)   display as free (green)

B5 A CRANE FINISHES MOVING TO PICK-UP COMPONENT

(i)   schedule finish of loading (B6)
(ii)   IF crane at output end THEN move to storage end
        AND subtract 1 from queue in storage
(iii) IF crane at storage end THEN move to output end
        AND schedule finish of clearing 9 or 16 (B3)
        AND display clearing 9 or 16 (yellow shape)

B6 A CRANE FINISHES LOADING

(i)   schedule finish of moving (B7)
(ii)   display crane loaded (white)

B7 A LOADED CRANE FINISHES MOVING

(i)   schedule finish of unloading (B4)
(ii)   move crane on display
(iii) schedule finish of loading of entry 13 or 20 if at that end (B2)

B8 AN OPERATOR BECOMES PERMISSIVE

(i)   schedule operator to become obstructive (B9)
(ii)   display operator permissive (black)

B9 AN OPERATOR BECOMES OBSTRUCTIVE

(i)   schedule operator to become permissive (B8)
(ii)   display operator obstructive (blue)

Fig. 4.16 B-activities of warehouse model (*continued*).

```
11000   REM   B1 NEW ARRIVAL
11005 AM% = EN - 28
11010 BN = 1:ET = AR%(AM%): GOSUB 500
11020 Q%(AM%) = Q%(AM%) + 1
11030   RETURN

12000   REM   B2 A LIFTING TABLE LOADED
12010 CL(EN) = OC%
12020 NS% = NS% + 1
12999   RETURN

13001   REM   B3 A LIFTING TABLE CLEARED
13010 CL(EN) = UC%
13020   RETURN

14000   REM   B4 A CRANE UNLOADED
14010 CL(EN) = ID%
14999   RETURN

15001   REM   B5 CRANE MOVED TO PICK UP
15010 BN = 6:ET = PU%: GOSUB 500
15015   REM   CRANE MOVED TO STORAGE END
15020   IF LY(EN) = 105 THEN LY(EN) = 15:I = EN - 26
15021   IF LY(EN) = 105 THEN Q(I) = Q(I) - 1: RETURN
15025   REM   CRANE MOVED FROM STORAGE END
15030 LY(EN) = 105: GOSUB 600
15040 LT = 9: IF EN = 28 THEN LT = 16
15050 EN = LT:BN = 3: GOSUB 500
15060 CL(EN) = CL%
15999   RETURN

16001   REM   B6 A CRANE LOADED
16010 BN = 7:ET = MV%: GOSUB 500
16020 CL(EN) = LO%
16030   RETURN

17000   REM   B7 CRANE MOVED LOADED
17010 BN = 4:ET = DR%: GOSUB 500
17020   IF LY(EN) = 105 THEN LY(EN) = 15: RETURN
17025   REM   CRANE MOVED TO STORAGE END
17030 LY(EN) = 105: GOSUB 600
17040 LT = 13: IF EN = 28 THEN LT = 20
17050 EN = LT:BN = 2: GOSUB 500
17999   RETURN

18001   REM   B8 OPERATOR BECOMES PERMISSIVE
18010 BN = 9:ET = WT%: GOSUB 500
18020 CL(EN) = PE%
18999   RETURN

19001   REM   B9 OPERATOR BECOMES OBSTRUCTIVE
19010 BN = 8:ET = IT%: GOSUB 500
19020 CL(EN) = OB%
19999   RETURN
```

Fig. 4.17 BASIC code of B-activities.

Table 4.2 Variables and constants used in warehouse model

AM%	'Arrival machine' number (1 to 3 for entities 29–31)
AR%(I)	Inter-arrival time for arrival machine I
*BN	B-activity number
*CL(I)	Colour of shape representing component displayed on table I
CL%	Colour yellow indicating lifting table being cleared
DR%	Crane unloading (drop) time
*EN	Entity number
*ET	Entity time
ID%	Colour green indicating idle crane
IT%	Idle (obstructive) time of operator
LO%	Colour white indicating crane loaded
LT	Identification number of lifting table interacting with crane
*LX(I) ⎫	Display position of shape representing component
*LY(I) ⎭	on entity I (see Sec. 2.2)
MV%	Crane moving time
NS%	Number of stationary components
OB%	Colour blue indicating operator obstructive
OC%	Colour blue indicating lifting table occupied by stationary component
PE%	Colour black (on white background) indicating operator permissive
PU%	Crane pick-up (loading) time
Q%(AM)	Queue from arrival machine AM% (entities 29–31)
*RT(I)	Rotation angle of shape on entity I
*TN	Current time
UC%	Colour black indicating lifting table unoccupied
WT%	Operator working (permissive) time

* Variables used by executive of Sec. 3.2

Model Initialization

The model is initialized with all tables clear and cranes idle at the lifting table end of their tracks. Each arrival machine (entities 29–31) is scheduled to produce an arrival at the first time increment (TN=1). The simulation user is asked to change the values of PU% (crane pick up time) and MV% (crane moving time) at the beginning of the run if he so wishes. All the other constants are assigned preselected values, including the array of times taken for all entity movements.

Picture initialization

As most of the screen is covered by a white background, the first step in initializing the picture is to draw a white block of colour all over the screen, using the executive's subroutine (GOSUB 800 in Sec. 3.2) with X = 0, A = 279, Y = 0, B = 191. For each entity from number 1 to 26, information is then read in from data statements for a new smaller block to rub out the previous white. These leave white lines between the table positions so each is distinct on the picture. Each crane track also has its block drawn in the same way.

The only shapes that need to be entered at this stage are those for the idle cranes which also have a colour assigned. The shape positions for tables 1–26, the cranes and the operators must all be defined with LX( ) and LY( ) (see Sec. 2.2). Only the cranes move from their initial positions so the rest of the LX,LY values are defined for the length of the simulation. The components are 'moved' by blacking out the shape associated with one table and drawing the next one. The rotation of the shapes at entities 13 and 20 are defined too. All the other entities, except table 1, take the rotation as a 'destination label' which is passed over with the component by activity C1. At entity 1 the rotation is assigned by activity C3 when it chooses the destination label.

Model experimentation

There are two critical factors in the model, the relationship between the times taken to move the components in different places in the system and the priority arrangements at junctions. The times given for the original equipment produced a bottleneck at table 21 and a subsequent blockage of all input. Output from crane 28 had priority over output from crane 27 which had priority over input to crane 28 (see Fig. 4.14). As no component could move into a junction unless its subsequent destination was free, components became stationary at entity 21 and then at 19, 20, and 17. When 21 cleared, 19 and 20 were cleared next and the component at 17 rarely moved. Crane 28 could supply components quickly as it was not taking any into storage. Entities 12 and 13 were cleared next after 17 (14 and 11 being junctions) and crane 27 could easily keep up sufficient outflow (with no inflow) to keep the component on entity 10 there for ever. This blocked 6 if its component was due for crane 28 and thus prevented any input coming in at all.

The operation of the warehouse as originally conceived allowed a change of destination at table 6 if the input path to crane 27 was busy but no possible change if entity 10 was busy. A change here allows input originally for crane 28, to go to crane 27 which slows down its rate of output from storage and unblocks the system. Without being able to watch the display, and see the system block up, it would be very hard to persuade anyone that such a change would be so significant in operation.

This model was used to demonstrate to the designers the flaws in their system, before it became a failure in operation.

129

4.3 Trucks model

Features included

1. Use of two screens to see picture as it changes at each time step.
2. Graphical historical picture as simulation runs.
3. Use of machine language programs to move graphs on screen and generate characters.
4. Interaction with the simulation via the paddles.
5. Choice of variables for the paddles.

Introduction

We wrote three separate versions of the trucks model. Two used the picture drawing executive (Sec. 3.2), one on the Apple II and another on the PET; the third employed the graph/paddle executive of Sec. 3.3, but only on the Apple. We first described the model without pictures, graphs or interaction, as it would run with the executive of Sec. 3.1.

Then we incorporate the picture. This we describe in full for the Apple version; for the PET it is so similar to this that the slight differences are only noted. A PET user who has tried out the executive of Sec. 3.2 will find most of these obvious from the slight variations in the BASIC on the two machines. For the final version of the model we return to the original to add the graphs and interactive subroutines on the Apple II.

The truck delivery system

Look at the cycle diagram in Fig. 4.18. Trucks are filled at loading bays and then go out on delivery rounds. When finished they may need to be repaired by repair gangs or they may return directly to the loading bays. Once repaired a truck rejoins the others at the loading bays.

Each loading bay and repair gang can handle only one truck at a time so queues will form when a facility is busy. At times the bays or gangs will be idle. They are then modelled as though they themselves were in queues waiting for trucks to use them. There are therefore four queues, two of trucks and one

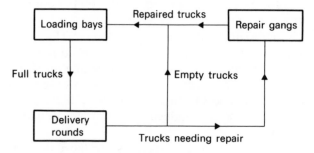

Fig. 4.18 Flow diagram of the trucks model.

each of loading bays and repair gangs. Each queue has a known upper limit, since maxima of 20 trucks, 3 bays, and 4 gangs are imposed.

Each truck is an entity which may be loading, out on delivery, being repaired, or queueing for loading or repair. The loading bays and repair gangs are also entities. They are either busy handling a truck or queueing for one. The simulation moves the entities between these states and keeps track of the number of completed delivery rounds and the idle times of the bays and gangs.

Model structure

There are five B- and two C-activities, which are shown in narrative form in Fig. 4.19. The corresponding BASIC code and a list of variables are in Fig. 4.20 and Table 4.3 respectively.

Each B-activity occurs with a scheduled change of state of one entity. B1, B3, and B4 release a truck from loading, delivery, and repair. B2 and B5 free a loading bay and repair gang.

Records are kept of the numbers of trucks, loading bays, and repair gangs in each queue.

The identity number of the entities actually in each queue at any time are held in arrays QB( ), QG( ), QR( ), and QL( ). The Nth entity in each queue has its identity number stored at $Q(N-1)$, e.g., the last truck queueing for loading is at $QL(NL-1)$. A new arrival enters at $QL(NL)$ before NL is updated as in activities B3 and B4.

B1 TRUCK IS LOADED AND STARTS DELIVERY

Schedule truck to return from delivery (B3)

B2 LOADING BAY SET FREE

Put loading bay into queue available for loading

B3 TRUCK DELIVERY ENDS

Add to delivery statistics.

IF truck needs repair, THEN add to queue for repair.

ELSE Add to queue for loading.

Fig. 4.19 The trucks model activity structure (*continues*).

131

B4 TRUCK IS REPAIRED

Put truck into queue for loading

B5 REPAIR GANG FREE

Put repair gang into queue available for repair

C1 LOADING

IF there is a truck queueing and a bay available for loading

THEN remove bay from queue

Schedule bay to finish loading (B2)
Collect loading bay statistics
Remove truck from queue
Schedule truck to finish loading (B1)

Repeat activity

C2 REPAIRING

IF there is a truck queueing and a repair gang available

THEN remove gang from queue

Schedule gang to finish repair (B5)
Collect repair gang statistics
Remove truck from queue
Schedule truck to be repaired (B4)

Repeat activity

Fig. 4.19 The trucks model activity structure (*continued*).

Because there is no interest in the movement of an individual truck, the queue discipline in the model is 'last-in–first-out', e.g., the last truck to come from loading is loaded first. When loading starts, NB (1020) is reduced by one so the entity number of the bay to be busy is held in QB(NB). This truck is scheduled to finish loading and start delivery LT time units later.

```
1000   REM   C1 LOADING
1010   IF NL = 0 OR NB = 0 THEN   RETURN
1020 NB = NB - 1:EN = QB(NB):BN = 2:ET = LT: GOSUB 500
1040   IF TN > TS THEN LB(EN) = LB(EN) + TN - BF(EN)
1050   IF TN + LT > TS THEN BF(EN) = TN + LT
1060 NL = NL - 1:EN = QL(NL):BN = 1: GOSUB 500
1080   GOTO 1010

2000   REM   C2 REPAIRING
2010   IF NR = 0 OR NG = 0 THEN   RETURN
2020 NG = NG - 1:EN = QG(NG):BN = 5:ET = RT +   INT (10 *   RND
   (1)): GOSUB 500
2040   IF TN > TS THEN I = EN - ER:RG(I) = RG(I) + TN - GF(I)
2050   IF TN + ET > TS THEN GF(EN - ER) = TN + ET
2060 NR = NR - 1:EN = QR(NR):BN = 4: GOSUB 500
2080   GOTO 2010

11000   REM   B1 TRUCK STARTS DELIVERY
11010 BN = 3:ET = 50 +   INT (10 *   RND (1)): GOSUB 500
11030   RETURN

12000   REM   B2 LOADING BAY FREE
12010 QB(NB) = EN:NB = NB + 1
12030   RETURN

13000   REM   B3 DELIVERY ENDS
13010 DT = DT + 1
13020   IF   RND (1) < 0.25 THEN 13060
13030 QL(NL) = EN:NL = NL + 1
13050   RETURN
13060 QR(NR) = EN:NR = NR + 1
13080   RETURN

14000   REM   B4 TRUCK IS REPAIRED
14010 QL(NL) = EN:NL = NL + 1
14030   RETURN

15000   REM   B5 REPAIR GANG FREE
15010 QG(NG) = EN:NG = NG + 1
15030   RETURN
```

Fig. 4.20 Code for activities of trucks model with no graphics.

Randomness

There are three sources of random change from RND(1).

1. Delivery Time = 50 + INT(10 + RND(1))

   This gives integer times uniformly distributed between 50 and 60, and is used in activity B1 (11010).

2. In B3(13020), when a truck returns from a delivery round, the probability of its needing repair is 0.25.

3. Repair Time = RT + INT(10 + RND(1))

See activity C2 (2020)

This gives a repair time between RT and RT + 10. RT is used, instead of a constant, in anticipation of its being a variable for interactive change in the later version.

Table 4.3 Variables used in the truck model coding

BF(I)	Latest time that loading Bay I became Free
*BN	B-activity Number
DT	Total number of Deliveries completed
*EN	Entity Number
*ET	Entity Time
GF(I)	Latest time that repair Gang I became Free
LB(I)	Idle time of Loading Bay (I)
LT	Loading Time
NB	Number of loading Bays in queue
*NC	Number of C-activities in the model
*NE	Number of Entities in the model
NG	Number of repair Gangs in queue
NL	Number of trucks queueing for Loading
NR	Number of trucks queueing for Repair
QB( )	Queue of loading Bays—holds identity numbers of entities
QG( )	Queue of repair Gangs—holds identity numbers of entities
QL( )	Queue of trucks for Loading—holds identity numbers of entities
QR( )	Queue of trucks for Repair—holds identity numbers of entities
RG(I)	Idle time of Repair Gang I
RT	Repair Time
*TN	Current simulation time (Time Now)
*TS	Time from which Statistics are required

* Variables used by the executive described in Sec. 3.1

Statistics

Statistics collected are the total time that each loading bay and repair gang is idle, and the total number of deliveries completed (DT). The idleness statistics are all handled in the two C-activities. The time TS gives the starting time for collection of statistics and provided that TS has passed, the latest idle interval is added to the total. The simulation starts with each entity having a 'freed time' set to TS. After TS is passed this is updated to each new time that the entity becomes free, e.g., loading bays become free at BF(EN) = TN + LT in C1 (1050). Each new idle interval is thus TN − BF(EN) when the bay starts loading (1040).

2040 and 2050 are similar for repair gangs, except for their two identity numbers. Each has an entity number (EN) and a repair gang number (I), to avoid wasteful, large arrays for RG and GF. EN is 23 larger than I. The loading bays have entity numbers 1–3 which cause no problems.

Initialization (Figs 4.21, 4.22)

The activities use the dimensions and data given in the first phase of the modeller's initialization (Fig. 4.21). There are 20 trucks, 3 loading bays, and 4 repair gangs—27 entities in all. The corresponding queue dimensions are one less, because the first place in each is at the zero position of the array.

```
45000   REM   MODEL DIMENSIONS AND DATA
45010 NE = 27:NC = 2
45020   DIM QB(2),QG(3),QR(19),QL(19),GF(4),BF(3),RG(4),LB(3)
45030 LT = 10:RT = 80:ER = 23
45040   RETURN
```

Fig. 4.21 Dimensions and data subroutine.

```
50000   REM   MODEL INITIALISATION
50020 NB = 3: FOR EN = 1 TO 3:QB(EN - 1) = EN:BF(EN) = TS: NEXT
50030 NL = 20: FOR EN = 4 TO 23:QL(EN - 4) = EN: NEXT
50040 NG = 4: FOR EN = 24 TO 27:QG(EN - 24) = EN:GF(EN - 23) =
    TS: NEXT
50050 NR = 0
50060   RETURN
```

Fig. 4.22 Model initialization subroutine.

The second phase (the BASIC statements of Fig. 4.22) sets the model ready for the simulation. No activities are scheduled, all the trucks are waiting to load and all the bays and repair gangs are idle. As noted earlier, the bays and gangs are given the value TS (the time statistics begin) for the start of their first idle time for recording purposes.

Model output

An example of the output is given in Fig. 4.23, produced by the code of Fig. 4.24, the finalization subroutine. The first check is that some statistics have been collected (i.e., TN > TS). For each loading bay and repair gang currently idle (e.g., BF(I) > = TN), the last bit of idle time needs adding on (55030, 55130). The percentage idle time is then calculated to two decimal places for the period of collecting the statistics (55040, 55140).

135

```
IDLE TIME OF LOADING BAYS

1 - 31.67%    2 - 30.17%

3 - 17.7%

IDLE TIME OF REPAIR GANGS

1 - 15.71%    2 - 12.96%

3 - 4.48%    4 - .24%

NO. OF DELIVERIES = 105

Å
```

Fig. 4.23 An example of output from trucks model.

```
55000   IF TN < TS THEN   END
55010   PRINT "IDLE TIME OF LOADING BAYS"
55020   FOR I = 1 TO 3
55030   IF BF(I) < TN THEN LB(I) = LB(I) + TN - BF(I)
55040 LB(I) =   INT (LB(I) / (TN - TS) * 10000) / 100
55050   NEXT
55060   PRINT : PRINT "1 - ";LB(1);"%    2 - ";LB(2);"%"
55070   PRINT : PRINT "3 - ";LB(3);"%"
55100   PRINT : PRINT : PRINT : PRINT
55110   PRINT "IDLE TIME OF REPAIR GANGS"
55120   FOR I = 1 TO 4
55130   IF GF(I) < TN THEN RG(I) = RG(I) + TN - GF(I)
55140 RG(I) =   INT (RG(I) / (TN - TS) * 10000) / 100
55150   NEXT
55160   PRINT : PRINT "1 - ";RG(1);"%    2 - ";RG(2);"%"
55170   PRINT : PRINT "3 - ";RG(3);"%    4 - ";RG(4);"%"
55190   PRINT : PRINT : PRINT
55200   PRINT "NO. OF DELIVERIES = ";DT
55210   END
```

Fig. 4.24 Finalization subroutine.

Picture drawing version on the Apple

This uses the executive of Sec. 3.2 to draw a picture of the states of the trucks, loading bays, and repair gangs as the simulation progresses, as in Fig. 4.25. The stars represent trucks, with their state being indicated by their position on the screen, i.e., at the bottom they are out on delivery, top left they are using or waiting for loading bays, and top right they are using or waiting for repair gangs. The symbol ■ represents a busy loading bay and 🔣 an idle one. Repair gangs are shown by vertical lines when busy and horizontal ones when idle. The queues of trucks are below and to the side of the facilities they are waiting to use. When loading or being repaired they are placed directly below the symbol for the loading bay or repair gang.

TRUCKS SIMULATION

TIME NOW IS 126

OUT ON DELIVERY

Fig. 4.25 Pictorial representation of the trucks simulation.

Figure 4.26 gives the additional lines to produce moving pictures from the activities of Fig. 4.20. The extra subroutine calls in the C-activities are to draw (GOSUB 600) and rub out (GOSUB 700) the symbols on the screen as described in Sec. 2.2.

Line 1030 resets the symbol number in RS(EN) for a loading bay to become busy (127) and stores the position for the truck to use the loading bay (repair gang) in variable M. 1070 rubs out the truck symbol in the queue for loading bays and draws a new one next to the appropriate bay. 2030 and 2070 deal with the repair gangs in a similar way. The busy repair gang has symbol number 124. The loading bays are placed across the screen at positions 3, 5, and 7 for EN = 1–3 with the repair gangs at 32, 34, 36, and 38, for EN = 24–28.

```
1030 RS(EN) = 127: GOSUB 600:M = 2 * EN + 1
1070  GOSUB 700:LX(EN) = M:LY(EN) = 2: GOSUB 600

2030 RS(EN) = 124: GOSUB 600:M = 2 * EN - 16
2070  GOSUB 700:LX(EN) = M:LY(EN) = 2: GOSUB 600

11020 LX(EN) = EN + 5:LY(EN) = 20

12020 RS(EN) = 4

13040 LX(EN) = 1:LY(EN) = 2 + NL
13070 LX(EN) = 40:LY(EN) = 2 + NR

14020 LX(EN) = 1:LY(EN) = 2 + NL

15020 RS(EN) = 45
```

Fig. 4.26 Additional lines in activities to produce picture changes.

For each B-activity rubbing out and redrawing the symbol of each associated entity is carried out automatically by the executive so only the symbol and its position need to be altered as necessary. 12020 changes a bay symbol to idle (4) and 15020 does the same for a repair gang. 11020, 13040, 13070, and 14020 reposition a truck by altering its X coordinate (LX) and its Y coordinate (LY). The trucks out on delivery (11020) are placed in a row at line 20 according to their entity numbers. The queue for loading is in column 1 (13040, 14020) and that for repair in column 40. Each vertical position is determined by the number in the queue.

Picture initialization

Picture initialization is carried out when the model writer initializes his model. There are no additional dimensions or data so the statements of Fig. 4.21, are sufficient for the first initialization phase. The arrays holding the graphical information on position (LX( ) and LY( )) and representative symbols (RS( )) of each entity are dimensioned by the executive.

The second phase (model initialization subroutine), complete with picture initialization statements, is given in Fig. 4.27. 50000–50050 label the different parts of the picture (shown in Fig. 4.25), positioning the labels horizontally with HTAB and vertically with VTAB. 50060, 50080, 50100, and 50120 are statements from Fig. 4.22 extended to produce a picture of the initial state of the model on the video display by lines 50070, 50090, and 50110. GOSUB 600 is used again to draw the entity (EN) once its position (given by LX(EN) and LY(EN)) and representative symbol (RS(EN)) have been defined.

To display the time at the right place at each event time, an information display subroutine is required (see Fig. 4.25):

```
20000 VTAB 13: HTAB 24: PRINT TN: RETURN
```

```
50000   REM   MODEL INITIALISATION
50010   VTAB 3: PRINT " LOADING";: HTAB 32: PRINT "REPAIR"
50020   PRINT "  BAYS";: HTAB 32: PRINT "GANGS"
50030   VTAB 9: HTAB 12: PRINT "TRUCKS SIMULATION"
50040   VTAB 13: HTAB 12: PRINT "TIME NOW IS 0"
50050   VTAB 19: HTAB 12: PRINT "OUT ON DELIVERY"
50060   NB = 3: FOR EN = 1 TO 3:QB(EN - 1) = EN:BF(EN) = TS
50070   LX(EN) = 2 * EN + 1:LY(EN) = 1:RS(EN) = 4: GOSUB 600: NE
        XT
50080   NL = 20: FOR EN = 4 TO 23:QL(EN - 4) = EN
50090   LX(EN) = 1:LY(EN) = EN - 2:RS(EN) = 42: GOSUB 600: NEXT
50100   NG = 4: FOR EN = 24 TO 27:QG(EN - 24) = EN:GF(EN - 23) =
        TS
50110   LX(EN) = 2 * EN - 16:LY(EN) = 1:RS(EN) = 45: GOSUB 600:
        NEXT
50120   NR = 0
50130   RETURN
```

Fig. 4.27 Model and picture initialization subroutine.

138

Running the picture version

The addition of pictures enables the user to sit back and watch the queues change as the simulation runs. He can see how quickly the initial queue for loading disappears and watch the queue for repair start and erratically build up. The statistics can now be collected for a chosen period after the effect of the initial conditions has been seen to have died away. They can also be considered in the light of the instability of the system which was not apparent before.

By switching to watch each entity being drawn separately each time step, the model can easily be verified. The position of each entity can be seen and checked relative to the other entities.

Picture drawing version on the PET

The code for the PET model is virtually the same as for the Apple. One difference is the use of RS$( ) to hold the representative symbol directly instead of using its number stored in RS( ). The only other ones are the use of cursor controls in the finalization subroutine instead of VTAB and HTAB to initialize the picture and update the time display. The executives are of course different as explained in Sec. 3.2 but the model subroutines for the activities and initialization, including picture drawing, have only these small differences.

Graph drawing version using paddles

Once the information from the picture version has been absorbed, there is a desire to change various parameters in the model. Experience has shown that a graphical display is more useful at this stage and the screen is used to show a graph of the changing number of trucks in each queue as these are good indicators of the state of the model. Also displayed graphically are the values of the variables currently being altered via the paddles. The numerical values of these paddle variables are also shown in the text lines at the bottom of the screen together with the current simulation time as in Fig. 4.28.

The paddle variables are chosen from the following:

Number of trucks
Loading time
Number of loading bays
Repair time
Number of repair gangs

Up to two of these may be varied by the paddles at any time. Three of these variables are numbers of entities, which leads to greater changes in the coding than the use of simple variables.

This simulation uses the same model structure as the picture drawing version, but the executive of Sec. 3.3 instead of Sec. 3.2. Again, there are a few extra statements required in the activities (of Fig. 4.20) to carry out the

139

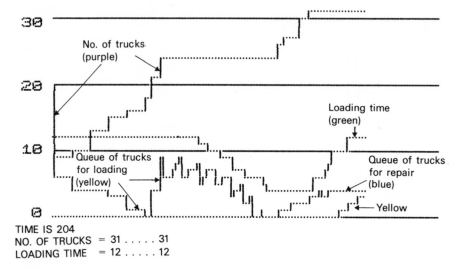

TIME IS 204
NO. OF TRUCKS = 31 31
LOADING TIME = 12 12

Fig. 4.28 Trucks model graphical display.

changes needed by the graphical display. These are the additions to and subtractions from the two queues chosen for display—i.e., trucks for loading (Q(1)) and trucks for repair (Q(2)). Figure 4.29 gives the additional lines of code and the statement (20000) to display the current time. This time information will not be displayed when the simulation is stopped to reset a paddle so the full sentence is required each time, unlike the picture version of the model.

The dimensions (see Fig. 4.30, line 45020) have been changed to allow the paddles to vary the number of entities as follows: trucks 0–30, loading bays 0–6, and repair gangs 0–8. This means the arrays for queues and statistics collected have to be large enough to cope with the maxima of these ranges. There are also additional arrays to hold the entity numbers of trucks, etc., which are waiting to take part in the system but are not currently in it; and for the ranges for the paddle variables. These are listed in Table 4.4 which gives the additional variables in the coding for the graph drawing version.

```
1070 Q(1) = Q(1) - 1

2070 Q(2) = Q(2) - 1

13040 Q(1) = Q(1) + 1

13070 Q(2) = Q(2) + 1

14020 Q(1) = Q(1) + 1

20000   VTAB 21: PRINT "TIME NOW IS "TN: RETURN
```

Fig. 4.29 Additional lines in activities to produce graph changes.

140

Table 4.4 Additional variables for graph drawing version

BW	Number of Loading Bays Waiting to take part
BW( )	Entity number of Loading Bays Waiting to take part
GN	Repair Gang Number (=EN−37)
GW	Number of Repair Gangs Waiting to take part
GW( )	Entity number of Repair Gangs Waiting to take part
LD	Latest Difference in paddle value
*NQ	Number of Queues to be displayed
+PDL(0)	Value returned by paddle two
+PDL(1)	Value returned by paddle one
*PP(I)	Number of variable currently on paddle I
*PV(I)	Previous value of variable on paddle I
*Q( )	Queues to be displayed
RA(J)	Range of paddle variable J
TW( )	Entity numbers of Trucks Waiting to take part
*VN	Number of paddle variables
*VV(J)	Default value of paddle variable
TW	Number of Trucks Waiting to take part
XX	Indicator (=1) that variable cannot be taken off paddle

* Variables used by the executive, described in Sec. 3.3

+ See Sec. 2.3

Model, paddles, and graph initialization (Figs 4.30, 4.31)

The number of paddle variables, the queues for display must be specified (45010), while the range of each variable is stored in array RA( ) (line 45040). The names of the paddle variables are given, in order, in data statements 45050 to 45090. These set variable one as the number of trucks, variable two as loading time, etc. The default values and scaling factors (for plotting) are given in the same order in the next two statements, followed by the queue scaling factor and graph labels.

Model initialization is as before (Fig. 4.31), but with additions arising from displays of queues and from the inclusion of the paddles. The queues are initialized in 50100.

The second system phase of initialization (described in Sec. 3.3) allows the user to choose starting values for his selected paddle variables. He may therefore have chosen numbers of trucks, loading bays, or repair gangs to be in the model at the start of the run different from the initialization of 50030–50100. These changes are best handled by the routines which enter paddle variable values into the model before the activities. To set this up correctly, PV(I) must be reset if paddle I has been associated with a number of entities. The executive has previously set PV(I) to the user's starting value to initialize the graphs accordingly. For a number of entities as a paddle variable this will mean that the model initialization does not correspond to the graph initialization. 50010 and 50020 test for a 'number of entities' on a

141

```
45000   REM   MODEL DIMENSIONS AND DATA
45010 NE = 45:NC = 2:VN = 5:NQ = 2
45020   DIM QB(5),QG(7),QR(30),QL(30),GF(8),BF(6),RG(8),LB(6),R
      A(5)
45021   DIM BW(5),GW(7),TW(30)
45030 LT = 10:RT = 80:ER = 37
45040 RA(1) = 31:RA(2) = 15:RA(3) = 6:RA(4) = 118:RA(5) = 8
45050   DATA "NO. OF TRUCKS"
45060   DATA  "   LOADING TIME"
45070   DATA  "NO. OF LOADING BAYS"
45080   DATA  "   REPAIR TIME"
45090   DATA  "NO. OF REPAIR GANGS"
45100   DATA  20,10,3,80,4: REM   DEFAULT VALUES
45110   DATA  5,5,5,1,5: REM   PADDLE SCALING FACTORS
45120   DATA  5,5: REM   QUEUE SCALING FACTORS
45130   DATA  "30","20","10": REM   GRAPH LABELS
45140   RETURN
```

Fig. 4.30 First model phase in initialization, graph/paddle version.

```
50000   REM   MODEL INITIALISATION
50010   FOR I = 1 TO 2
50011   IF PP(I) = 1 OR PP(I) = 3 OR PP(I) = 5 THEN PV(I) = VV(P
      P(I))
50020   NEXT
50030 NB = 3: FOR EN = 1 TO 3:QB(EN - 1) = EN:BF(EN) = TS: NEXT
50040 BW = 3: FOR EN = 4 TO 6:BW(EN - 4) = EN:BF(EN) = TS: NEXT
50050 NL = 20: FOR EN = 7 TO 26:QL(EN - 7) = EN: NEXT
50060 TW = 11: FOR EN = 27 TO 37:TW(EN - 27) = EN: NEXT
50070 NG = 4: FOR EN = 38 TO 41:QG(EN - 38) = EN:GF(EN - 37) =
      TS: NEXT
50080 GW = 4: FOR EN = 42 TO 45:GW(EN - 42) = EN:GF(EN - 37) =
      TS: NEXT
50090 NR = 0
50100 Q(1) = 20:Q(2) = 0
50110   RETURN
```

Fig. 4.31 Model initialization subroutine for graph drawing version.

paddle $(PP(I)) = 1$, 3, or 5) and, if there is one, reset $PV(I)$ to the default value $(VV(PP(I)))$ which agrees with the model initialization (50030–50100), e.g., $VV(1) = 20$ (45100 Fig. 4.30) and 20 trucks are in the model initially (50050).

The arrays for the entities waiting to take part are used in the same way as the queues in the original model. The last entity in is the first one out; the first one is stored in the zero position; and the indicator (BW,TW or GW) is set to the number waiting. Loading bays now have entity numbers 1–6, trucks 7–37, and repair gangs 38–45 but apart from these factors the rest of the model initialization is the same as before (Fig. 4.22).

```
40000   REM   NEW VARIABLE ONTO PADDLE
40001   REM
40100   IF IP = 1 THEN   DEF   FN F1(I) =   INT ( PDL (1) * (RA(1) + 1) / 256
    ): RETURN
40110   DEF   FN F2(I) =   INT ( PDL (0) * (RA(1) + 1) / 256): RETURN
40111   REM
40200   IF IP = 1 THEN   DEF   FN F1(I) = 5 +   INT ( PDL (1) * (RA(2) + 1) /
    256): RETURN
40210   DEF   FN F2(I) = 5 +   INT ( PDL (0) * (RA(2) + 1) / 256): RETURN
40211   REM
40300   IF IP = 1 THEN   DEF   FN F1(I) =   INT ( PDL (1) * (RA(3) + 1) / 256
    ): RETURN
40310   DEF   FN F2(I) =   INT ( PDL (0) * (RA(3) + 1) / 256): RETURN
40311   REM
40400   IF IP = 1 THEN   DEF   FN F1(I) = 40 +   INT ( PDL (1) * (RA(4) + 1) /
    256): RETURN
40410   DEF   FN F2(I) = 40 +   INT ( PDL (0) * (RA(4) + 1) / 256): RETURN
40411   REM
40500   IF IP = 1 THEN   DEF   FN F1(I) =   INT ( PDL (1) * (RA(5) + 1) / 256
    ): RETURN
40510   DEF   FN F2(I) =   INT ( PDL (0) * (RA(5) + 1) / 256): RETURN
```

Fig. 4.32 Subroutines to put a new variable on a paddle.

Paddle variable subroutines

As described in Secs 2.3 and 4.1, there are three sets of subroutines required to put a new variable onto a paddle, to take an old one off, and to enter values from the paddles into the model. Figure 4.32 shows how a new variable is put on. Each subroutine defines function F1 or F2 (for paddle 1 or 2) using IP set by the executive to the paddle number. The form of the equations used for the definition is discussed in Sec. 2.3. For variables 1, 3, and 5 each gives an integer between 0 and a maximum of RA(J) (according to the paddle setting) where J is the variable number. For 2 the numbers lie between 5 and 5 + RA(2), while 4 has a minimum of 40 and range of RA(4).

The other two sets of subroutines are more complicated because variables 1, 3, and 5 represent numbers of entities. When a variable is removed from a paddle it reverts to its default so there may be a change in the number of entities in the system. When this is an increase, the trucks are added to the queue for loading, and the loading bays and repair gangs to those waiting for trucks. Decreases occur in the same queues but may not be possible if there are insufficient entities in the appropriate state. For example, there may be 25 trucks in the system, while variable 1 is on a paddle but this must drop to 20 when it is taken off. This can only be allowed when there are at least 5 trucks queueing for loading.

Figure 4.33 gives the coding for the subroutines to take variables off paddles. For variables 2 and 4, the loading and repair times are simply set to their default values (30200, 30400).

For the other three, being numbers of entities, the first check (30100, 30310, 30510) is whether there is any difference between the default and the last value used in the activities. With zero difference there is nothing to be

143

done. With the default higher than the previous value, entities must be added to the system, from the 'waiting' arrays (30180–30195). To keep the record straight for collection of statistics, each loading bay and repair gang entering has its latest becoming-free-time updated (30390, 30590). For new trucks, the queue for loading must have its display updated (30185).

When the default is less than the previous value (negative LD), and there are not sufficient entities in the appropriate queue, control is returned with the indicator (XX) set so the executive can proceed with no change of variable on the paddle (e.g., 30130). Otherwise entities are removed one at a time until the default value is achieved (e.g., 30140–30170). Again the display of the queue for loading must be updated (30150) and also the idle time statistics (30360, 30560). Time waiting out of the system is not included as idle time.

The set of subroutines which put the values of the paddle variables into the model are very similar to those of Fig. 4.33. Indeed, to save recoding the parts which are the same, there are jumps from those subroutines putting in the paddle value to those removing a variable from a paddle. They start differently as can be seen from Fig. 4.34 (25100, 25200, etc). Instead of the default VV(J) the new value for the variable is the latest on the paddle, V(IP). FN F1(I) or FN F2(I) is not used directly because the paddle value may be changing and the same value needs to be used for both the model and for plotting as explained in Sec. 2.3.

The major difference comes for variables 1, 3, and 5 when the requested reduction in entities cannot be achieved. When the reduction was needed in order to take the variable off the paddle, the executive had to be informed. In this case some acceptable value has to be found for each paddle variable. The user is first told that the current paddle value is impossible with a delay, so he has time to read it (25140, 251500). Then system subroutines are called to ask the user for a new value (GOSUB 27160) and to reset V(IP) (GOSUB 27500). The process is then started all over again—determining the new change in value and acting accordingly.

```
30000   REM   OLD VARIABLE OFF PADDLE

30100 LD = VV(1) - PV(IP): REM    TRUCKS
30110   IF LD = 0 THEN   RETURN
30120   IF LD > 0 THEN 30180
30130   IF NL < - LD THEN XX = 1: RETURN
30140   FOR J = 1 TO  - LD: REM  REMOVE TRUCKS
30150 NL = NL - 1:Q(1) = Q(1) - 1
30160 TW(TW) = QL(NL):TW = TW + 1
30170   NEXT : RETURN
30180   FOR J = 1 TO LD: REM  ADD TRUCKS
30185 TW = TW - 1:Q(1) = Q(1) + 1
30190 QL(NL) = TW(TW):NL = NL + 1
30195   NEXT : RETURN

30200 LT = VV(2): RETURN : REM  LOADING TIME
```

```
30300 LD = VV(3) - PV(IP): REM    LOADING BAYS
30310  IF LD = O THEN  RETURN
30320  IF LD > O THEN 30380
30330  IF NB < - LD THEN XX = 1: RETURN
30340  FOR J = 1 TO - LD: REM   REMOVE LOADING BAYS
30350 NB = NB - 1:EN = QB(NB)
30360  IF TN > TS THEN LB(EN) = LB(EN) + TN - BF(EN)
30370 BW(BW) = EN: BW = BW + 1
30375  NEXT : RETURN
30380  FOR J = 1 TO LD: REM   ADD LOADING BAYS
30385 BW = BW - 1:QB(NB) = BW(BW)
30390  IF TN > TS THEN BF(QB(NB)) = TN
30395 NB = NB + 1: NEXT : RETURN

30400 RT = VV(4): RETURN : REM   REPAIR TIME

30500 LD = VV(5) - PV(IP): REM    REPAIR GANGS
30510  IF LD = O THEN  RETURN
30520  IF LD > O THEN 30580
30530  IF NG < - LD THEN XX = 1: RETURN
30540  FOR J = 1 TO - LD: REM   REMOVE REPAIR GANGS
30550 NG = NG - 1:GN = QG(NG) - 37
30560  IF TN > TS THEN RG(GN) = RG(GN) + TN - GF(GN)
30570 GW(GW) = QG(NG):GW = GW + 1
30575  NEXT : RETURN
30580  FOR J = 1 TO LD: REM   ADD REPAIR GANGS
30585 GW = GW - 1:QG(NG) = GW(GW):GN = QG(NG) - ER
30590  IF TN > TS THEN GF(GN) = TN
30595 NG = NG + 1: NEXT : RETURN
```

Fig. 4.33 Subroutines to take old variable off paddle.

A large number of different experiments can be performed. One challenging exercise is to maximize the deliveries made in a set time without any high idle times or long queues. The output from the model is similar to that previously described but will include idle times for more loading bays and repair gangs. A typical output is given in Fig. 4.35 and the code to produce it in Fig. 4.36. This too is similar to the previous one (Fig. 4.24) apart from the need to keep track of entities which are out of the system at the end of the run. These entities are identified through their entity numbers in the arrays BW( )

```
25000  REM  PADDLE VALUES INTO MODEL

25100 LD = V(IP) - PV(IP): REM   TRUCKS
25110  IF LD = O THEN  RETURN
25120  IF LD > O THEN 30180
25130  IF NL > = - LD THEN 30140
25140  VTAB 21: PRINT "NO. OF TRUCKS IMPOSSIBLE"
25150  FOR J = 1 TO 2000: NEXT : REM   DELAY
25160   GOSUB 27160: GOSUB 27500: CALL - 936: REM CHOOSE ANOTHE
    R VALUE
25170  GOTO 25100: REM   TRY AGAIN
```

```
25200 LT = V(IP): RETURN : REM    LOADING TIME

25300 LD = V(IP) - PV(IP): REM    LOADING BAYS
25310  IF LD = 0 THEN  RETURN
25320  IF LD > 0 THEN 30380
25330  IF NB >  = - LD THEN 30340
25340  VTAB 21: PRINT "NO. OF LOADING BAYS IMPOSSIBLE"
25350  FOR J = 1 TO 2000: NEXT : REM   DELAY
25360  REM  CHOOSE ANOTHER VALUE
25361   GOSUB 27160: GOSUB 27500: CALL  - 936
25370   GOTO 25300: REM  TRY AGAIN

25400 RT = V(IP): RETURN : REM    REPAIR TIME

25500 LD = V(IP) - PV(IP): REM    REPAIR GANGS
25510  IF LD = 0 THEN  RETURN
25520  IF LD > 0 THEN 30580
25530  IF NG >  = - LD THEN 30540
25540  VTAB 21: PRINT "NO. OF REPAIR GANGS IMPOSSIBLE"
25550  FOR J = 1 TO 2000: NEXT : REM   DELAY
25560   GOSUB 27160: GOSUB 27500: CALL  - 936: REM CHOOSE ANOTHE
   R VALUE
25570   GOTO 25500: REM  TRY AGAIN
```

Fig. 4.34 Subroutine to enter paddle value into model.

IDLE TIME OF LOADING BAYS

1 — 10.26%	2 — 5.34%	3 — 6.79%
4 — 0%	5 — 0%	6 — 1.21%

IDLE TIME OF REPAIR GANGS

1 — 11.30%	2 — 8.29%	3 — 5.47%
4 — 8.71%	5 — 0%	6 — 0%
7 — 3.29%	8 — 1.62%	

NO. OF DELIVERIES = 65

Fig. 4.35 An example of statistics produced.

```
55000  REM  FINAL OUTPUT
55010  IF TN <  = TS THEN  RETURN
55020  PRINT : PRINT "IDLE TIME OF LOADING BAYS"
55030  FOR I = 1 TO RA(3)
55040  FOR J = 0 TO BW: IF BW(J) = I THEN BF(I) = TN: GOTO 5508
   0
55050  NEXT J
55070  IF BF(I) < TN THEN LB(I) = LB(I) + TN - BF(I)
55080 LB(I) =  INT (LB(I) / (TN - TS) * 10000) / 100
55090  NEXT I
55100  PRINT
55101  PRINT "1 -  ";LB(1);"%   2 -  ";LB(2)"%   3 -  ";LB(3);"
   %"
```

```
55110   PRINT
55111   PRINT "4 -   ";LB(4);"%   5 -   ";LB(5)"%   6 -   ";LB(6);"
        %"
55115   PRINT : PRINT : PRINT : PRINT
55120   PRINT "IDLE TIME OF REPAIR GANGS"
55130   FOR I = 1 TO RA(5):EN = I + 37
55140   FOR J = 0 TO GW: IF GW(J) = EN THEN GF(I) = TN: GOTO 551
        80
55150   NEXT J
55170   IF GF(I) < TN THEN RG(I) = RG(I) + TN - GF(I)
55180 RG(I) =   INT (RG(I) / (TN - TS) * 10000) / 100
55190   NEXT I
55200   PRINT
55201   PRINT "1 -   ";RG(1);"%   2 -   ";RG(2)"%   3 -   ";RG(3);"
        %"
55210   PRINT
55211   PRINT "4 -   ";RG(4);"%   5 -   ";RG(5)"%   6 -   ";RG(6);"
        %"
55220   PRINT : PRINT "7 -   ";RG(7);"%   8 -   ";RG(8)"%"
55230   PRINT : PRINT : PRINT : PRINT "NO. OF DELIVERIES = ";DT:
        PRINT
55240   RETURN
```

Fig. 4.36 Subroutine to produce final statistics.

and GW( ) (55040, 55050). Each entity found has the current time (TN) entered as its time last becoming free. They are thus brought into the system for output purposes as the run ends.

4.4 Reactor model

Features included

Use of combined executive and activity.
Observing the system as it changes using graphs and drawings.
Automatic screen moving by machine language program.
Use of noise for attracting attention.

Introduction

Pritsker's chemical reactor model (Pritsker, 1974) has become a popular bench-mark for combined simulation executives. Until now, all versions of this model have been developed on mainframe computers; indeed, the original reactor model was programmed in GASP IV, an event-based language, with output on line printer—including 'static' graphs. This section shows that the model is easily written on a microcomputer, using the BASIC combined executive we discussed in Sec. 3.4. We display the 'semi-static' picture of the reactors filling and discharging, and also moving graphs of the state variables involved. We present a slight modification of the original Pritsker model, using a simpler method for keeping track of the reactors. The complete model has also been programmed but the simplification avoids cluttering the code and thus distraction from the main points—the illustration of B- and C-activities for a combined simulation, with moving graphical output.

The four reactors

A hydrogen reaction is conducted in four reactors operating in parallel (Fig. 4.37). Each reactor may be started, stopped, or discharged and cleaned independently of the others. A compressor with a constant molal flow rate supplies hydrogen to the reactors through a surge pressure tank and individual valves for each reactor. These valves ensure the effective pressure in each reactor is the minimum of surge tank pressure and the critical pressure, i.e., the pressure in the reactors must not exceed 100. Initially the surge tank pressure is 500. Reactor 1 is fully charged and started at time 0. The other three are in the process of being cleaned and recharged and are restarted at half-hour intervals. As they react their concentration (and their thirst for hydrogen) drops exponentially (each is governed by its own differential equation). When the concentration of a reactor falls to 10 per cent of its

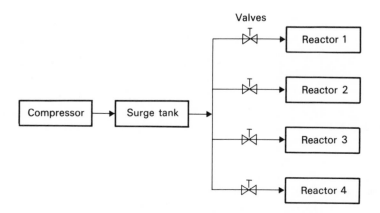

Fig. 4.37 Pritsker's reactor model—layout of plant.

$$\frac{dY_i}{dt} = \begin{cases} -R_i\,P_E\,Y_i & i \text{ is on} \\ 0 & i \text{ is off} \end{cases} \quad i = 1, \ldots, 4$$

$$\frac{dY_5}{dt} = R_T(F_C - S_F)$$

$$\text{where } S_F = -\sum_{i=1}^{4} \frac{dY_i}{dt}\, V_i$$

$$P_E = \min(P_c, Y_5)$$

148

CONSTANTS

R_i = (.03466, .00866, .01155, .00770)
V_i = (10, 15, 20, 25)
R_T = 120.
P_C = 100.
P_N = 150.
F_C = 4.35

INITIAL VALUES

Y_1 = .1   T=0
Y_2 = .4   at   T=.5   and whenever
Y_3 = .2   T=1.0   restarted
Y_4 = .5   T=1.5
Y_5 = 500   at   T=0

Fig. 4.38 Equation definition for reactor model.

original value, it is withdrawn, discharged, cleaned, recharged, and finally restarted. Our model, unlike Pritsker's, assumes that the time for discharging and cleaning is constant. The operating policy for the system entails that the last reactor started will be immediately stopped whenever the surge tank pressure falls below the critical value of 100. All the others on at that time will continue. Reactors can only be started when surge tank pressure is above a nominal 150.

Description of model

Figure 4.38 gives the definition of the equations, and Table 4.5 describes the variables and constants used. As explained in Sec. 2.4, the BASIC array YN(I) is used for the differential equation variables and F(I) for their derivatives. The concentrations, YN(1) to YN(4), and surge tank pressure, YN(5), are thus continuous variables, though of course there will be discontinuities in their derivatives as reactors are started and stopped. That is, the equations for the four reactors, when in operation, describe exponential falls in the concentrations, and they are switched to a constant value when not. The fifth equation (for the pressure) depends on each of these concentrations through the SF term. The stopping and starting of the reactors and the resulting discontinuities are easily handled by the combined executive. The BASIC coding of them is in lines 100–210 of Fig. 4.40.

Table 4.5 Definition of BASIC variables for reactors model

*BN	Number of B-activity to be scheduled
CLNTIM	Length of time for cleaning reactor
CP	Critical Pressure
*EN	Number of Entity being scheduled
*ET	Elapsed Time before scheduled event
*EVNT	Flag indicating a discrete or state event
FC	Flow constant
*F(I)	Derivative of Ith state variable
I	Reactor number.

IC(I)	Initial concentration for reactor I
J	Position of reactor in waiting to start queue
LAST	Number of last reactor started
NRCT	Total number of reactors stopped when finished
NP	Nominal pressure
NWTNG	Total number of reactors waiting to start
PE	Effective pressure
REACT/OFF	Flag indicating reactor is REACTING (1) or OFF (0)
RO(I)	On/off indicator for reactor I
RT	Reaction constant
R(I)	Reaction constant for reactor I
SF	Total flow of hydrogen to reactors
*THRESH	Flag indicating threshold is reached
*TV(I)	Value of threshold to be obtained by state variable I
V(I)	Volume of reactor I
*VN(ACT,J)	Index of Jth state variable involved in activity ACT
*YN(I)	Value of state variable I, 1–4 are reactor concentrations and 5 is surge tank pressure

* Variables used by executive

Activities

The C- and B-activities are summarized in Fig. 4.39 with the corresponding BASIC code in Fig. 4.40.

First, a few general remarks about them. There is a queue of reactors waiting to start—how many of them is recorded in NWTNG (lines 1090 and 11030). As each is started, the time is noted. This is for use in determining which is the last one started, so it can be the first one stopped if the pressure falls below the critical value. REACT and OFF are used as mnemonics, their values being 1 and 0 respectively. The counter NRCT records how many reactors finish reacting at the same time—this is of course almost always 1, but the possibility of its being greater must be allowed for. Each of the three C-activities has a threshold test and only C2: START REACTOR has a discrete test: is there a reactor waiting to start?

C1 STOP WHEN LOW

If surge tank pressure < critical pressure

(i) add 1 to number of reactors waiting
(ii) put last reactor started into waiting line
(iii) switch reactor off
(iv) draw asterisk and bleep

```
C2  START REACTOR

    If there is a reactor waiting to start
    and if surge tank pressure > nominal pressure

    for each waiting reactor

    (i)    take out of waiting queue
    (ii)   start the reactor
    (iii)  black out asterisk and bleep

    set number waiting to zero
```

```
C3  STOP WHEN FINISHED

    for each reactor

    if concentration < 10% of initial
        concentration

    (i)    schedule cleaning
    (ii)   switch reactor off
    (iii)  reset concentration to initial value
    (iv)   black out reactor and bleep
```

```
B1  END CLEANING

    (i)    add one to number of reactors waiting
    (ii)   put in waiting queue
    (iii)  fill reactor with colour
```

Fig. 4.39 C- and B-activities for reactor model.

```
100   REM ***********************
101   REM   EQUATIONS
102   REM ***********************
105 SF = 0
125 PE = YN(5): IF CP < YN(5) THEN PE = CP
150   FOR I = 1 TO 4
160 F(I) =  - R(I) * YN(I) * RO(I) * PE
170 SF = SF - F(I) * V(I)
190   NEXT
200 F(5) = RT * (FC - SF)
210   RETURN
```

151

```
1000   REM *********************
1020   REM   C1  STOP WHEN LOW
1030   REM *********************
1050   IF YN(5) >  = CP THEN   RETURN
1060 VN(1,1) = 5:TV(5) = CP:THRESH = TRUE
1070   IF EVNT = FALSE THEN   RETURN
1080   REM ---------------------------
1090 NWTNG = NWTNG + 1
1100   GOSUB 1200: REM   PUT LAST REACTOR INTO WAITING QUEUE
1110 RO(LAST) = OFF
1120   GOSUB 1300: REM   DRAW ASTERISK AND BLEEP
1190   RETURN

2000   REM *********************
2010   REM    C2   START REACTOR
2020   REM *********************
2030   IF NWTNG = 0 THEN   RETURN
2040   IF YN(5) <  = NP THEN   RETURN
2050 VN(2,1) = 5:TV(5) = NP:THRESH = TRUE
2060   IF EVNT = FALSE THEN   RETURN
2065   REM ---------------------------
2085   FOR J = 1 TO NWTNG
2090   GOSUB 2200: REM   TAKE OUT OF WAITING QUEUE
2100 RO(I) = REACT
2110   GOSUB 2300: REM   BLACK OUT ASTERISK AND BLEEP
2150   NEXT
2155 NWTNG = 0
2160   RETURN

3000   REM *********************
3010   REM   C3   STOP WHEN FINISHED
3020   REM *********************
3030 NRCT = 0
3040   FOR I = 1 TO 4
3050   IF YN(I) > .1 * IC(I) THEN   GOTO 3170
3060 TV(I) = .1 * IC(I):THRESH = TRUE
3070 NRCT = NRCT + 1
3080 VN(3,NRCT) = I
3090   IF EVNT = FALSE THEN   GOTO 3170
3100   REM -----------------------
3110 EN = 2:ET = CLNTIM:BN = 1: GOSUB 500: REM   SCHEDULE CLEANI
     NG
3120 RO(I) = OFF
3130 YN(I) = IC
3160   GOSUB 3300: REM   BLEEP AND BLACK OUT REACTOR
3170   NEXT
3180   RETURN

11000   REM *********************
11010   REM   B1   END CLEANING
11020   REM *********************
11030 NWTNG = NWTNG + 1
11040   GOSUB 1200: REM   PUT IN WAITING QUEUE
11050   GOSUB 51000: REM   FILL REACTOR WITH COLOUR (FIG 1.5.3)
11060   RETURN
```

Fig. 4.40 Equations, C- and B-activities.

Let us consider C1 in more detail—the others should then be clear, with the help of Fig. 4.40. C1: STOP WHEN LOW stops the reactor last started when the surge tank pressure falls below the critical pressure (CP = 100). The threshold test (written in negative form with a RETURN) is in line 1050 of the BASIC program. The following line if reached tells the executive that the fifth variable (surge tank pressure) is the one (and only one) involved in the threshold test (VN(1,1)=5); that the threshold value is CP (TV(5)=CP); and that a threshold has been detected (see Sec. 2.4). After the executive has accurately located the associated state event it sets EVNT = TRUE, so that the body (lines 1090–1190) is executed when the C-activity is entered during the C-phase.

Note the arrangements for passing this information in an activity like C3, which is written for several reactors differentiated by an index I. If EVNT is false for one reactor, then instead of RETURN, the activity is repeated (GOTO 3170) for the next reactor, until all have been tried in turn.

Returning to the body of C1, NWTNG (1090), as mentioned above, records the number waiting to start. RO(LAST) = OFF indicates that the reactor last started is switched off, and is used in evaluating the equations in line 160. Finally, an asterisk is drawn to indicate which reactor is off, along with the appropriate number of bleeps to draw attention to it. (One bleep for reactor one, etc.)

There is only one B-activity needed and this ends the cleaning and recharging of a reactor by transferring it from the 'cleaning' to 'waiting to start' queue. This B-activity is scheduled for a particular reactor in the third C-activity C3: STOP WHEN FINISHED.

Initialization

Initialization is straightforward and merits little comment. We must define model constants and variables (such as CP, V(I), etc.) and define the initial states of the reactors: Reactor '1' starts reacting at time 0; 2, 3, and 4 are ready to start at half-hour intervals, after they have finished being cleaned.

Pictures and graphs and things

The output of this model, of course, differs rather vividly from the static display produced by GASP IV; full use is made of the television and even the speaker (to emit attention-drawing squeaks and blips). As already emphasized, to have a display unfolding before you on a TV set is much more informative and interesting than a static paper display, or tables of numbers which only have much significance when laboriously plotted.

Figure 4.41 shows the layout of the reactors and graphs of the variables at a typical stage in the simulation. A number of 'frames' are shown, reproduced from the TV screen, via a line printer. They were chosen to illustrate the appearance of the curves on the TV screen; the moving of the graphs when the end of the screen is reached; and, of course, the various states of the system.

The picture of the layout of the plant is perhaps not as useful as in, say, that of the warehouse example (Sec. 4.2). There the only changes to the picture arise from discrete events which, of course, are the essence of that simulation. In the reactors problem the discrete events are much less frequent. Initially, the four reactors are filled, with different colours. As reaction proceeds the colours are blacked out accordingly, until a reactor is being cleaned when it is completely black—see the top reactor in Fig. 4.41(a). When the last reactor started is stopped a small rectangle appears alongside accompanied by a

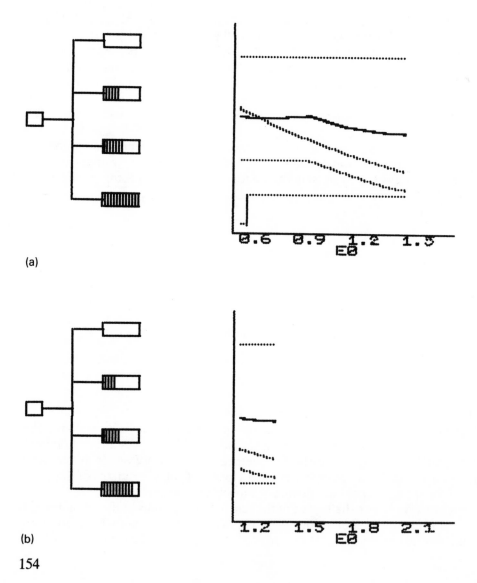

(a)

(b)

154

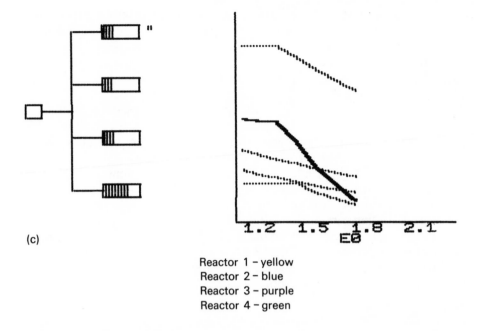

(c)

Reactor 1 – yellow
Reactor 2 – blue
Reactor 3 – purple
Reactor 4 – green

Fig. 4.41 Stills from reactor model.

corresponding number of squeaks from the speaker to draw attention. The only discrete event, of course, is the recharging of a reactor (filling with colour in the display). The reactor drawing is done in a subroutine written by the modeller and called by the executive.

The layout picture then was produced during the building of the model before the graphics display was developed. What, then, are the benefits of it? It provides a colourful display of the plant being discussed and is therefore useful in introducing the model to an audience. It is an alternative to the graphs display and summarizes the information in a different format. It can be very useful in debugging, though, of course, defects it reveals would also show up quickly in the graph displays.

Let us turn now to the graphs, already described in general in Sec. 1.6. These are drawn by the executive from information provided in the parameter arrays by the modeller, immediately after an acceptable integration step and also after the C-phase (see Sec. 3.4). If this last update is omitted, the switching off of a reactor, for example, will appear as a displeasing sloping line, instead of a vertical one—it corresponds of course to the step-like nature of the discrete plots of Secs 4.1 and 4.3.

There are five curves plotted; four concentrations and the surge tank pressure (in five different colours). The blacking out and redrawing when the end of the screen is reached can be seen from Fig. 4.41(a) and (b), which are consecutive stills; (c) is a few time steps later. In (a) even though reactor 1 (at the top) is off, the curve is drawn (at the bottom) as though the reactor is

155

recharged and waiting to start—this of course, is not strictly correct, but if drawn at zero level, the eye is confused by lack of continuity of the display. You can see the various state events: in (a) at time 0.6, reactor 1 finishes, and 3 (second one up) is switched on at 0.9. Again, in (c), 4 (at the top) is switched on and then 1. The latter is stopped when the pressure has fallen to below the critical value at time 1.8.

Noises, as seen in Sec. 3.4, are easily produced. We used an appropriate number of short, medium, and long notes to denote start up, finish reacting, and close down due to low pressure. Noises are not essential, but are useful for drawing attention to significant events. We introduced them during debugging as an aid. To display TEXT, one loses the graphical display and with it the ability to follow the events of the simulation. Adding 'coded' noises helps to restore some of this lost information.

This model when run for a simulation time of 2 hours takes about 3 minutes; thus for 150 hours it would take approximately 5 hours running time—this is to be compared with the 0.5 second on a CDC 7600 for the same model with no display using GASP IV. We mention some ways of trying to improve this running speed in Appendix 2.

4.5 Tank and tanker model

Features included

Use of combined executive and activities.
Paddle control of continuous and discrete parameters.
Optimization using paddles and graphs.
Discontinuities in derivative and variable values.

Introduction

As we reported in Chapter 1, we concocted an example which would test the speed of development of a simulation program on microcomputer. We developed the 'same' model on a mainframe machine (CDC 7600) and also on the Apple and compared the times taken and the costs incurred. In addition we wanted to incorporate the paddles, as introduced in the Hospital Model, to control not just a discrete parameter, but also some continuous ones, and so we plumped for optimizing something—that something is described in the next section. Since it is not possible (for mere mortals) to connect a games paddle to a CDC 7600, it is very difficult, if not impossible, to achieve the same optimization on a mainframe machine. Below we describe the extended model.

We have tried to indicate in the following description that model building is not instantaneous—i.e., at the first attempt one cannot produce a fully debugged and correctly working model. We mention that there is still scope

156

for improvement, and that some of the changes we made were as a result of running the developing model. This is the way of simulation. Thus, the tank and tanker model could still be improved; read it and see if you can think of defects and their cures. However, we must point out that in many hours of running the model, it performed as we would wish.

Description of system

A frugal chemical company produces liquid X which it distributes to its customers by a tanker. The company's sole aim is to maximize its weekly profit by delivering as much of liquid X as possible. They are frustrated in this aim by fouling of pipes and the possession of only one tanker.

At the end of the production stage liquid X pours through an inlet pipe into a storage tank, which has two outlet pipes. The tanker is filled from one or both of these. Unfortunately, liquid X fouls the outlets over time. Diluting liquid X with water controls the rate of fouling to some extent and a faster speed through the pipes also has the same effect. When completely blocked, a pipe is shut off automatically. When both are blocked cleaning commences immediately. The level of the fluid in the tank is important: if the head rises above a critical value, the production of liquid X must cease to avoid disaster and this incurs a stiff financial penalty. Production restarts only when the level drops sufficiently. Similarly, if the head drops too low, the outlet pipes are shut off automatically and only reopened when the level rises sufficiently.

To afford the tank operator some control, he can open or close pipe number two as he thinks best. Thus, for example, he can choose to waste liquid X while the tanker is on delivery to try to avoid the more stringent overflow penalty. The aim of the simulation is to devise a strategy to maximize the profit from the delivery of liquid X over a period of one week.

Paddles

We connected one paddle to the second pipe, allowing it to be opened or closed; and the other to the concentrations of liquid X, a continuous variable, ranging from 0 to 1. Both these affect the continuous part of the model.

Equations

Figure 4.42 along with the variable definitions in Table 4.6 show, in non-dimensionalized form, the five differential equations to be solved. Bernoulli's equation of fluid flow leads to the first governing the height of fluid (water +

$$\frac{dR_i}{dT} = -\rho / (V_s + \sqrt{Z}) \delta i$$

$$\frac{dZ}{dT} = \tau - \lambda R^2 \sqrt{Z}$$

Fig. 4.42 (*continues*).

157

$$\frac{d\phi}{dT} = \pm \lambda^* \rho R^2 \sqrt{Z}$$

$$\frac{d\psi}{dT} = \left.\begin{matrix} \lambda^* R^2 \sqrt{Z} \\ 0 \end{matrix}\right\} \text{ tanker } \left\{\begin{matrix} \text{present} \\ \text{absent} \end{matrix}\right.$$

with $R^2 = \delta_1 R_1{}^2 + \delta_2 R_2{}^2$

$$\delta_i = \begin{matrix} 1 & \text{pipe on} \\ 0 & \text{pipe off} \end{matrix}$$

ϕ reduced by ϕ_C on overflow

Initial Conditions

$$\left.\begin{matrix} Z &=& .5 \\ R_i &=& 1.0 \\ \phi &=& 0 \end{matrix}\right\} \quad \text{at } T = 0$$

$\psi \;\; = 0$ at every tanker return

Constants

$$\begin{matrix} \tau &=& 15.98 \\ \lambda &=& 15.98 \\ \rho &=& .50 \\ V_s &=& 1.07 \\ \lambda^* &=& .250 \end{matrix}$$

Fig. 4.42 Definition of equations for tank–tanker model (*continued*).

Table 4.6 Definition of equation variables for tank–tanker model

T	Time
$R_i(T)$	$i = 1,2$ useful radius of exit pipe
$Z(T)$	Height of surface at time T
$\phi(T)$	Profit from liquid X to time T
$\psi(T)$	Total volume of liquid in tanker at time T
τ	Rate of flow
$\rho(T)$	Concentration of liquid X
λ,λ^*,V	Constants depending on size of tank, tanker fouling rates, etc.

liquid X) in the tank; τ represents the rate of inflow, and the other term outflow through an orifice (the two outlet pipes, in our case). The next equation determines the rate of fouling in the outlet pipes, which is directly proportional to the concentration of liquid X and inversely to the velocity of flow. V_s reflects a deposit occurring in motionless fluid. We have assumed liquid X has the same density as water The fourth equation describes the rate of change of profit from liquid X. This change depends on the concentration of liquid X in the outflow and on its flow rate. R^2 is a term defining the area of the exit orifice, depending on how many pipes are switched on. When the tanker is away and the pipes are on, fluid will run to waste, leading to a loss of profit; hence the negative sign. Similarly, on overflow, profit is instantly reduced by a fixed amount Φ_c. The fourth equation is simply the rate of increase in volume of fluid in the tanker and is related directly to the flow rate. If the tanker is away, this is set to zero.

The values of the constants were chosen such that the pipes foul in approximately 2 days and the tanker fills in 1 hour and is away for 1 hour. Cleaning time is 12 hours.

These equations are subject to discontinuities in both derivative and variable values as a result of changes arising from switching pipes on and off. Two B- and seven C-activities are needed to describe the system. These are described in a summarized form in Fig. 4.43 while an example of the BASIC code for some of them, the paddles, and the equations is to be found in Fig. 4.44 with an explanation of symbols in Table 4.7. The correspondence of the two should be self-evident.

C1 TANKER FULL	C2 TANK OVERFLOW
If volume in tanker > tanker capacity	If not already overflowing and
	If height in tank > overflow level
(i) reset volume in tanker to zero	
(ii) dispatch tanker for distribution time	(i) set overflow true
(iii) switch pipes off	(ii) switch inlet pipe off
(iv) monitor tanker's leaving	(iii) reduce value by penalty

C3 TANK UNDERFLOW	C4 OVERFLOW RECOVERY
If not already underflowing and	If overflowing and
If height in tank < underflow level	If height in tank < recovery level
(i) set underflow true	(i) set overflow false
(ii) switch outlet pipes off	(ii) switch inlet pipe on

Fig. 4.43 C- and B-activities for tank–tanker model (*continues*).

159

```
C5  UNDERFLOW RECOVERY

If underflowing and

If height in tank > recovery level

(i)    set underflow false
(ii)   switch outlet pipes on
(iii)  limit step size
```

```
C6  PIPE FOULS

For each pipe (i)

if pipe (i) is on and

if radius (i) < 0

(i)    switch pipe (i) off
(ii)   increase number of blocked pipes by 1
```

```
C7  BOTH PIPES BLOCKED

If both pipes blocked

(i)    schedule end of cleaning
```

```
B1  FINISH CLEANING

(i)    switch both pipes on together
(ii)   set radii to initial values
```

```
B2  TANKER ARRIVES

(i)    switch both pipes on
(ii)   set tanker to 'back'
(iii)  monitor arrival
```

Fig. 4.43 C- and B-activities for tank-tanker model (*continued*).

```
100   REM   EQUATIONS
102   REM   *********************
103   REM   THE F'S ARE DERIVATIVES OF THE YN'S
104   REM   YN (1) - RADIUS OF PIPE 1
105   REM   YN (2) - RADIUS OF PIPE 2
106   REM   YN (3) - HEIGHT IN TANK
107   REM   YN(4)  - VOLUME IN TANKER
108   REM   YN (5) - PROFIT FROM LIQUID DELIVERED
109   REM   PI      - INLET PIPE ON/OFF INDICATOR
110   REM   *********************
130 R = PO(1) * YN(1) ^ 2 + PO(2) * YN(2) ^ 2:ZE =  SQR (YN(3))
140 F(4) = LS * R * ZE:F(5) = F(4) * RO
150 F(3) = TU * PI - LA * R * ZE
160   IF TKR = AWAY THEN F(4) = 0:F(5) =  - F(5)
170   FOR II = 1 TO 2
180 F(II) =  - PO(II) * RO / (VS + ZE)
190   NEXT
200   RETURN

900   REM   PLOT VARIABLES
910   FOR Z9 = 1 TO 5:V2(Z9) = YN(Z9): NEXT Z9:T2 = T
912   IF PO(1) = OFF THEN V2(1) = MIN(1)
914   IF PO(2) = OFF THEN V2(2) = MIN(2)
920   RETURN

1000   REM   *************************
1010   REM   C-ACTIVITY £1 (TANKER FULL)
1020   REM   *************************
1030   IF YN(4) < TV THEN  RETURN
1040   VN(1,1) = 4:TV(4) = TV:THRESH = TRUE
1050   IF EVNT = FALSE THEN  RETURN
1060   REM   --------------------------
1070   IF PR = 1 THEN  PRINT "TANKER FULL"
1080 YN(4) = 0
1090 TKR = AWAY
1095 EN = 2:ET = TDIS:BN = 2: GOSUB 500: REM   SCHEDULE TANKER
1100 PO(1) = OFF:PO(2) = OFF
1120   FLASH
1130   VTAB (23): HTAB (26): PRINT "TANKER LEFT      "
1140   NORMAL
1150 N1 = 1:N2 = 10:N3 = 10: GOSUB 300: REM   MAKE NOISE
1160   RETURN

2000   REM   *************************
2010   REM   C-ACTIVITY £4 (TANK OVERFLOW)
2020   REM   *************************
2030   IF OVERFLOW = TRUE THEN  RETURN
2040   IF YN(3) < L2 THEN  RETURN
2050   VN(2,1) = 3:TV(3) = L2:THRESH = TRUE
2060   IF EVNT = FALSE THEN  RETURN
2070   REM   --------------------------
2080   IF PR = 1 THEN  PRINT "2080 OVERFLOW"
2090 OVERFLOW = TRUE
2100 PI = OFF: REM   INLET PIPE OFF
2110 YN(5) = YN(5) - PE
2120   RETURN
```

Fig. 4.44 Equations, plot variables, activities, and paddles code for tank–tanker model.
(*continues*)

```
3000   REM   *************************
3010   REM   C-ACTIVITY £3 (TANK UNDERFLOW)
3020   REM   *************************
3030   IF UNDRFLOW = TRUE THEN   RETURN
3040   IF YN(3) > L1 THEN   RETURN
3050 VN(3,1) = 3:TV(3) = L1:THRESH = TRUE
3060   IF EVNT = FALSE THEN   RETURN
3070   REM   ------------------------
3080   IF PR = 1 THEN   PRINT "3080 UNDERFLOW"
3090 UNDRFLOW = TRUE
3100 PO(1) = OFF:PO(2) = OFF
3110   RETURN

4000   REM   *************************
4010   REM   C-ACTIVITY £4 (OVERFLOW RECOVERY)
4020   REM   *************************
4030   IF OVERFLOW = FALSE THEN   RETURN
4040   IF YN(3) > L4 THEN   RETURN
4050 VN(4,1) = 3:TV(3) = L4:THRESH = TRUE
4060   IF EVNT = FALSE THEN   RETURN
4070   REM   ------------------------
4080   IF PR = 1 THEN   PRINT "4080 OVERFLOW RECOVERY"
4090 OVERFLOW = FALSE
4100 PI = OPEN: REM   SWITCH INLET ON
4110   RETURN

5000   REM   *************************
5010   REM   C-ACTIVITY £5 (UNDERFLOW RECOVERY)
5020   REM   *************************
5030   IF UNDERFLOW = FALSE THEN   RETURN
5040   IF YN(3) < L3 THEN   RETURN
5050 VN(5,1) = 3:TV(3) = L3:THRESH = TRUE
5060   IF EVNT = FALSE THEN   RETURN
5070   REM   ------------------------
5080   IF PR = 1 THEN   PRINT "5080 UNDERFLOW RECOVERY"
5090 UNDRFLOW = FALSE
5100 PO(1) = OPEN:PO(2) = OPEN: REM   SWITCH OUTLETS ON
5110   REM   LIMIT STEP SIZE
5120 H = .8 *   SQR (YN(3)) / (2 * LA * (R(1) ^ 2 + R(2) ^ 2))
5130   RETURN

6000   REM   *************************
6010   REM   C-ACTIVITY £6 (PIPE BLOCKED)
6020   REM   *************************
6030 IJ = 0
6040   FOR I9 = 1 TO 2
6050   IF PO(I9) = OFF GOTO 6150
6060   IF YN(I9) > 0 THEN   GOTO 6150
6070 TV(I9) = 0:THRESH = TRUE
6090 IJ = IJ + 1:VN(6,IJ) = I9
6100   IF EVNT = FALSE THEN   GOTO 6150
6110   REM   ------------------------
6120   IF PR = 1 THEN   PRINT "6120 PIPE BLOCKED"
6130 PO(I9) = OFF: REM   SWITCH PIPE OFF
6140 BL = BL + 1: REM   COUNT BLOCKED PIPES
6150   NEXT
6160   RETURN
```

Fig 4.44 (*continued*).

162

```
7000    REM    ****************************
7010    REM    C-ACTIVITY £7 (BOTH PIPES BLOCKED)
7020    REM    ****************************
7030    IF BL < > 2 THEN    RETURN
7040    REM    ----------------------
7050    EN = 1:ET = CLNTIME:BN = 1: GOSUB 500: REM    SCHEDULE PI
    PE CLEANING
7060 BL = 0
7070    RETURN


11000    REM    *****************************
11010    REM    B-ACTIVITY £1 (FINISH CLEANING PIPES)
11020    REM    *****************************
11030 PO(1) = OPEN:PO(2) = OPEN
11040 YN(1) = R(1):YN(2) = R(2)
11050    RETURN


12000    REM    *****************************
12002    REM    B-ACTIVITY £2 (TANKER ARRIVES)
12005    REM    *****************************
12010 PO(1) = OPEN:PO(2) = OPEN
12015 TKR = BACK
12020    VTAB (23): HTAB (26):: PRINT "TANKER ARRIVAL"
12030 N1 = 1:N2 = 10:N3 = 10: GOSUB 300: REM    MAKE NOISES
12040    RETURN


27000    REM    PADDLE FOR DISCRETE VARS
27050    RETURN


27500    REM    PADDLE FOR CONT VARS
27502    REM    CHECK IF PADDLES HAVE CHANGED
27503    REM    ***************************
27505 PO =    PDL (0):P1 =    PDL (1)
27510    IF (PO < > P2) OR (P1 < > P3) THEN PADCH = TRUE
27515 P2 = PO:P3 = P1

27520 RO = PO / 255: REM    PADDLE 1 FOR CONCENTRATION
27525    IF UNDERFLOW = FALSE AND YN(2) > 0 THEN    GOSUB 27600:
    REM    PADDLE 2 WHEN PIPE 2 NOT BLOCKED

27530    REM    DISPLAY PADDLE VARIABLES
27535    VTAB (23): HTAB (8)
27540    IF PO(2) = OFF THEN    PRINT "PIPE OFF"
27545    IF PO(2) = OPEN THEN    PRINT "PIPE ON "
27546    VTAB (23)
27550    HTAB (18): PRINT "RHO    "; INT (.01 + RO * 9.9) / 10
27555    RETURN


27600    REM    PIPE 2
27605 PO(2) =    INT (P1 * 1.99 / 255)
27610    REM    LIMIT STEP LENGTH
27615 R = PO(1) * YN(1) ^ 2 + PO(2) * YN(2) ^ 2:ZE =    SQR (YN(
    3))
27620    IF TU * PI < LA * R * ZE THEN H = .8 *    SQR (YN(3)) / (
    2 * LA * R)

27625    RETURN
```

Fig. 4.44 (*conclusion*).

Table 4.7 Definition of BASIC variables for tank–tanker model

AWAY	Tanker is away indicator
BACK	Tanker is back indicator
BL	Number of blocked pipes
*BN	Number of B-activities
CLNTIME	Length of time to clean pipes
*EN	Number of entities
*ET	Elapsed time to next scheduled event
*EVNT	Flag indicating a discrete or state event
*H	Step length
L1,2,3,4	Levels of underflow, overflow, and their recoveries, respectively
LA	λ
LS	$\lambda*$
*MIN(I)	The minimum value of variable I chosen for display (see Fig. 1.14)
N1, N2, N3	Parameters to noise routines
OPEN/OFF	Flag indicating pipe is OPEN (1) or OFF (0)
OVRFLOW	Flag indicating overflow
*PADCH	Flag indicating a paddle change has occurred
PO(I)	Pipe I on/off indicator
PE	Penalty for overflow
PI	Inlet pipe on/off switch
PR	Print switch
P0,P2	Old/new values of Paddle 1
P1,P3	Old/new values of Paddle 2
R	Effective cross-sectional area of outlet pipes
R(I)	Radius of clean pipe I
RO	ρ concentration of liquid X
*T2	Current time (for plotting subroutine, Fig. 1.14)
TDIS	Delivery time
*THRESH	Flag indicating a threshold is reached
TKR	State of tanker—AWAY or BACK
TU	τ rate of inflow
TV	Tanker volume
*TV(I)	Value of threshold to be attained by state variable I
UNDRFLOW	Flag indicating underflow
*V2(IC)	Array for plot variables
*VN(ACT,I)	Index of Ith state variable involved in activity ACT
VS	V_s
*YN(1) to YN(5)	$R1, R2, Z, \psi, \phi$
ZE	$\sqrt{Z}$

* Used by executive

Activities

Each of the first six C-activities has a threshold test and the bodies, when reached, affect the differential equations through the switching on/off of inlet/outlet pipes (through τ and R respectively). The B-activities also switch the pipes. Further, C2: TANK OVERFLOW produces a discontinuity in the variable 'profit from liquid X'. All these discontinuities are efficiently handled without problem by the combined executive.

B2: TANKER ARRIVES might need a few words of clarification. 12010 would appear to switch both pipes on when the tanker returns even if one or more of them was blocked when it left. However, as soon as the B-activities have been completed, all C's are tried (and recall from Sec. 2.4 that EVNT is set TRUE by the executive for the C-phase), so that C6: PIPE BLOCKED will reblock the appropriate pipes. While this mechanism works for the present model, it is shaky and one can well imagine situations in which it goes awry. Better modelling practice would be to have a status recorder for each pipe, which 'remembers' the old state before the tanker leaves and then restores it in B2.

Indeed, to illustrate this a word about simultaneity is perhaps in order. The executive uses real time, so the coincidence of two events, such as C1: TANKER FULL and C3: TANK UNDERFLOW, is remote (see Sec. 2.4). Does the model as presented deal correctly with this circumstance? C3 will of course switch both pipes off and the return of the tanker switches them on again. C3 will not then switch them off again, as you might expect from the description of the mechanism of the last paragraph. Why not? Because in 3030 underflow is still TRUE and thus C3 is not entered. This 'incorrect' modelling would be avoided by the use of the pipe status recorders of the last paragraph. However, it is fair to point out that in many hours of running this model no such coincidence of events has been observed; the model performs as one would wish.

The C-activities each contain a line which prints a message if PR is set to '1' (cf. 1070 etc.). This is a device useful in debugging to check the logical sequencing of the C-activities as the simulation runs.

We have already given examples of the information which the executive needs to locate threshold accurately in the Reactor model above.

In C1, 1090 is for use in the equations section (160). The tanker is entity 2, the tank 1. 1120 to 1140 flash the message 'TANKER LEFT' to attract attention. The NORMAL ensures subsequent PRINT statements are as usual, i.e., no flashing. N1 to N3 are parameters of the noise subroutine (Sec. 3.4) which determine the length and frequency of the sound emitted.

In C5 UNDERFLOW RECOVERY, we discovered in developing the model that we had to limit the step size (5120), otherwise, during the next integration, the tank would drain in less than one time step, i.e., the height of the liquid (YN(3)) became negative. The model would then stop abruptly at 130, in finding the square root (during the same integration step—remember from Sec. 3.4 that the equations section (100-) is entered several times in each integration step). We were able to derive the step limit analytically, from the

165

equations describing an emptying tank. The same problem can arise in using the paddles.

Paddles code (27000–27625)

No discrete variable is altered via a paddle so this subroutine (27000–27050) just returns. (The discrete parameter, PO(2) affects the equations section.) As we remarked in Sec. 3.4, we need to tell the executive if any 'continuous' paddle has changed its value (27502–27515). Paddle 1 (concentration) ranges from 0 to 1 (27520); Paddle 2 (pipe open/closed) is not so straightforward (27525). If the tank has underflowed or the second pipe is blocked (i.e., radius < 0), the user is not allowed to change pipe 2 to open. 27605 fixes the pipes open or closed (1 or 0). If re-opened, the step length must be limited to avoid the height of liquid becoming negative (27615–27620). It might be thought that paddle 2 should be a 'discrete' paddle. However, this is not the case, as the effect of changing the paddle is on the continuous part of the model.

Plot variables (900–920)

The variables chosen for display are numbers 1–5; the radii of the pipes, the height of the tank, the volume in the tanker, and the profit, respectively. 912 and 914 display a pipe as 'zero' radius whenever it is switched off.

Running the model

Figure 4.45 shows a 'still' from a typical colour display produced while running the model. For clarity of presentation the curves have been drawn in two groups: the lower three (profit and the two effective radii of the outlet pipes) have their zero on the time axis; the upper two (heights of liquid in the tank and in the tanker) have their zero on the line indicated (which is not actually part of the TV display). The topmost dashed line (purple) roughly indicates to the user when the tanker is full. Looking at the tanker curve (purple), one can clearly see when the tanker becomes full, leaves and returns. When it first leaves (8 h), the tank overflows while it is away, giving the sudden penalty drop in the profit. Realizing this, the user, for the second occasion, took steps to avoid this penalty, by opening the second pipe, via the paddle control, allowing some liquid to go to waste. The opening and closing of the pipes are reflected in the radii plots. The second pipe is closed as indicated by the arrow and remains so until opened (as shown by the second arrow). This opening happens to coincide with the return of the tanker, which in any case would occasion the opening of both pipes, via the C-activity: TANKER RETURN. Though not to be seen from this particular still, one quickly finds a fairly delicate balance of the height of the head, especially when the pipes are clean; it needs to be as high as possible for fast filling and low fouling rate; but, when the tanker leaves it needs to be low to avoid overflow, and this is more important as the pipes become increasingly fouled. However, if the level drops below the minimum the outlets are automatically

166

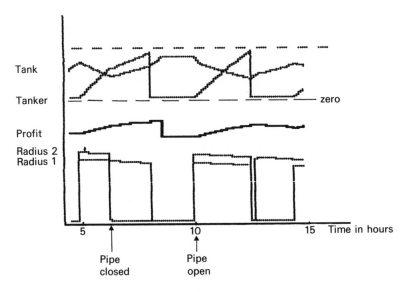

Fig. 4.45 A still from the tank–tanker display. Colours used: tank—green; tanker—purple; profit—white; radius 2—blue; radius 1—yellow.

shut off, until the level rises sufficiently, thus delaying the tanker in its dispatch.

The second paddle was connected to the concentration and the effect of varying this was greater as the pipe became fouled—a rule of thumb discovered after a few runs was to decrease the concentration with time to increase the profit within a specified period (e.g. one week). Such a rule would be very difficult to find on a mainframe machine on which one cannot continuously vary the concentration, but can only keep re-running with different fixed rules each time. However, it must be said that one week's simulated time took approximately 30 minutes Apple run-time, and at the end of this, negative profits were the only result! This was because the pipes, being so fouled, could not deliver liquid quickly enough. Thus a system of cleaning the pipes when desired, rather than waiting till completely fouled, should be introduced. This entails a device for stopping the program at will and scheduling an event (the cleaning). This is easily done using a keyboard interrupt, within the test of a C-activity to schedule cleaning.

There is an error apparent in Fig. 4.45—that is, when the tanker leaves on the second occasion, the pipes are (correctly) shut off (by the C-activity TANKER FULL). The second pipe should then be opened immediately (the paddle still stays OPEN), but this is in fact not done till after another integration step. This is a fine example of how a bug can manifest itself on the screen quite glaringly, but could be easily overlooked without such a display. The cure was quite simple. The call to the GOSUB 27500 was originally incorrectly placed after the integration instead of before it (see Sec. 3.4). We have, on occasions, also found evidence of errors such as curves crossing axes or the plotting starting to go backwards which again could be very difficult to spot from tables of numbers. Using interactive BASIC, the program can be immediately stopped and values of variables instantly printed out—a great boon in finding errors.

Reference

PRITSKER, A.A.B. (1974) *The GASP IV Simulation Language*, Wiley.

Appendix I: The BASIC used in this book

Standard BASIC, like a universal standard of FORTRAN, does not exist. Or, more correctly, certain standards have been laid down by certain august bodies, but as everyone seeks to improve or disagree with such standards they are not standard for long. The standard BASIC was designed with mainframe computers in mind; microcomputers have since come to fruition and each type has its own BASIC, with its own idiosyncracies. They differ from mainframe BASICs chiefly in that they have, in general, no matrix manipulation facilities and that they allow names with many symbols, while recognizing only the first two as significant. However, microcomputer BASICs have extras—for example, for handling discs, tapes, and graphics, and so on.

The BASIC we exploit in this book is mainly Applesoft, with reference also to PET BASIC. This should work on other microcomputers with small and usually 'obvious' changes. The 'obvious' differences will be found in your microcomputer's manual. A useful summary of 'standard' BASIC on microcomputers can be found in Parr (1981).

However, the following Applesoft commands, used by the simulation executive of Chapter 3, may need some explanation:

DEF FN name (parameter) = expression

allows you to define your own functions, with one parameter. They can be redefined within the program. For example DEF FN A(B) = B*H/2 would give 5 times the current value of H when called as FN A(10). The parameter must be included even if it is not used by the function.

PEEK (expression)

gives you the content of the memory at the address of the expression. PEEK (−16384), for example, will indicate whether or not a key has been depressed since address −16384 is reserved for that information. Similarly the addresses −16286, −16287 indicate whether or not the paddle buttons are depressed.

POKE expression 1, expression 2

allows you to enter a value (expression 2) into a memory location (expression 1). For example POKE −16368,0 zeroes the indicator representing a keyboard depression.

PDL (expression)

gives the integer value (in the range 0–255) set by the position of the knob, on the paddle whose number is given by the expression. The knob position is checked each time PDL( ) is encountered in the program. We use the two paddles provided whose numbers are 0 and 1.

ON expression GOSUB linenumber 1, linenumber 2, linenumber 3, . . . linenumber *n*

ON expression GOTO linenumber 1, linenumber 2, linenumber 3, . . . linenumber *n*

This transfers control to one of the specified line numbers depending on the integer value of the expression, for example,

40 ON N GOTO 50, 60 70

will transfer to 60, 50, 70 for N = 2, 1, 3 respectively.

The GOSUB version returns as a normal GOSUB would do. If the expression has a value for which there is no linenumber the following statement is executed.

HTAB expression
VTAB expression

HTAB moves the cursor horizontally to the position on the screen given by the expression. Position 1 is at the left-hand side and 40 at the right.

VTAB moves the cursor vertically to the screen linenumber given by the expression. Line 1 is at the top and 24 is at the bottom.

CALL expression

makes the program execute a machine-language subroutine at the address specified by the expression. For example, CALL 39074 will transfer control to the subroutine beginning at the decimal address 39074.

Reference

PARR, M. (1981) 'BASIC BASIC', *Personal Computer World*, Sept., p. 54.

Appendix 2:
Assembly language/
machine code subroutines

It may happen that your program is very slow running. If you are lucky you may be able to isolate a small part which is the culprit and by rewriting it in assembly language speed it up. You do not have to be an expert to do this—you may write crude assembly language but it will almost certainly run more quickly than the BASIC. How much more quickly? It all depends . . . .

Increases of a factor of two or three hundred or more are possible—the screen shifting routine (described in Sec. 1.8) is one such example. In BASIC it takes one and a half minutes; in machine code, the twinkling of an eye (0.02 sec!) Despite this subroutine being called only occasionally, one and a half minutes is an intolerable time to wait for graph redrawing.

In contrast our efforts with rewriting the integration routine (described in Sec. 3.4) were less fruitful. The tanker example of Sec. 4.5 was programmed on the Apple and a CDC 7600, with respective run times of 55 min and 0.25 sec! This must be interpreted as meaning that the 7600 is very powerful (but produces no moving display), not that you cannot do anything useful with an Apple. We did some preliminary checks which indicated that by rewriting the integration routine, which lies at the innermost sanctum of the combined executive, we could expect a threefold increase in running speed. So we spent some time doing this to achieve a factor of only 1.3! In this case, it is precisely because the integration does lie at the heart of the executive that the rest of the program swamps any gain from the machine code—the BASIC interpreter spends so much time in searching for GOSUB line numbers.

Let us give some advice on writing assembly language. First, keep the code simple, to do the task demanded of it. Second, do not be afraid of writing in assembly language—simple programs are fairly straightforward, with a bit of practice and experience. Third, again, learn from looking at (and possibly adapting) working examples.

Assembly language, machine code, and computer architecture

Before we can understand the graph moving example below we need to explain a little about assembly language, machine code, and how the hearts of microcomputers function.

Machine language is a set of numerical codes that control the functioning of the computer. For a user to write other than small programs in machine code is tedious and slow. Hence assembly language was invented to help in this—it is a set of alphabetic characters (mnemonics) used as substitutes for machine code. Thus, for example, if you examine part of a microcomputer program in machine code you might see:

A9 00 8D 00 94 60

In assembly language this may be:

LDA # $00
STA $9400
RTS

which says take the number '0' and store it in memory at location $9400 and then return to the calling subroutine. The $ denotes a hexadecimal number (i.e., base 16 instead of base $10 - 9 \times 16^3 + 4 \times 16^2 + 0 \times 16 + 0$). Mnemonic LDA is equivalent to machine code A9; STA to 8D; and RTS to 60.

However, we must explain something of the functioning of the micro-computer before we return to discuss more assembly language. The brief look we give does not cover all aspects but is sufficient to explain the graph moving example. For those who wish to read more about microprocessors and assembly language we recommend French (1980).

A classical computer and most microcomputers are centred on three basic building blocks:

The central processing unit (CPU)

The memory unit

The input/output unit.

The CPU controls the interpretation and execution of instructions. It may consist of some seven or eight elements, of which the arithmetic logic unit (ALU) and accumulator are our main concern at present.

The ALU carries out the basic arithmetic and also logical decision-making necessary for the computer to function as a computer. For example, it can:

ADD two numbers

SUBTRACT one number from another

COMPARE two numbers

Logically ADD two numbers together

along with several other such tasks.

An accumulator is a register of the ALU used as intermediate storage during certain logical and arithmetic operations. A register is a temporary storage area usually consisting of one single computer word (see below). The Apple has just one 8-bit accumulator which can be quickly accessed for temporary storage. It is used with some but not all of the assembly instructions.

If, while adding two numbers, the sum is greater than the word length can hold the ALU sets a carry flag. Thus, suppose we are adding 254 and 13 which are respectively

11111110 and 1101 in binary. Then the addition is

```
11111110
00001101
00001011   carry 1
```

which is 11 plus 256, in decimal, with the carry representing 256. Just a similar process to decimal arithmetic, really.

Thus one should constantly be aware of the status of the carry flag, since many instructions set or reset it. In subtracting two numbers, for example, one should set carry (SEC) before the operation and check it is set/reset afterwards and act accordingly.

The memory unit stores not only the computer program but also data that may be needed. Each instruction or datum is assigned a unique address which is used by the CPU when fetching information or storing it in the memory. An address is a number identifying that memory location. The main memory consists of many thousands of bits—single binary digits, which have the value either 0 or 1. The computer processes a number of contiguous bits at a time in a group known as a byte. A word is also a set of bits and is used to represent the primary unit of information handled by the computer. A byte may or may not be different from a word; for example, if a byte consists of 8 bits, a 16-bit word is 2 bytes; an Apple word is 8 bits and thus is only 1 byte. Typically, each memory location contains one word. The longer the word length of a computer the greater is the precision obtainable and also the larger the variety of its basic instruction set. With an 8-bit Apple, word numbers from 0 to 255 can be stored; with 16 bits, 0 to 65 535. Machine code instructions may require 1, 2, or 3 bytes in order to represent them. Such instructions from a program are stored by 'address' in the main computer memory. These addresses are the hexadecimal number of the storage location of the first byte of the instruction.

Thus in Fig. A2.1 the address of the first byte of LDA # $00 is $9412, of STA $9400, $9414; of RTS, $9417.

The first instruction requires two bytes ($9412, $9413), the second three, ($9414–$9416) and the last just one. In LDA # $00 the # denotes absolute

Address	Assembler Code	Machine Code
.	.	.
.	.	.
.	.	.
$9412	LDA # $00	A9 00
$9414	STA $9400	8D 00 94
$9417	RTS	60
.	.	.
.	.	.
.	.	.

Fig. A2.1 A fragment of memory.

173

address: that is, the hexadecimal number $00 is loaded into the accumulator (and not the contents of address $00). STA $9400 stores the contents of the accumulator in the storage location starting at $9400. Note, in the machine code the order of the address $9400 is changed around: 00 94. The reason for this is straightforward; it takes two bytes (in the Apple or PET) to represent an address. This means addresses can range from decimal 0 to 65 535 (hexadecimal 0000 to FFFF); with one byte this range is 0 to 255 only. The computer recognizes the least significant part of the address first, the most significant second.

In passing it is perhaps worth mentioning that the machine code 8D 00 94 would appear as

8	D	0	0	9	4
1000	1100	0000	0000	1001	0100
1st byte		2nd byte		3rd byte	

to the computer.

The Input/Output unit looks after feeding data into or out of the CPU and will not concern us further.

Graph redrawing example

Now we are in a position to explain the graph redrawing example.

In Sec. 1.6 we describe a device for shifting part of a high resolution graphics screen. The essential details of the BASIC program are:

```
FOR H = 0 TO 80 STEP 40
FOR I = I1 TO 12 STEP 128
FOR J = 0 TO 7168 STEP 1024
FOR K = K1 TO K2
AD = I + J + K + H
POKE AD-SH, PEEK (AD)
NEXT K
NEXT J
NEXT I
NEXT H
```

The strange numbers arise from the way the HGR screen is stored in an Apple—some details can be found in the Apple II Reference Manual. I1, I2, K1, K2 are given constants. This BASIC routine takes one and a half minutes to run. The corresponding machine code is in Fig. A2.2. The few addresses with just NOPs (no operation) do nothing; they are padding only and the computer glances over them. They may have appeared as the code was developed, to fill in otherwise incorrect code.

We see that the program consists essentially of 4 FOR loops, some additions, a subtraction, and a PEEK and a POKE.

174

94	00	01	02	03	04	05	06	07	08	09	0A	0B	0C	0D	0E	0F	10
	H		I LS	I MS	J	K			I1 LS	I1 MS	I2 LS	I2 MS	K1		K2		SH

Fig. A2.2(a) Variable addresses (screen redrawing).

	Address	M/c code		Assembly code	
				Address M/c code	Assembly code
H-loop start	9412–	A9 00		LDA	#$00
H-loop start	9414–	8D 00 94		STA	$9400
	9417–	AD 08 94		LDA	$9408
	941A–	8D 02 94		STA	$9402
	941D–	AD 09 94		LDA	$9409
	9420–	8D 03 94		STA	$9403
I-loop start	9423–	A9 00		LDA	#$00
	9425–	18		CLC	
	9426–	EA		NOP	
	9427–	EA		NOP	
	9428–	EA		NOP	
	9429–	8D 05 94		STA	$9405
J-loop start	942C–	AD 0C 94		LDA	$940C
K-loop start	942F–	8D 06 94		STA	$9406

	9432–	AD 00 94	LDA	$9400	
	9435–	6D 06 94	ADC	$9406	LS
	9438–	6D 02 94	ADC	$9402	
	943B–	85 F9	STA	$F9	
AD=H+I+J+K	943D–	EA	NOP		
	943E–	EA	NOP		
	943F–	AD 05 94	LDA	$9405	MS
	9442–	6D 03 94	ADC	$9403	
	9445–	85 FA	STA	$FA	

	9447–	38	SEC		
	9448–	85 FC	STA	$FC	LS
	944A–	A5 F9	LDA	$F9	no borrow
	944C–	ED 10 94	SBC	$9410	MS
	944F–	85 FB	STA	$FB	
	9451–	B0 0E	BCS	$9461	
	9453–	69 FF	ADC	#$FF	LS
AD–SH	9455–	69 01	ADC	#$01	
	9457–	85 FB	STA	$FB	borrow
	9459–	A5 FA	LDA	$FA	
	945B–	38	SEC		MS
	945C–	E9 01	SBC	#$01	
	945E–	18	CLC		
	945F–	85 FC	STA	$FC	
PEEK AD	9461–	A0 00	LDY	#$00	
POKE AD+H,AD	9463–	B1 F9	LDA	($F9),Y	
	9465–	91 FB	STA	($FB),Y	
	9467–	EA	NOP		
	9468–	EA	NOP		
	9469–	EA	NOP		
	946A–	EA	NOP		
	946B–	EA	NOP		
	946C–	18	CLC		

	Address M/c code		Assembly code		
	946D–	AD 06 94	LDA	$9406	K
	9470–	69 01	ADC	#$01	+1
K-loop end	9472–	CD 0E 94	CMP	$940E	
	9475–	18	CLC		
	9476–	30 B7	BMI	$942F	
	9478–	F0 B5	BEQ	$942F	
	947A–	EA	NOP		
	947B–	AD 05 94	LDA	$9405	J
	947E–	69 04	ADC	#$04	+1024
J-loop end	9480–	8D 05 94	STA	$9405	
	9483–	C9 1C	CMP	#$1C	
	9485–	18	CLC		
	9486–	30 A4	BMI	$942C	
	9488–	F0 A2	BEQ	S942C	
	948A–	18	CLC		
	948B–	AD 02 94	LDA	$9402	
	948E–	69 80	ADC	#$80	
	9490–	8D 02 94	STA	$9402	
	9493–	90 0D	BCC	$94A2	
	9495–	AD 03 94	LDA	$9403	
	9498–	69 00	ADC	#$00	
	949A–	8D 03 94	STA	$9403	
	949D–	18	CLC		
	949E–	EA	NOP		
	949F–	EA	NOP		
I-loop end	94A0–	EA	NOP		
	94A1–	EA	NOP		
	94A2–	AD 03 94	LDA	$9403	
	94A5–	CD 0B 94	CMP	$940B	
	94A8–	F0 05	BEQ	$94AF	
	94AA–	30 1A	BMI	$94C6	
	94AC–	4C BB 94	JMP	$94BB	
	94AF–	AD 02 94	LDA	$9402	
	94B2–	CD 0A 94	CMP	$940A	
	94B5–	30 0F	BMI	$94C6	
	94B7–	F0 0D	BEQ	$94C6	
	94B9–	18	CLC		
	94BA–	EA	NOP		
	94BB–	18	CLC		
	94BC–	AD 00 94	LDA	$9400	H
H-loop end	94BF–	69 28	ADC	#$28	+40
	94C1–	C9 78	CMP	#$78	128
	94C3–	D0 05	BNE	$94CA	
Return	94C5–	60	RTS		
	94C6–	18	CLC		
	94C7–	4C 23 94	JMP	$9423	
	94CA–	18	CLC		
	94CB–	4C 14 94	JMP	$9414	

Fig. A2.2(b) Machine/assembly code for screen redrawing.

FOR loops

These can be handled as follows:

load start of loop into accumulator
store loop count in address 1
1st line of body

.   .   .

.

.

last line of body

Recall value in address 1
add step to it
if this $<$ = end value repeat loop

otherwise do rest of program

Thus, for example, with K1 and K2 stored in \$940C, \$940E respectively, FOR K = K1 TO K2 (which is extracted from Fig. A2.2) becomes:

942C	LDA \$940C	:	load accumulator with K1 from 940C
942F	STA \$9406	:	store K in 9406

.

.

.

.

946C	CLC	:	clear carry
946D	LDA \$9406	:	load K
9470	ADC # \$01	:	add step 1 to K
9472	CMP \$940E	:	compare it with K2
9475	CLC		
9476	BMI \$942F	:	if K $<$
9478	BEQ \$942F	:	or = K2 repeat loop.

The value of K has to be stored before the body is entered since the accumulator will undoubtedly be overwritten. The first clear carry makes sure all is fine for the addition ADC which adds to the value of the carry as well.

CMP compares the value in the accumulator with that in the address given (940E, in this case) and a flag is set to indicate the result. This flag can be acted upon by various Branch instructions, which jump to the address specified if a certain condition is met: thus BMI \$942F jumps to the instruction at address \$942F if the value of the flag is minus, i.e., if the flag indicates the previous (the CMP in this case) operation produced a negative result. Similarly BEQ jumps if the result was equal.

This explains a straightforward loop; the one for H is similar, except the step is 40 (\$28—line 94BF of Fig. A2.2); and for the J loop the step is 1024 to 7188 which is equivalent to a step 4×256 to 28×256. The I loop is slightly more complicated as it goes beyond the abilities of one word, i.e., its value exceeds 256. Thus the counter is dealt with in two words; and when the first overflows, the carry is included in the second. Appropriate tests are carried out on each to detect the loop ending.

POKE AD-SH, PEEK (AD)

Let us assume that AD and AD-SH have been found and stored in the consecutive addresses, FA F9, FC FB, i.e., since AD is greater than 256, 2 bytes are required for its storage; the most significant part goes in address FA, the least in F9. Similarly for AD-SH in FC,FB. For example, if the value of AD is 269 (=1*256 + 13) then FA contains $1 and F9, $D. We then have to look after the arithmetic of each byte ourselves—the ALU does not do it for us. PEEK and POKE are straightforward, being no more than LDA and STA respectively. However, the address part needs a bit of explanation. So far, with LDA we have loaded an 8-bit number into the accumulator. The screen addresses, however require larger numbers than 8 bits can represent (in the range 8000–16000 K, roughly), so how can we achieve this? By using 16-bit addressing which is a feature provided for you in the central processor. With 16 bits available one can address from 0 to 65 536. There are certain areas of memory (known as zero page) which allow you to store such a 'double length' address. By using the correct form for the address part of the instruction you can make use of this. For example.

LDY # $00
LDA ($F9),Y

stores values 0 in the index register Y, which is then used in the special LDA instruction to indicate that a double-length address (F9,FA) is to be used. This address contains an 8-bit piece of data which is transferred to the accumulator. Similarly STA ($FB),Y will put into the address FCFB, the value in the accumulator. So the effect of the three instructions is to transfer the contents of address AD into address AD-SH: i.e., POKE AD-SH, PEEK AD.

AD = I + J + K + H and AD − SH

The rest of the program is mostly concerned with finding AD and AD − SH. We are summing four quantities and must use two words.

MS and LS refer to the most and least significant parts of the double word value respectively. Thus we just add the LS parts of H, K, and I (J has none since it increases in steps of 1024); and then the MS parts of J + I (H and K have none).

The subtraction AD −. SH is also done in two parts, and care has to be exercised in dealing with any borrow. Before a subtraction is done carry must be set. This is a consequence of the way the processor does subtraction; if afterwards it is clear, there was no borrow; otherwise one has to take care of the borrow, for the LS parts, by adding 256 and then subtracting 1 from the MS.

Blacking out example—Fig. A2.3

94	0C	0E	10	EE	F0	F2
	K1	K2	SH	loop variable	upper limit of loop	current shift

Fig. A2.3(a) Variable addresses (blacking out).

94F4–	18		CLC		9512–	8D 10 94	STA	$9410
94F5–	A9 27		LDA	#$27	9515–	EA	NOP	
94F7–	8D 0C 94		STA	$940C	9516–	EA	NOP	
94FA–	8D 0E 94		STA	$940E	9517–	20 12 94	JSR	$9412
94FD–	A9 00		LDA	#$00	951A–	18	CLC	
94FF–	8D F2 94		STA	$94F2	951B–	AD EE 94	LDA	$94EE
9502–	A9 01		LDA	#$01	951E–	69 01	ADC	#$01
9504–	8D EE 94		STA	$94EE	9520–	8D EE 94	STA	$94EE
9507–	EA		NOP		9523–	CD F0 94	CMP	$94F0
9508–	EA		NOP		9526–	18	CLC	
9509–	EA		NOP		9527–	30 E1	BMI	$950A
950A–	AD F2 94		LDA	$94F2	9529–	F0 DF	BEQ	$950A
950D–	69 01		ADC	#$01	952B–	60	RTS	
950F–	8D F2 94		STA	$94F2				

Fig. A2.3(b) Machine/assembly code for blacking out.

Once the graphs have been redrawn, the unwanted portion is blacked out, by repeatedly shifting the 39th column, increasing SH by one each time. The 39th column is kept black, apart from the stub of the X-axis and the horizontal lines of the discrete executive, for this purpose. Thus, at first it is shifted 1 column; then 2; then 3 and so on until the newly redrawn graph is reached. By this means, the unwanted portion is blacked out and the X-axis redrawn.

The machine code program for this is in Fig. A2.3, and consists of a repeated call (9517) to the shift program above (9412), with the appropriate values for the parameters, the loop limits for K, and the shift.

The former are kept at 39 (94F7,94FA); the shift increases by 1 each time through (950A–9512). The loop variable is in 94EE and is checked in lines 951B to 9529. The upper limit is set by the calling BASIC program, using a POKE.

Both these programs, graph redrawing and blacking out, are loaded as one unit, RAPID, in the executive of Secs 3.3 and 3.4.

Copying screen—Fig. A2.4

The use of this is described in Sec. 3.2. It allows the visible screen to be updated apparently instantaneously at each time step and is used in the executive of Sec. 3.2. It copies the information stored in memory in the addresses $4000–$5999 (screen changed directly by program) to the addresses $2000–$3999 (screen changed each time step). The X register is used to hold the number of pages (each 256 locations) which is 32 or $20 ($9503). The Y register holds the current position of the page (0 to 256). $9507–$950E transfer one page at a time with $9510–$9517 moving the operation to the next page.

INY increases Y by one and INC increases the contents of the accompanying address by one. The 40 and 20 of $9509 and $950C are thus changed as the program runs and have to be reset before it is used again.

On the PET the screen copying program is very similar and is loaded via DATA statements in the BASIC program of Fig. 3.20. The additions at each end make the screen totally blank during the copying.

```
9503-    A2 20        LDX    #$20
9505-    A0 00        LDY    #$00
9507-    B9 00 40     LDA    $4000,Y
950A-    99 00 20     STA    $2000,Y
950D-    C8           INY
950E-    D0 F7        BNE    $9507
9510-    EE 09 95     INC    $9509
9513-    EE 0C 95     INC    $950C
9516-    CA           DEX
9517-    D0 EC        BNE    $9505
9519-    20 3F FF     JSR    $FF3F
951C-    60           RTS
```

Fig. A2.4 Machine/assembly code for copying screens.

Shape specification—Fig. A2.5

The first byte (number 0) gives the number of shapes (01). Byte numbers 2 and 3 give the index of the first shape relative to the start (0400). The actual shape definition starts at byte 4 (C0) and specifies the shape of Fig. 1.5. This is used in the warehouse example of Sec. 4.2 and is stored at $9470 where it is accessed by the executive of Sec. 3.2.

```
9470-  01 00 04 00 C0 37 36 2E
9478-  2D 25 24 3C 36 3E 27 24
9480-  15 00 00 49 FF FF 00 00
```

Fig. A2.5 Shape specification.

Character generator

This machine language program is used by the executives of Secs 3.2 and 3.3. It is not listed here as it is available through Apple suppliers. It must be stored at $0C00 to be initiated by:

POKE 54,0: POKE 55,12

$(12 \times 256 = \$0C00)$.

Access to characters not available on the keyboard can be made via the system function CHR$(N) where N is an integer specifying the character to be generated. For example, PRINT CHR$ (127) puts a ■ on the screen.

Conclusion

There are two reasons for giving you these machine language programs. Firstly, you will need them to use the executives of Chapter 3. But perhaps more importantly we hope you will use them as working examples on which you can base your own machine language programs. Try modifying one of them to do a slightly different task, then you will gain confidence in handling the language. Full details of the instructions set for your micro will be in the appropriate manual. If you have a 6502 Apple or PET then the above programs will only need the addresses altering if the storage position changes. For a different micro, translation will be required.

References

Apple II Reference Manual, Apple Computer Inc., 1979.
FRENCH, G.S. (1980) *Computer Science*, D.P. Publications.

Glossary

Accumulator
A register of the central processing unit (CPU) for intermediate storage during logical and arithmetical operations.

Activity based simulation
A simulation approach in which the modeller breaks up his real-world system into a number of activities. An activity is a set of instructions governing certain actions which change the state of the model.

Address
A unique name or number identifying a memory location.

A-phase
The time advance phase in an activity-based simulation in which the clock time is advanced to that of the next event.

Assembler
A systems program to convert an assembly language program into an executable machine code program.

Assembly language
A symbolic/mnemonic language for writing programs, which are translated by the assembler into machine code. Assembly language is more easily written and understood than machine code.

B-activity
A Bound-activity is one scheduled to occur, and is often used for generating arrivals into the simulation. A B-activity has no testhead. (cf. C-activity).

B-phase
The phase of the simulation during which all B-activities scheduled for that time are performed.

Bit
A binary digit; the smallest unit of data in a computer.

Branch
An instruction which can cause a jump in the order of execution of program instructions. Normally the order is sequential.

Buttons (paddle)
A button on a games paddle can be pressed to interrupt the flow of a running program. The user must ensure that suitable BASIC tests are incorporated in his program to achieve this.

Byte
A set of (usually 8) contiguous bits, which the computer operates on as a unit. A byte is sometimes a subset of a word.

C-activity
The performance of a C-activity requires the cooperation of a number of

entities. If any of these is not available, the activity is passed over. C-activities thus consist of a number of tests followed by a body, in which further events may be scheduled, entities removed from or added to queues, and so on. (cf. B-activity).

C-phase
The phase in a simulation when all C-activities are tried in turn and those whose every test is satisfied are peformed.

Character generator
A systems program for placing text (letters, numbers, symbols, etc.) any-where on an Apple graphics screen.

Combined simulation
A simulation which is a combination of discrete and continuous parts. Between consecutive discrete events, continuous (or 'state') events may occur, defined by some continuous variable reaching a threshold value.

Compiler
A systems program to translate a user's program in a high-level language (such as BASIC or FORTRAN) into a machine code program. The user's program is translated as a whole (cf. interpreter) in preparation for its execution.

Continuous simulation
A simulation chiefly involving continuous variables, often in the form of differential equations.

CPU
Central Processing Unit. This controls the interpretation and execution of computer instructions.

Dimension
The size of an array, which must be defined in a dimension statement if greater than 10.

Disc
A circular plate coated with a magnetic material, used for high-speed bulk storage of data. The disc is rotated at a constant speed by a disc drive.

Discrete simulation
A simulation involving discrete variables in which events are scheduled to occur at discrete points in time—nothing in the model changes between these times (events).

DOS
Disc Operating System—A system program controlling the storage of data on a disc: its location, type, its input and output, etc.

Editor
A systems program which aids preparation of source programs, by allowing text manipulation (insertion, deletion, etc., of symbols, words, sentences, etc.).

Entity

An object taking part in a simulation. The movement of entities from activity to activity determines the course of the simulation.

Event-based simulation

A simulation approach in which the modeller breaks up his real-world system into a number of events. Each event is a description of the steps that occur consequent to a change in the state of an entity.

Event time

The time (in the simulation) at which some event(s) occurs in the model.

Executive

A program which controls the running of a simulation. It organizes initialization, time advance, the carrying out of events and activities, and finalization.

Finalization

That part of a simulation which outputs final results.

Function

A function takes some numbers and operates on them to produce a simple value. The user cán define a function in a program line and, once that line has been executed, can use the function in any arithmetic expression. The function can then be redefined by another program line if desired, e.g., 10 DEF FN DBL(W) = 2 * W + 2.

Graphical display

Output from the computer program in the form of graphs on a VDU.

Hexadecimal

A number system using 0,1,2,. . .,9,A,B,C,D,E,F (equivalent to decimal 0 to 15) to represent all possible values of a 4-bit digit.

High-level language

A computer language using symbols and command statements (often English words) which are easily read and understood. Each statement represents several machine code instructions. Examples are BASIC, FORTRAN, and ALGOL.

High-resolution graphics

The definition of the VDU for use in drawing (as opposed to text) as an area of 280 × 192 dots (or part of it as 280 × 160). Each dot can be allocated one of six colours, BUT on the Apple II colours can be distorted by adjacent dots unless they are coloured in horizontal pairs.

Initialization

A section of a simulation program; (1) defining the number of entities and activities etc.; and (2) defining the initial state of the system: which activities are in progress and in which queues the entities are.

Instruction

A set of bits defining a computer command which is understood and acted on by the CPU. It may move data, do arithmetic and logic functions, control input and output operations, or decide which instruction to perform next.

Interpreter

A systems program to translate a user's program in a high-level language (such as BASIC) into a machine code program. The user's program is translated and executed one line at a time. (cf. Compiler).

Knob (paddle)

The knob on the paddle can be turned to output to the computer a value in the range 0 to 255. A BASIC program can read this value and act upon it according to the value.

Machine code

The lowest level of computer languages, usually written in bits (0 or 1), which can be immediately executed by the computer without further translation. It is very hard to program in machine code.

Mainframe machine

A large computer with many users, as opposed to a mini- or microcomputer.

Memory unit

The part of a computer which holds data and instructions.

Microcomputer

A complete computer system including a microprocessor (CPU), memory unit, and input/output controller.

Microprocessor

A simple large-scale integrated circuit performing the functions of a CPU. It has a small size and cost.

Model

The representation of a real-life organization or system by logical statements of relevant happenings in the organization.

Module

A more or less self-contained segment of a program, often written as a subroutine.

Paddle

A black plastics box with a knob and pushbutton to allow control of associated parameters of a model as it runs. Each paddle is basically a potentiometer.

Picture display, dynamic

The use of the VDU to show the state of the model in simulation time by the position on the screen of the entities and the colour/symbol used to represent them.

Picture display, static

The use of the VDU to show the state of the model, in which there are no entities moving round the screen. Useful for showing tanks filling and emptying, etc.

Pseudocode

A structured form of English to express the logical statements of the 'program' before translating them into a progamming language for use on the computer.

RAM
Random Access Memory. A type of computer memory in which the time to access any data stored is the same as for any other.

Redraw graph
Shift graph (see below) and blank out the rest (right-hand) of the graph.

Register
A single computer word used for temporary storage of data.

Schedule
The associating of an entity with a B-activity at a particular simulation time so that the appropriate happenings of the activity occur automatically at that time in the simulation.

Screen 1 and 2
Two areas of computer memory reserved for producing displays on the VDU. In a simulation, machine code programs are used to clear the VDU and display one screen, while the other is being prepared for display. Thus changes can be made to appear instantaneous.

Shape table
The definition by vectors of shape(s) used in a program for display on the VDU. It is written in hexadecimal and can be stored on disc for 'loading' into the computer memory when needed in a BASIC program.

Shift graph
The movement via a machine code program of the right-hand part of the simulation graph to the left hand side of the screen graph space. This allows the graph plotting to continue with some of the old graph displayed for continuity.

Software
Programs to control the operation of computer hardware: e.g., operating system, monitor, compiler, editor, and user's program, etc.

State equation
A continuous equation which is integrated to obtain successive values of the state variable.

State event
A continuous variable crossing some threshold value, which happening may activate other happenings in the model.

Step length
The length of the integration step. This will change in value to maintain accuracy of the solution.

Storage location
A word of memory at a specified address.

Subroutine
A group of program instructions which may be called from more than one place in the program. Subroutines are often used to segment a large program into easily comprehended blocks of program.

186

Subroutine tree
A diagram showing the interdependence of the subroutines in a program.

Threshold
A value which a continuous variable may cross. This crossing usually determines the time of a state event.

Time advance
The process of moving on simulation time. In discrete simulation, time is moved to that of the next discrete event; in combined simulation, time is advanced in relatively small integration steps until the next event is reached—this could be a discrete or a state event.

Variable
   Model: Some quantity in the model whose value may change as the simulation runs.
   Display: Some quantity in the model which is chosen to have its value graphed as the simulation runs.
   Paddle: Some quantity in the model whose value can be changed by turning the knob on the paddle.
   State: A continuous quantity in the model whose value is found by integration.

VDU
Visual Display Unit—A television or monitor for communicating with a computer.

Word
A set of bits handled by a computer as a primary unit of information. Its length is determined by hardware design. The longer the word, the richer the instruction set. Each memory location usually consists of 1 word.

Index

DATE DUE

HIGHSMITH 45-220